OFF THE BEATEN PATH®
NORTH CAROLINA →

Help Us Keep This Guide Up to Date

Every effort has been made by the author and editors to make this guide as accurate and useful as possible. However, many changes can occur after a guide is published—establishments close, phone numbers change, facilities come under new management, and so on.

We would love to hear from you concerning your experiences with this guide and how you feel it could be improved and be kept up to date. While we may not be able to respond to all comments and suggestions, we'll take them to heart, and we'll make certain to share them with the author. Please send your comments and suggestions to the following address:

The Globe Pequot Press
Reader Response/Editorial Department
P.O. Box 480
Guilford, CT 06437

Or you may e-mail us at: editorial@GlobePequot.com

Thanks for your input, and happy travels!

NINTH EDITION

OFF THE BEATEN PATH®
NORTH CAROLINA ➡

A GUIDE TO UNIQUE PLACES

SARA PITZER

travel

Guilford, Connecticut

The prices, rates, and hours listed in this guidebook were confirmed at press time. We recommend, however, that you call establishments to obtain current information before traveling.

Text design by Linda R. Loiewski
Maps by Equator Graphics © Morris Book Publishing, LLC
Illustrations by Carole Drong
Drawing of Town Creek Indian Mound on p. 123 based on photograph by Sara Pitzer. Drawing of Grove Arcade Building on p. 160 based on photograph by Jeannine J. Wynne.
Spot photography throughout © Jeffery Stone/Shutterstock

ISSN 1539-7769
ISBN 978-0-7627-4875-4

Printed in the United States of America
10 9 8 7 6 5 4 3 2 1

This one's for the whippersnapper, Drew—carboy lifter, mattress flipper, kitchen companion, kindred spirit. Thanks from the O.F.

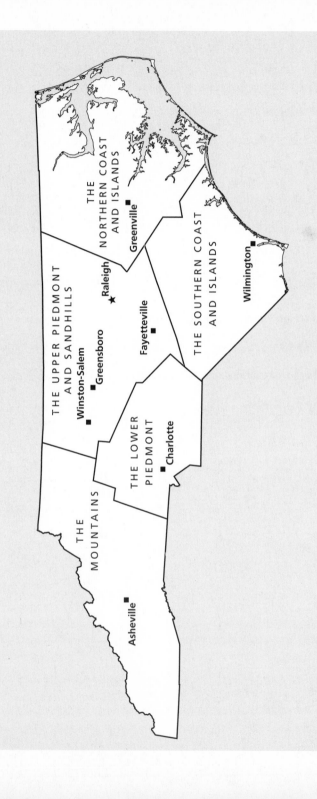

THE MOUNTAINS

Asheville

THE UPPER PIEDMONT AND SANDHILLS

THE LOWER PIEDMONT

Winston-Salem

Greensboro

Charlotte

Raleigh

Fayetteville

THE NORTHERN COAST AND ISLANDS

Greenville

THE SOUTHERN COAST AND ISLANDS

Wilmington

Contents

Introduction

I was lost—again—somewhere around Raleigh, but nowhere near the place I wanted to be. I'd already pulled into the entrance of a large industrial park, where an executive stopped on his way out to ask if he could help me. I'd already walked along the sidewalk in front of North Carolina State University, where a professor leaving campus gave me detailed instructions on getting out of the city in the direction I wanted to go. And I was pretty sure I was going to get it right, if I could just find the beltway. Seeing that the car in the next lane had both windows down as we waited for a light to turn, I called across to the driver, "Is this road going to take me to the beltway?"

"Where do you want to go?" he yelled back. I told him. "Follow me," he shouted, and when the light changed, took off in a cloud of exhaust. I followed him nearly 10 miles. At the proper entrance onto the beltway, he blinked his turn signal and also pointed emphatically with his left hand, just in case I missed the signal. I turned. He was already gone, leaving me with a grin and a wave.

And that's how people in North Carolina are.

For me, living in North Carolina is no accident of birth or whim of corporate transfer; it's a studied choice. When my husband and I decided that we should both work freelance, it meant that we could live pretty much wherever we wanted to. We spent the better part of a year looking for a place where the topography was appealing, the climate was sunny and temperate, the economy was thriving, and the people were nice. We found North Carolina.

In the years since we moved here in 1983, life has been one joyful discovery about the state after another. Indeed, sometimes it seems too good to believe. Many mornings I wake up thinking: Today's the day I'm going to be disappointed. But I never am.

In 1993 my husband, Croy, died of ALS (Lou Gehrig's disease). In a way it was the happiest year of his life. Although his body deteriorated, his mind did not, so he knew and understood every day the remarkable friendship and love that our North Carolina friends, neighbors, and business associates showered upon him without restraint. The last photograph ever taken of Croy, a week before he died, shows him sitting by our pool in the sun at the edge of the woods, surrounded by his friends. The sky was Carolina blue, the people were joking, and everybody, including Croy, was laughing. He often said, "This is the most wonderful place on earth." And that day, after sharing a decade of discoveries in North Carolina, we knew it was true more than ever.

I'm making the discoveries on my own now. It tells you a lot about North Carolina that there are still lots of laughing friends around and that the experience continues to delight me.

Barbecue, Pottery, Wine

Take the barbecue, for instance. Two authors writing an article on southern barbecue for *Cook's* magazine traveled through several states looking for the best barbecue restaurants, but they were not able to get to North Carolina. They apologized in their article, because, they said, in comparison, nothing else is barbecue at all. (North Carolina barbecue is always pork cooked over a wood fire, never prepared in a sauce, and usually served with slaw and hush puppies.)

Then there's the pottery. This state has scores and scores of potters, working in the historic old production styles and in contemporary studio modes, producing such a variety of work that a collection could easily crowd everything else from a room.

Wineries are catching on, too, more opening every year, with vineyards thriving in the sunny climate.

Rich History

Historically important, North Carolina, one of the thirteen original colonies, played key roles in the Revolutionary War, the Civil War, and World Wars I and II. The area is rich in Native American history; blacks made many early significant advances here; and the Moravians created a historic settlement at Old Salem. The Wright brothers first accomplished powered flight in North Carolina, on a site that is popular today with hang gliders more interested in playing than in setting records.

The Shape of the Land

As for topography, North Carolina has some of the oldest mountains in the world, the largest natural sand dune on the East Coast, and some of the most unspoiled beaches and islands in the country. The rich soil of the Piedmont and foothills grows apples, vegetables, Christmas trees, cotton, and tobacco, a problematic crop with much historic significance.

Each of the three major geographic areas of the state—the coastal plain, the Piedmont, and the mountains—differs radically from the others. It's almost like traveling through three smaller states. The nature of each region influenced the kinds of commerce that flourished historically and that continue to flourish, and also left a mark on the people. As you travel you'll hear fascinating changes in the music of the accents of people native to each region.

The coastal plain accounts for almost two-fifths of the state's area. The North Carolina coast has been considered dangerous since the first settlers tried to cope with its ever-changing beaches, currents, and waterways. There was no guarantee that just because you had safely sailed into a particular port once, you would find it safe, or even open, the next time you tried. That's at least one reason why English colonization shifted up toward the Chesapeake and why North Carolina was settled more sparsely and slowly than some other colonies were. Even today you'll find areas that are remarkably sparsely settled compared to most states' coastal regions. For vacationers the main activities and sightseeing highlights are related to the same activities that have long supported the area economically—fishing, boating, and beachgoing.

In the Piedmont, which makes up about another two-fifths of the state, you'll find mostly rolling hills and red clay. Although the clay is harder to work than the sandy soil of the coast, it seems to have held its fertility better against some pretty bad early farming habits. (Wherever they are grown, cotton and tobacco are notorious for wearing out the soil.) Since the Piedmont doesn't have many large stretches of flat land, it didn't invite the huge plantations that had to be worked with many slaves. Smaller family farms were often worked by the people who owned them, perhaps with some hired help. The historians Hugh Talmage Lefler and Albert Ray Newsome point out in their classic *The History of a State: North Carolina* that the narrow, swift streams of the Piedmont, which weren't worth much for transportation, were great for generating power. And that, along with the presence of hardwoods and other resources, accounts for the great number of manufacturing activities that flourish in the Piedmont. Here you find lots of attractions related to manufacturing—tobacco museums, furniture showrooms, and more outlet stores than you can count. Probably because of the past concentration of moneyed manufacturers and merchants, you'll also find rich lodes of cultural attractions and arts here.

The mountains make up the smallest part of the state, but they compensate in interest and beauty for what they lack in area. Some of the highest mountains in the Appalachians are here. As anyone who drives in the mountains knows, transportation is difficult. In earlier times it was nearly impossible; hence the development of small pockets of civilization separated by stretches of wilderness, creating those tough, independent, resourceful, self-sufficient folks—mountain people. This kind of early self-sufficiency and distance from major metropolitan areas made the growth of all kinds of crafts almost inevitable. The mountains are still the richest source of handcrafts in the state.

Although tourism and technology have homogenized somewhat the state's regional populations, you can still find lots of those tall, thin, rangy people. It remains a pretty good joke in the Piedmont for a young woman marrying outside the area to claim she's found herself a mountain man.

Recreation and Travel

As a place to play, the state offers hiking and white-water rafting, waterskiing and snow skiing, freshwater and saltwater fishing and boating, athletics, auto racing, horseback riding, and golf on some of the most famous courses in the country.

Face it—you're not going to be able to do it all or see it all in one trip, or even in ten trips. Don't try to squeeze too much into a single trip, or you'll end up driving a lot and not doing much else. But the driving you do shouldn't be unpleasant if you avoid the interstates around major cities at rush hour and accept the fact that the two-lane roads tend to be well maintained but slow, since there are few good places for passing slow drivers and tractors. To understand the roads and decide when to travel on a major highway and when to get onto secondary roads, you'll definitely need a state map. The best one is the North Carolina transportation map, issued by the North Carolina Department of Transportation and the Division of Travel and Tourism (800-847-4862). You may pick one up free at a welcome center or receive it by writing to the North Carolina Division of Travel and Tourism, 430 North Salisbury Street, Raleigh 27611.

If you or those traveling with you are in any way physically challenged, you should also request a copy of the book, *Access North Carolina: A Guide to Travel Site Accessibility.* This is a remarkably good book published by the North Carolina Department of Human Resources, the Division of Vocational Rehabilitation Services, and the Division of Travel and Tourism. It briefly describes historic sites, state and national parks and forests, and general-interest attractions, focusing on their accessibility of parking, entrance, interior rooms, exterior areas, and restrooms. The book is free. Call the aforementioned tourism number, or check the Web site: http://dvr.dhhs.state.nc.us/DVR/pubs/accessnc/accessnc.htm.

More Stuff to Read

A state with so many resources inevitably becomes the subject of many books. Depending on your interests, you may find several of them useful along with this guide. The University of North Carolina Press publishes *Turners and Burners: The Folk Potters of North Carolina,* by Charles G. Zug III, the most complete explication of the subject available. The press also publishes many books about North Carolina history. For further information, write University of North Carolina Press, P.O. Box 2288, Chapel Hill 27514.

If you are a devotee of back roads, you may enjoy Earl Thollander's *Back Roads of the Carolinas,* devoted entirely to "nonhighway" drives along roads that often aren't on regular maps. Thollander designed the book, lettered the text in calligraphy, and drew the maps and wash illustrations himself. Often Thollander suggests a dirt road or other obscure route from one historic point to another, which you could use as a much, much slower alternative to the routes I suggest. It is published by Clarkson N. Potter. Finally, the North Carolina publisher John F. Blair offers several books about the history and ecology of the North Carolina coast. It's especially fun to read such books ahead of time and then carry them with you to consult, because the material comes alive as you see the subject matter firsthand.

Good People

With or without the books, though, North Carolina comes alive when you travel here because of its people. Significant history, appealing countryside, even good food can be part of any well-planned trip. Adding helpful, friendly, almost uniformly cheerful people changes the mix from plain cake to an angel food celebration. In the years I've been traveling almost continuously about the state, I've not had a single unpleasant experience with a North Carolinian. Unless you carry a chip the size of one of Mount Mitchell's ancient trees on your shoulder, you won't either. And if you're in that bad a mood, don't come. If you can't have fun in North Carolina, you can't enjoy yourself anywhere. Might as well stay home.

Rapid Growth

Maybe I shouldn't have talked so loud. Maybe I shouldn't have been so enthusiastic. Maybe I shot myself in the foot, big time, because North Carolina has been discovered. It happened fast. Not long ago the state was pretty much all off the beaten path, except for development around Raleigh and Durham, Greensboro, and, more recently, Charlotte. But within the past few years, North Carolina has become the sixth-fastest-growing state in the country, attracting people from the colder areas of the Northeast as well as many people who've decided they don't like life in Florida anymore. Housing developments and shopping malls circle not only the major cities but many of the smaller towns as well. Suddenly there's a Wendy's and a car wash at every intersection. Ever-widening highways cover great expanses that used to be woods or farmland or fishing holes with concrete and macadam. Let's face it, we're talking about sprawl here, just as it's happened, for instance, in places like parts of California; around Atlanta, Georgia; and in the Pocono Mountains of Pennsylvania. That's the bad news.

But it's the good news, too, because with the rush of growth, some people are getting worried about losing what makes this place special, and they're acting decisively to preserve some of it. Two examples come to mind at once: the little town of Hillsborough, up near the Virginia border, and the city of Salisbury at the center of the state. In places like this and in other communities, residents are emphasizing historic preservation and working to keep their downtowns vital.

NORTH CAROLINA GENERAL WEB SITES

North Carolina Division of Tourism
www.visitnc.com

African-American Heritage
www.ncculturetour.org

Golf in North Carolina
www.visitnc.com/golf

Sports in North Carolina
www.nccommerce.com/sports

North Carolina Crafts
www.discovercraftnc.org

Native American Culture
www.cherokeeheritagetrails.org

North Carolina Association of Festivals and Events
www.ncfestivals.com

North Carolina Ferry Systems
www.ncferry.org

A Changing Population

Along with this development, another new dimension has changed North Carolina—the immigration of Hispanic and Asian people as well as people from European countries, a result of the evolving global economy. Many Hispanics have come to find jobs better than those at home. They've often started out in the jobs nobody else seemed willing to do, like the hot, heavy work of making bricks and quarrying granite and cleaning shopping malls. But as their hard work pays off and their children move up in school, the Hispanic population is becoming a force in the state. Mexican restaurants and stores selling the kinds of ingredients with which Hispanics cook dot most communities, while supermarkets try to keep up with the new customers, too. Similarly, Asian immigrants have brought their influence, reflected in Thai, Vietnamese, Korean, and Chinese restaurants, even in smaller towns. Add to that the influence of transplanted Yankees with their demands for bagels and Philadelphia cheese steaks, Italians who like their prosciutto and salami, and vegetarian Muslims, and you've got the core of a surprisingly sophisticated population in an area that once consisted almost entirely of down-home Southerners. Their shops and restaurants have become part of the state and worthy of off-the-beaten-path status.

What it means is that even if you've been here before, visiting North Carolina now is a whole new experience.

NORTH CAROLINA WELCOME CENTERS

North Carolina Welcome Centers
4324 Mail Service Center
Raleigh 27699-4324
(800) 847-4862
www.nccommerce.com

Interstate 26 East
Columbus
(828) 894-2120

Interstate 26 West
Mars Hill
(828) 689-4257

Interstate 40 West
Waynesville
(828) 627-6206

Interstate 77 North
Dobson
(336) 320-2181

Interstate 77 South
Charlotte
(704) 588-2660

Interstate 85 North
Norlina
(252) 456-3236

Interstate 85 South
Kings Mountain
(704) 937-7861

Interstate 95 North
Roanoke Rapids
(252) 537-3365

Interstate 95 South
Rowland
(910) 422-8314

North Carolina has state parks and recreation areas that are visited by twelve million visitors every year. Many have camping, fishing, and hiking. Some offer special educational programs. Some are developed, while others remain wild. For full details, check the Web site: www.ncparks.gov.

North Carolina State Parks

IN THE MOUNTAINS

Burnsville
Mount Mitchell
(828) 675-4611

Connelly Springs
South Mountains
(828) 433-4772

Jefferson
Mount Jefferson State
Natural Area
(336) 246-9653

Jefferson
New River
(336) 982-2587

Nebo
Lake James
(828) 652-5047

Roaring Gap
Stone Mountain
(336) 957-8185

Sapphire
Gorges
(828) 966-9099

IN THE PIEDMONT AND SANDHILLS

Albemarle
Morrow Mountain
(704) 982-4402

Apex
Jordan Lake State
Recreation Area
(919) 362-0586

Danbury
Hanging Rock
(336) 593-8480

Durham
Eno River
(919) 383-1686

Henderson
Kerr Lake State
Recreation Area
(252) 438-7791

Hillsborough
Occoneechee
Mountain
(919) 383-1686

Hollister
Medoc Mountain
(252) 586-6588

Kings Mountain
Crowders Mountain
(704) 853-5375

Lillington
Raven Rock
(910) 893-4888

Orrum
Lumber River
(910) 628-9844

Pinnacle
Pilot Mountain
(336) 325-2355

Raleigh
William B. Umstead
Crabtree
(919) 571-4170

Raleigh
William B. Umstead
Reedy Creek
(919) 571-4170

Seven Springs
Cliffs of the Neuse
(919) 778-6234

Southern Pines
Weymouth Woods
(910) 692-2167

Troutman
Lake Norman
(704) 528-6350

Wake Forest
Falls Lake State
Recreation Area
(919) 676-1027

AT THE COAST

Atlantic Beach
Fort Macon
(252) 726-3775

Carolina Beach
Carolina Beach
(910) 458-8206

Creswell
Pettigrew
(252) 797-4475

Elizabethtown
Jones Lake
(910) 588-4550

Gatesville
Merchants Millpond
(252) 357-1191

Kelly
Singletary Lake
(910) 669-2928

Kure Beach
Fort Fisher State
Recreation Area
(910) 458-5798

Lake Waccamaw
Lake Waccamaw
(910) 646-4748

Nags Head
Jockey's Ridge
(252) 441-7132

Pine Knoll Shores
Theodore Roosevelt
Natural Area
(252) 726-3775

Swansboro
Hammocks Beach
(910) 326-4881

Washington
Goose Creek
(252) 923-2191

Wineries

The wine industry in North Carolina has taken off. Every year more wineries open across the state, often in remote places, as grapes begin to replace tobacco as a crop, and cotton mills as businesses. Many of the wines produced are sweet, from scuppernong and other muscadine grapes, which have historically done well here. But growers and vintners are also beginning to make such dry wines as cabernet sauvignon and pinot grigio, as well as such specialties as blueberry wine. Some of the wines are available in grocery stores and wine shops; others are sold mainly out of the winery's shop, often at the vineyard. Wine tours and tastings are becoming an increasingly popular activity (www.visitncwine.com).

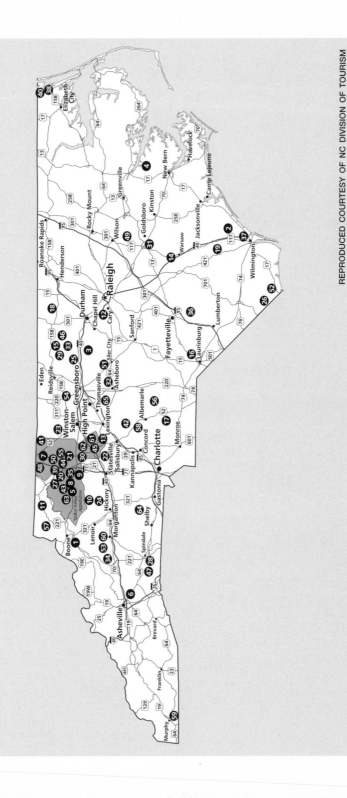

Wineries in North Carolina

Numbers correspond to map on page xvii.

Banner Elk Winery (1)
Banner Elk, NC
(828) 260-1790
www.bannerelkwinery.com

Bannerman Vineyard (2)
Burgaw, NC
(910) 259-5474
www.bannermanvineyard
.com

Benjamin Vineyards & Winery (3)
Graham, NC
(336) 376-1080
www.benjaminvineyards
.com

Bennett Vineyards (4)
Edward, NC
(877) 762-9463
www.ncwines.com

Benny Parsons Rendezvous Ridge (5)
Wilkesboro, NC
(336) 973-7375
www.rendezvousridge.com

Biltmore Estate Wine Company (6)
Asheville, NC
(800) 624-1575
www.biltmore.com

Black Wolf Vineyards (7)
Dobson, NC
(336) 374-2532
www.blackwolfvineyards
.com

Brushy Mountain Winery (8)
Elkin, NC
(336) 835-1313
www.brushymountainwine
.com

Buck Shoals Vineyard (9)
Hamptonville, NC
(336) 468-9274
www.buckshoalsvineyard
.com

Cerminaro Vineyard (10)
Boomer, NC
(828) 754-9306
www.cerminarovineyard
.com

Chateau Laurinda (11)
Sparta, NC
(800) 650-3236
chateaulaurindavineyards
.com

Chatham Hill Winery (12)
Morrisville, NC
(800) 808-6768
www.chathamhillwine.com

Childress Vineyards (13)
Lexington, NC
(336) 236-9463
www.childressvineyards
.com

Country Squire Winery (14)
Warsaw, NC
(910) 296-1727
www.countrysquirewinery
.com

Creek Side Winery (15)
Elon, NC
(336) 584-4117
www.creeksidewinery.com

Cypress Bend Vineyards (16)
Wagram, NC
(910) 369-0411
www.cypressbend
vineyards.com

Dennis Vineyards (17)
Albemarle, NC
(800) 230-1743
www.dennisvineyards.com

Desi's Dew Meadery (18)
Rougemont, NC
(919) 632-4770
www.desidew.com

Duplin Winery (19)
Rose Hill, NC
(800) 774-9634
www.duplinwinery.com

Elkin Creek Vineyard (20)
Elkin, NC
(336) 526-5119
www.elkincreekvineyard
.com

Flint Hill Vineyards (21)
East Bend, NC
(336) 699-4455
www.flinthillvineyards.com

Garden Gate Vineyards (22)
Mocksville, NC
(336) 751-3794
www.gardengatevineyards
.com

Germanton Vineyard & Winery (23)
Germanton, NC
(336) 969-2075
www.germantongallery
.com

Ginger Creek Vineyards (24)
Taylorsville, NC
(828) 312-4362

Glen Marie Vineyards & Winery (25)
Burlington, NC
(336) 578-3938
www.glenmariewinery.com

Grapefull Sisters Vineyard (26)
Tabor City, NC
(910) 653-2944
www.grapefullsisters
vineyard.com

Grassy Creek Vineyard & Winery (27)
State Road, NC
(336) 835-4230
www.grassycreekvineyard
.com

Green Creek Winery (28)
Columbus, NC
(828) 863-2182
www.greencreekwinery
.com

Grove Winery (29)
Osceola, NC
(336) 584-4060
www.grovewinery.com

Hanover Park Vineyard (30)
Yadkinville, NC
(336) 463-2875
www.hanoverparkwines
.com

Hinnant Family Vineyards (31)
Pine Level, NC
(919) 965-3350
www.hinnantvineyards.com

Horizon Cellars (32)
Siler City, NC
(919) 742-1404
www.horizoncellars.com

Iron Gate Vineyards & Winery (33)
Mebane, NC
(919) 304-9463
www.irongatevineyards
.com

Lake James Cellars (34)
Glen Alpine, NC
(828) 584-4551
www.lakejamescellars.com

Laurel Gray Vineyards (35)
Hamptonville, NC
(336) GOT-WINE
www.laurelgray.com

LuMil Vineyard (36)
Dublin, NC
(800) 545-2293
www.taylormfg.com

Lumina Winery (37)
Wilmington, NC
(910) 793-5299
www.luminawine.com

Martin Vineyards (38)
Knotts Island, NC
(252) 429-3542
www.martinvineyards
.com

McRitchie Winery & Ciderworks (39)
Thurmond, NC
(336) 874-3003
www.mcritchiewine.com

Moonrise Bay Vineyard (40)
Knotts Island, NC
(866) 888-9463
www.moonrisebaywine
.com

Old North State Winery (41)
Mt. Airy, NC
(336) 789-WINE
www.oldnorthstatewinery
.com

Old Stone Vineyard & Winery (42)
Salisbury, NC
(704) 279-0930
www.osvwinery.com

Raffaldini Vineyards (43)
Ronda, NC
(336) 835-9463
www.raffaldini.com

RagApple Lassie Vineyards (44)
Boonville, NC
(866) RAGAPPLE
www.ragapplelassie.com

RayLen Vineyards & Winery (45)
Mocksville, NC
(336) 998-3100
www.raylenvineyards.com

Rock of Ages Winery & Vineyard (46)
Hurdle Mills, NC
(336) 364-7625
www.rockofageswinery
.com

Rockhouse Vineyards (47)
Tryon, NC
(828) 863-2784
www.rockhousevineyards
.com

Round Peak Vineyards (48)
Mt. Airy, NC
(336) 352-5595
www.roundpeak.com

A Secret Garden Winery (49)
Pikeville, NC
(919) 734-0260
www.asecretgardenwinery
.com

Shelton Vineyards (50)
Dobson, NC
(336) 366-4724
www.sheltonvineyards.com

SilkHope Winery (51)
Pittsboro, NC
(919) 742-4601
www.silkhopewinery.com

Silver Coast Winery (52)
Ocean Isle Beach, NC
(910) 287-2800
www.silvercoastwinery.com

South Creek Vineyards & Winery (53)
Nebo, NC
(828) 652-5729
www.southcreekwinery
.com

**Stonefield Cellars
Winery (54)**
Stokesdale, NC
(336) 644-9908
www.stonefieldcellars.com

**Stony Knoll
Vineyards (55)**
Dobson, NC
(336) 374-5752
www.stonyknollvineyards
.com

**Stony Mountain
Vineyards (56)**
Albemarle, NC
(704) 982-0922
www.stonymountain
vineyards.com

**Thistle Meadow
Winery (57)**
Laurel Springs, NC
(800) 233-1505
www.thistlemeadowwinery
.com

Uwharrie Vineyards (58)
Albemarle, NC
(704) 982-WINE
www.uwharrievineyards
.com

**Valley River
Vineyards (59)**
Murphy, NC
(828) 321-5333

**Waldensian Heritage
Wines (60)**
Valdese, NC
(828) 879-3202
www.waldensian
heritagewines.com

Weathervane Winery (61)
Winston-Salem, NC
(336) 775-9717
www.weathervanewinery
.com

Westbend Vineyards (62)
Lewisville, NC
(336) 945-5032
www.westbendvineyards
.com

Windy Gap Vineyards (63)
Ronda, NC
(336) 984-3926
www.windygapwine.com

Woodmill Winery (64)
Vale, NC
(704) 276-2288
www.woodmillwinery.com

**Zimmerman Vineyards
(65)**
Trinity, NC
(336) 861-1414
www.zimmermanvineyards
.net

The Southern Coast and Islands

Along the Grand Strand

Like most of this country's coastal areas, the beaches of North Carolina attract plenty of tourists, but some have so far managed to avoid the near honky-tonk atmosphere of the better-known places such as Myrtle Beach, just below the North Carolina–South Carolina border.

Close enough to the border to confuse anyone who misses the North Carolina Welcome Center on U.S. Highway 17, the community of **Calabash** has been known for generations as the "Seafood Capital of the World." In the early years, a couple of families in what was just a fishing village set up tents and later enclosed buildings to sell the local catch, cooked "Calabash style." That meant then, and still means today, seafood very lightly battered and fried, almost like tempura. The stuff has become wildly popular in the area, and though the town now has all kinds of restaurants and tourist shops, you can still order Calabash-style seafood in many restaurants. One that's been around since the 1950s is *Ella's of Calabash,* at 1148 River Road (910-579-6728), open every day but Christmas from 11:00 a.m. to 9:00 p.m.

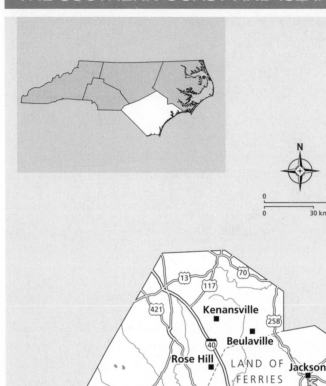

N

0 — 30 mi
0 — 30 km

Kenansville

Beulaville

Rose Hill

LAND OF
FERRIES
AND FORTS

Jacksonville

S. Black R.

Whiteville

Wilmington

ALONG THE
GRAND
STRAND

HWY
17

N. CAROLINA
S. CAROLINA

ATLANTIC
OCEAN

Southport

Calabash

Ocean Isle
Beach

Sunset
Beach

SOUTH
BRUNSWICK
ISLANDS

ANNUAL EVENTS IN THE SOUTHERN COAST AND ISLANDS

**Holden Beach
Day at the Docks**
(late March)
(910) 842-3828

**Nags Head
Nags Head Independence Day
Fireworks**
(252) 441-5508

**Ocean Isle Beach
Annual N.C. Oyster Festival**
(mid-October)
(800) 426-6644

**Shallote Point
Annual Flounder Tournament**
(early June)
(910) 579-3757

**Southport
N.C. Fourth of July Festival**
www.nc4thofjuly.com

**Wilmington
Riverfest**
(early October)
(910) 452-6862
www.wilmingtonriverfest.com

N.C. Azalea Festival
(early March)
(910) 754-7177

In addition to fried fish, some Calabash restaurants offer an oyster roast, which is a huge kettle full of oysters steamed just until they open, a shucking knife to prod the oysters from their shells, a bowl of the steaming broth, a dish of melted butter, a roll of paper towels, and a wastebasket for your discarded shells. These are rock oysters, not the kind you get when you order oysters on the half shell—neatly arranged on a bed of ice. Rock oysters come in clumps, with large, medium, and small oysters all stuck together. Eating them, you usually just skip those no bigger than your thumbnail, start with the largest ones first and work your way down to the smaller ones. It's messy and fun and good, if you like oysters.

As Calabash has grown, a variety of other restaurants have moved in, offering everything from German to Italian cuisine. Some of them make it, some don't. But your true local experience is in an older seafood restaurant.

In summer Calabash is busy, attracting tourists from Myrtle Beach as well as from the beaches to the north, so the best time to visit is in the slower seasons.

goodnight,jimmy

If you're old enough to remember Jimmy Durante, you may recall that he started closing his radio and TV shows by saying, "Good night, Mrs. Calabash, wherever you are." Local people swear it's because he ate in Calabash and liked it so much that he acknowledged it with those words for Mrs. Calabash, whoever she was.

Talkin' the Talk

In North Carolina what we say is sometimes just the opposite of what we mean, but other North Carolinians get the point. For instance, when a comment begins, "Bless his heart" or "Bless her heart," it sounds as if you're about to say something nice, but it's actually a signal that what's coming next is critical: "Bless his heart, his elevator doesn't go all the way to the top." Or "Bless her heart, she can't even boil water in a microwave." On the other hand, we show affection with the seemingly negative statement, "She's a mess." Or, even more affectionately, "She's a real mess."

And when someone says something with which we agree, we don't say so. Instead we say, "You got that right."

It all makes perfect sense. You just have to know the code.

The South Brunswick Islands

Driving north on US 17 just over 10 miles takes you to the beginning of the South Brunswick Islands. Sunset Beach, Ocean Isle Beach, and Holden Beach differ from one another as much as the siblings in most families. Part of the chain of barrier islands off the coast that stretches both north and south, the South Brunswick Islands have no boardwalks and relatively little commercial development except for beach houses and a few small grocery stores.

In the fall of 1989, Hurricane Hugo accentuated an interesting phenomenon along Holden Beach, Ocean Isle Beach, and Sunset Beach. The hurricane didn't do any more damage than any good storm does, breaking up some docks, flooding some first-floor rooms in cabins, and lifting off a piece of roof here and there. But it changed the beaches, hastening an erosion process that was already obvious, moving sand and dunes from the east and depositing them farther west. As more storms have hit the area, the changes continue. This means that beachfront at Holden Beach grows noticeably more narrow with each storm, as does the east end of Ocean Isle's beachfront, leading to such black-humor jokes as the one suggesting that the way to get cheap oceanfront property here is to buy third row and wait. Meanwhile, the beaches on the west end of Ocean Isle Beach and those on Sunset Beach are growing visibly broader. It takes regular dredging to keep the waterway between Ocean Isle Beach and Sunset Beach open because the currents continue to dump sand there. Beaches have broadened so much at Sunset Beach that when you stand at water's edge, you can't see the first-row cottages behind the dunes. It sounds like good, forward-thinking planning; actually, it's nature.

AUTHOR'S FAVORITE PLACES IN THE SOUTHERN COAST AND ISLANDS

Sunset Beach	Historic Wilmington District
Southport	Poplar Grove Plantation
Orton Plantation Gardens	Cedar Point

This shifting creates some problems for developers and homeowners but does not in any way spoil the pleasure of visiting any of the islands. Indeed, if you're interested in the ecology of coastlines, try to find a copy of *The Beaches Are Moving* by Wallace Kaufman and Orrin H. Pilkey Jr., published by Duke University Press in 1979. The book is rich in historical data and information about how tides, storms, and so on work. Even though it focuses on beaches along both the east and west coasts and doesn't talk specifically about the South Brunswick Islands, it describes, explains, and predicts coastline activity. Browsing through the book while you stay in the South Brunswick Islands is like having your very own little nature model to study as you read. It's great fun and genuinely instructive.

Access to **Sunset Beach** still depends on a one-lane swing bridge across the Intracoastal Waterway. A swing bridge differs from a drawbridge in that the movable part of the bridge swings to the side rather than lifting up to allow tall ships to pass under. It's rare in these times. It's also threatened. Developers have plans to replace it with a higher, modern bridge that would accommodate more and faster traffic. However, at the time of this update, nobody seems to have any idea when that might happen. So for at least the immediate future, this is a place with only a few paved roads and sidewalks, no high-rise condos, and no pink giraffes, waterslides, or beachfront grills. What the island does have is glorious, wide, flat beaches and clean white sand. From most of the beach area, you can't see any buildings at all. The beach homes, most of which are available for rent, sit hidden behind the dunes.

Just south of Sunset Beach, by water, not by road, lies **Bird Island.** It is one of the last undeveloped, privately owned barrier islands on the East Coast. It is a popular place for birding and just spending time in a spot that people have not managed to change. It used to be that the only way to get to that island was to swim, take a boat, or wade across at low tide, making sure to get back to Sunset before high tide. That has changed with recent storms, and now you can walk across any time, regardless of the tide, on sand that's been deposited here.

Spanish Moss

Not Spanish. Not moss. This gray-green epiphyte thrives almost anywhere in the South where warm air and high humidity are present.

Legend has it that an Indian princess cut her hair on her wedding day, as was traditional, and hung it over an oak tree. But the newlyweds were killed the day they married and buried under the same oak. The princess's hair turned gray, started to grow, and has been spreading among the trees ever since.

Southerners have been trying to figure out a use for Spanish moss for generations. In Louisiana it was used to stuff mattresses in the 1800s. Those that survive are decidedly stiff and crinkly. More recently it's been bagged as a decorative item for florists, but it's only pretty as long as it's exposed to moisture in the air. Take it inland and it turns gray and brittle and crumbles.

My college roommate, back in my Pennsylvania days, kept a bunch, tied with pink ribbon, hanging on a nozzle in the shower room. It did very well there until somebody stole it.

If you want to take Spanish moss home with you, keep it damp as you travel. At home, hang it in a steamy place, such as a shower stall.

On Sunset Island, *The Sunset Inn,* 9 North Shore Drive (910-575-1000 or toll-free 888-575-1001; www.thesunsetinn.net), is one place to stay where the innkeepers, Dave Nelson and Andrea Price, fully appreciate the beauty of the island and have taken maximum advantage of it. This fourteen-room inn has the comfort of new construction with the relaxed feeling of an old style. Except for rental houses and an older motel, it is the only place to stay on Sunset Beach, and the location is prime, with views of the salt marsh and the Intracoastal Waterway. Just a few steps take you to the ocean. One of the most popular rooms in the house is the Bird Island room.

Because Sunset Beach is not heavily developed, it has an air of calm and closeness to nature that has long since been lost from other beaches in the area. The Sunset Inn not only fits in quietly, but it also helps to prevent inappropriate kinds of development by occupying commercial space that otherwise might have gone to waterslides or souvenir shops. Each room has a private bath, TV, small refrigerator, wet bar, and private screened porch. Andrea Price emphasizes that it is not "kid-friendly."

More appropriate for families with children, the houses on the island can be rented through *Sunset Properties,* 419 South Sunset Boulevard (919-579-9900 or toll-free 888-339-2670; www.sunsetbeachnc.com); or *Sunset Vacations,* 401 Sunset Boulevard (910-579-5400 or toll-free 800-331-6428; www.sunsetvacations.com).

The next island north is ***Ocean Isle Beach.*** To get there, drive north on US 17 about 5 miles and turn right onto Highway 179 South, which takes you directly to the Odell Williamson Bridge, across the Intracoastal Waterway. This island is more fully developed, with sidewalks, all paved roads, some cluster homes on the west end, and more traditional beach homes on the east end. Also on the east end, a series of paved and natural canals, where homes have docks, can accommodate boats or just provide pleasant off-ocean outdoor lounging space. Some people live on the island year-round, but many of the accommodations are used by the owners part of the year and rented to vacationers the rest of the time. You can arrange to rent a place to stay through several agencies, each handling different properties. Three of these are: ***Cooke Realtors,*** 1 Causeway Drive (910-579-3535 or toll-free 800-622-3224; www .cookerealty.com); ***R. H. McClure Realty, Inc.,*** 24 Causeway Drive SW (910-579-3586; www.rhmcclurerealty.com); and ***Williamson Realty,*** 119 Causeway Drive (910-579-2373 or toll-free 800-727-9222; www.williamsonrealty.com). The private homes are mingled among those used strictly for vacation and rental. It's a nice mix, and especially if you do not stay in beachfront properties, you can learn a lot about the island from local people and form friendships that continue past your visit. In recent years the relatively new ***Museum of Coastal Carolina,*** 21 East Second Street (910-579-1016; www.museumofcc.org), has attracted vacationing children and school groups. The museum of natural history concentrates on the Carolina coast, with dioramas and Civil War artifacts, as well as Native American artifacts and a fine collection of seashells and fossils. The museum is open from 9:00 a.m. to 5:00 p.m. Friday and Saturday, 1:00 to 5:00 p.m. Sunday. The hours are shorter in the off-season. Admission is $8 for adults, $6 for senior citizens and students, $4 for children ages three to five.

A Little Beach Music and a Seaside Shuffle

The Shag is a dance popular along the coast with origins going back at least to the 1940s, with a surge in popularity at Carolina beaches in the 1960s. Today it's a popular recreation all along the coast. Depending on their state loyalties, shaggers pinpoint either Atlantic Beach, North Carolina, or Myrtle Beach, South Carolina, which is barely an hour from the North Carolina–South Carolina border, as a place where shagging really got going. The music to which one shags ranges from old-time swing to the twist. Shaggers now take lessons, join clubs, and maintain Web sites. If you're interested in the history and how-to, a good place to start is www.beachshag.com, but some native Carolinians simplify it: "Just imagine that you're dancing barefoot in the sand with a beer in one hand, kick back, and have a good time."

Ocean Isle Inn, 37 West First Street (800-352-5988; www.oceanisleinn .com), has seventy rooms on the waterfront. Facilities include an outdoor swimming pool and sundeck, an indoor heated pool and hot tub, and the use of boats, rafts, and canoes. The inn serves a complimentary continental breakfast.

Standing on the west end of Ocean Isle Beach, you can see Sunset Beach. It looks close enough to wade to, which old-timers remember doing before erosion and currents changed the shape of the islands. Standing on the east end of Ocean Isle Beach, you see ***Holden Beach,*** also seeming almost close enough to wade to. Without a boat, though, getting to Holden Beach requires a drive of about fifteen minutes. Richard Mubel once wrote for the *Brunswick Magazine* that Holden is a place where "old meets new, where tradition bisects progress and where history intersects the path of the future." He's talking about the contrasts between the back side of the island, along the Atlantic Intracoastal Waterway and the Lockwood Folly River Inlet, and the oceanfront. Shrimpers and anglers descended from families who settled the area still work along the waterway and inlet, as well as in the open sea, but the oceanfront is strictly a vacationland of white beaches and summer cottages. Holden is a family beach, not a party beach, with between 8 and 9 miles of oceanfront sand. One of its notable features is that it is a sea-turtle nesting place and a bird habitat, and when it comes to nightlife, you can stay up late during hatching season, May through October, to watch the tiny turtles come up out of the sand and head for the ocean. Most people who come here stay either in cottages or condos. For information about rental agencies, of which there are

Heads Up! Heads On!

If you've never seen shrimp with their heads and legs on, you're in for a surprise, because they look like squirmy, swimming critters, not the neat, pink C-shaped bits surrounding a cup of cocktail sauce.

Local shrimpers sell some of their catch by the sides of most of the roads in the coastal area. They may set up in a crude shelter or off the back of a truck or simply sit there in lawn chairs. They keep the shrimp iced down in coolers.

When you buy shrimp this way, the price per pound is lower than in markets because the shrimp still have their heads on. They seem so loosely attached you can't help but marvel that they haven't come off during some underwater activity! You can pop the heads off easily.

If you have any worries about the freshness of the shrimp, just ask to smell them. If they smell briny, they're fine. If you catch a whiff of ammonia (which has never happened to me at a roadside stand), don't buy them.

A Birdie at the Beach

Sand makes great beaches. It also makes devilish sand traps. It takes another golfing enthusiast to understand why you'd go to the beach and spend the time playing golf, but if you do, you'll be in good company. New golf courses spring up faster than dandelions.

North Carolina has approximately 600 golf courses dotted across the state, designed by such masters as Donald Ross, Tom Fazio, Arnold Palmer, Rees Jones, and Jack Nicklaus.

North Carolina golf courses have hosted the Ryder Cup, the U.S. Open, the U.S. Senior Open, the U.S. Women's Open, and regular PGA tour events.

For a free copy of the *North Carolina Golf Guide,* a comprehensive listing of courses in the state, call (800) VISIT-NC or check the Web site: www.visitncgolf.com.

many, visit www.hbtownhall.com. One well-known agency is *Alan Holden Vacations,* 128 Ocean Boulevard West (910-842-6061 or toll-free 800-720-2200; www.holden-beach.com).

Campgrounds also serve the island: *Green Oaks Campground,* 3342 Holden Beach Road SW, (910) 842-2844; and *Holden Beach Pier Campground,* 441 Ocean Boulevard West, (910) 842-6483.

If you enjoy local festivals and if you lo-o-o-o-ve seafood, try to schedule your Brunswick Islands trip for the third weekend in October, during the annual *North Carolina Oyster Festival.* This festival began as a small oyster roast in the late 1970s. Every year the party got a little better, and in three years got itself proclaimed the official oyster festival of North Carolina. It takes a couple hundred community volunteers to run the event, which now includes a beach run, a bullshooting (tall-tale-telling) contest, and the North Carolina Oyster Shucking Championship. This contest is no small potatoes. It has produced not only a national oyster shucking champion but also the top female oyster shucker in the world. With all that shucking going on, it stands to reason somebody's got to be doing some eating. That's where you come in. Steamed oysters, fried oysters, oysters on the half shell, boiled shrimp, fried flounder, and of course the ubiquitous hush puppies are available in abundance. In addition to the food and contests, the festival features two days of live music that includes beach music (shag), top forty, country and western, and gospel. Also artists and craftspeople display their wares for sale. For further details and firm dates in any year, call (800) 426-6644; www.ncbrunswick.com.

From the Ocean Isle Beach area, if you drive north for about an hour or less on Highway 130 to U.S. Highway 701, you'll come to *Whiteville.* At 101

Let's Pedal!

Ocean Isle Beach is a great place to take your bicycle. The streets are paved, which makes for easy riding, and traffic is heavy only during the standard coming and leaving day, Saturday. The island is about 12 miles long, end to end, a nice ride on nearly flat planes. It's also fun to ride up and down the canal streets, looking at the houses and their kitschy names. My favorite for years was THE STONED CRAB. The house had a picture of an out-of-kilter crab with a silly grin. New owners, with a less 1970s sense of humor, painted out the letter "d," and now the house is just THE STONE CRAB.

You'll find several places where you can take a bike down onto the beach, too. Riding there is good at low tide, when the sand is damp and hard. Sand that the water doesn't reach, even at high tide, is soft and hard to manage, better for walking. For a perfect early-morning workout, you can ride on the beach, then park the bike and walk for a while.

North Madison Street, ***The Madison House*** (910-640-2132; www.whiteville nc.com/madison house) is the only bed-and-breakfast in town. Innkeeper Yvonne Ellis says The Madison House and Whiteville are the best-kept secrets in North Carolina. She'd like that to change. Yvonne, who was born here, says Whiteville, the county seat of Columbus County, has small-town ambience and city sophistication. Unfortunately, many people know it only as a town they pass on US 701 on the way to the beach, but the area has enough natural attractions to warrant staying for a while, including Lake Waccamaw, the Lumber River, and the ***North Carolina Museum of Forestry*** (910-914-4185; www.naturalsciences.org). The Madison House is a beauty—a Victorian of nearly 7,000 square feet, it features a fireplace in the parlor and two kitchens, one of which is a full commercial kitchen. Yvonne and her husband, Jack, have a background in the restaurant business. In addition to preparing breakfasts, they cater special events, and often can provide not only breakfast but also dinner for their guests.

Jack Ellis has a passion for restoring old cars, which fascinates some guests and sometimes becomes part of the inn's service, providing special transportation for a special occasion. The inn has five rooms, furnished in understated elegance with antiques and warm colors. Three have private baths, while two share a bath, and each has wireless Internet access. There's also an outdoor swimming pool. Jack and Yvonne ended up with this house in September 2001 because the people who were selling specifically wanted them to have it. "It was perfect," Yvonne says. "All we had to do was move in." So the Ellises are happy; Yvonne thinks their guests are too. "If they're not happy, they're fooling us."

Highway 17

The Brunswick Isles are served by businesses in the town of *Shallotte,* a few miles inland on US 17. This is the place to stop when you need to do laundry or pick up a bicycle pump from the hardware store or get a prescription filled in a good-size pharmacy. From Shallotte, driving north on US 17 brings you to *Southport,* on the western bank of the Cape Fear River where the river joins the Atlantic Ocean. The harbor accommodates yachts, charter boats, and fishing piers. The town, rich in military and maritime history, was first called Smithville after Benjamin Smith, who became governor of North Carolina, but in 1887 the name was changed to Southport. To get into town from US 17, turn right onto Highway 211. Shortly you'll be driving into what is obviously still a real fishing village with stores and gas stations and marinas, although growing numbers of tourist-oriented shops are opening. Many of the homes in Southport are listed on the National Register of Historic Places. The old twelve-bed *Fort Johnston Hospital,* dating back to about 1852, has been moved and turned into a private residence; the *Old Brunswick Jail,* dating back to the early 1900s, now houses the Southport Historical Society. In *Keziah Memorial Park* you'll find a tree that the Cape Fear Indians bent over as a marker when it was just a sapling. It may be more than 800 years old. Half a century ago children could crawl under its arch.

The *A. E. Stevens House,* circa 1894, is noted as the home built for Mr. Stevens and his betrothed. She changed her mind and married his best friend. They built a house across from Mr. Stevens, who remained a bachelor the rest of his life. There's lots more, equally human and interesting, all mapped out on a 1-mile, self-guided walking tour called *Southport Trail.* You'll find a nice assortment of restaurants, antiques shops, and specialty stores in the area, too. Their names and sometimes their proprietors may change from year to year, but they're always fun. A shopping guide with a map, as well as the free self-guided walking-tour brochure of Southport's historic sites, is available

BETTER-KNOWN ATTRACTIONS IN THE SOUTHERN COAST AND ISLANDS

Wilmington
Battleship *North Carolina*
(910) 251-5797

Cape Fear Museum
(910) 798-4350

Cape Fear Coastal Beaches
Wrightsville, Carolina, Kure
(800) 222-4757;
www.capefear.nc.us

at the visitor center, 113 West Moore Street. Hours vary seasonally. Call (800) 388-9635; www.cityofsouthport.com.

Southport used to be the special province of people with boats and people who fish. Even those who docked their boats in Southport and lived inland didn't expect much in the way of elaborate accommodations or shopping. This is all changing—that's the good news *and* the bad news. As specialty shops and antiques shops open, more tourists come in, making the place not quite so off-the-beaten-path as it used to be. But the good news is that you can find more places to stay and eat.

Lois Jane's Riverview Inn (106 West Bay Street; 800-457-1152; www.loisjanes.com) is a small bed-and-breakfast in an 1891 home that is owned and operated by fourth-generation direct descendants of the builder. Although it was carefully restored in 1995, the house retains much of its original character and furniture. One of the guest rooms, called "Lois Jane's Room," is furnished and decorated exactly as she kept it in her lifetime, right down to a collection of Wedgwood plates on the wall. Guests gather around a table in the crimson dining room to share breakfast and conversation. The inn is directly across from the river.

Another small B&B is *The Brunswick Inn Bed and Breakfast* (301 East Bay Street; 910-457-5278; www.brunswickinn.com). Here you'll stay in spacious rooms in a Federal-style mansion dating back to about 1896. The place has wonderful views of the water, and each room has a working fireplace. A home-cooked gourmet breakfast is included in your daily room rate.

And for a special occasion, you can book a *"Boat and Breakfast"* stay aboard the **Stephania** sailboat. You don't actually have to sail anywhere. The boat is docked while you sleep, and breakfast prepared at a local restaurant is delivered to you in the morning. When the 37-foot, twin-cabin boat isn't being used for an overnight interlude, you can book it for morning, afternoon, sunset, and moonlight sails. You can also book an overnight stay in combination with a morning or evening sail. No morning cruise is scheduled for the day after a B&B booking. When you do sail, you'll be encouraged to take the helm for a picture of yourself in position. Jay Harvey is captain and his wife, Jackie, is admiral, but she says that's just another word for gofer. Check the *Stephania*'s Web site: www.windsofcarolina.com. To make reservations or book a sail, call (910) 278-7249 or (910) 232-3003.

The 38-foot sloop **Endless Summer** also takes cruises from Southport. Call (910) 253-0531 to make arrangements.

Another popular excursion from Southport takes you to *Bald Head Island* by private ferry. Only a couple hundred people live here, and future plans for the island call for tightly limited new construction. The first lighthouse in North

Carolina was built on this island. ***Old Baldy Lighthouse and Smith House Museum*** (910-457-5003; www.baldheadisland.com) commemorate the island's history. The most notable aspect of the island now is that no motor vehicles are allowed, which means you move about in golf carts, or on bicycles, or you walk. Overnight accommodations on the island include ***Marsh Harbour Inn*** (21 Keelson Row; 910-454-0451 or 800-680-3322; www.marshharbourinn.com) with fifteen rooms; and ***Theodosia's Bed and Breakfast*** (2 Keelson Row; 910-457-6563 or 800-656-1812; www.theodosias.com), of similar size.

Tours of the island and its museum, complete with lunch, originate at Southport. For details call (910) 457-5003.

North of Southport via Highway 133, ***Brunswick Town State Historic Site*** marks the first settlement in the Cape Fear area. Here you can study the remains of the colonial port town of Brunswick and the earth mounds of Fort Anderson that the Confederate Army built about one hundred years later. Some of the old foundations have been excavated and are uncovered as archaeological exhibits. The mounds have survived pretty much intact since the Civil War and actually make a good spot from which to see the older ruins. A visitor center on the site has slide presentations and exhibits about the colonial town and the artifacts excavated from the ruins. This is one of those well-managed sites where you can learn about both colonial life and the Civil War and get a sense of the continuity from one time to the other. Brunswick Town is open Tuesday through Saturday 9:00 a.m. to 5:00 p.m. (910-371-6613). Admission is free.

About 10 miles north of Southport, still on Highway 133, you come to ***Orton Plantation Gardens,*** a delight for anyone who loves flowers and grand old trees. The first owners were James and Luola Sprunk, who built terraces and ornamental gardens with live oaks lining the walkways. Later, with the help of a landscape architect, additional gardens and water features were added, and the gardens were opened to the public. Blooms extend over a long season, beginning with camellias in late winter; azaleas in spring; oleander, crape myrtle, and magnolias in summer and fall. Plantings of annuals add extra splashes of color. Orton House, a good example of Southern antebellum architecture, is an impressive feature on the property, too, but it is a private residence, so you must content yourself with admiring the exterior and visiting the small family chapel that is open to the public. The gardens are open daily March through August from 8:00 a.m. to 6:00 p.m., September and November from 10:00 a.m. to 5:00 p.m. Admission is $9 for adults, $8 for senior citizens, and $3 for children (910-371-6851; www.ortongardens.com).

After this, the easiest thing to do is return to US 17 to drive on up to ***Wilmington.*** People who live here call Wilmington the best-kept secret in North Carolina. They're of two minds as to whether that's good or bad. The thriving, historic community has a full share of entrepreneurial types who've done much to revitalize waterfront areas and old downtown buildings. They welcome tourists and new businesses. Some of the old-timers would rather the community's cultural and historical attractions not become too well known, lest all the new traffic spoil the ambience.

In 1989 Wilmington, which was settled before the Revolutionary War and was the last Atlantic port open to blockade runners during the Civil War, celebrated its 250th anniversary.

There are two buildings in the area worth seeing inside. The beautifully restored *1770 Burgwin-Wright House* (910-762-0570; www.burgwinwright house.com) stands at the corner of Third and Market Streets. It was built in 1770 on the foundation of the abandoned Wilmington City Jail. One reason the owner chose this site and kept the foundation was because it had a tunnel running down to the water, so he could get to the boats without going outside. Open Tuesday through Saturday 10:00 a.m. to 4:00 p.m. Closed on major holidays. Admission is $8 for adults, $4 for full-time students. The *Zebulon Latimer House* (910-762-0492; www.latimerhouse.org) at 126 South Third Street is one of the few remaining examples of a town house of the time. The same family inhabited it from its completion in 1852 until the historical society took it over in the 1960s. About 60 percent of the furnishings are the family's original belongings. Three of the four floors are open, so you can see everything from beds to china. The house also has archives and a library for those who want to study further, with a researcher available on Tuesday and Thursday. The house is open Monday through Friday from 10:00 a.m. to 4:00 p.m., Saturday from noon to 5:00 p.m. Closed on major holidays. Admission is $8 for adults, $4 for full-time students.

Both the Burgwin-Wright House and the Zebulon Latimer House have gardens, largely maintained by volunteers, within the confines of their original brick, masonry, and stucco walls, planted with flora that would have been typical of the area and such homes in the 1800s.

Another pleasant way to see the Wilmington District is to take a *Springbrook Farms* sightseeing tour (910-251-8889; www.horsedrawntours .com) by horse-drawn carriage, with a costumed driver who narrates as you pass the historic sites. At Christmas a nice touch is that you ride in a closed reindeer-drawn carriage, snuggled in a lap rug, for a tour narrated by Santa. Tours leave from the corner of Water and Market Streets. Hours vary with the season, weather, and day of the week. To plan a tour, call ahead. If no one is there, you can still learn current tour hours by listening to a recording. Sometimes tours may be arranged for different times by appointment. Rates are $11 for adults, $5 for children under twelve.

The Daughters of the Confederacy are responsible for creating the oldest history museum in the state. In 1898 they announced their intention to establish a "creditable museum of confederate relics." The **Cape Fear Museum of History and Science** was the result. For years it was moved from place to place, looking for a home. Since 1992 it's been housed in a large structure built just for the museum at 814 Market Street.

Not all the exhibits are about the Civil War. One comes from a tad before the Civil War—the reproduction of the 20-foot-long Wilmington ground sloth, believed to have lived one and a half million years ago. The creature had fur and hand-shaped appendages with claws, and it stood 15 feet tall. The original was found during construction on a dam basin at Randall Parkway, Wilmington, in 1991. The state gave the original to the North Carolina Museum of Natural Sciences in Raleigh, which in turn created the reproduction of urethane foam and steel for the Cape Fear Museum. Experts say the creature was not a dinosaur, but an ice age mammal.

The Michael Jordan Discovery Gallery features natural history of the upland forests, bottomland, and maritime forest in interactive exhibits for children and also includes some artifacts from Jordan's years growing up in Wilmington.

Yet another part of the museum shows one-third-scale wood carvings of bride figures by Frank Haines, with costumes researched and sewed by Elizabeth Haines. The brides range from Pocahontas to Queen Nefertiti.

But all that doesn't mean the museum has abandoned the Civil War. Along with military artifacts and representations of the Wilmington waterfront as it was in 1863, you'll find a diorama of the second battle of Fort Fisher in 1865.

The museum is open Monday through Saturday 9:00 a.m. to 5:00 p.m., Sunday 1:00 to 5:00 p.m.; from Labor Day to Memorial Day, the museum is closed Mondays. Admission is $5 for adults, $4 for senior citizens and college students with valid ID, and $1 for children ages three to seventeen. Children under three are free (910-798-4350; www.capefearmuseum.com).

If you are traveling with children, or with grown-up model railroad nuts, go to the **Wilmington Railroad Museum,** 501 Nutt Street, which spells out a major part of the town's history. Although Wilmington is known now for being the state's main deepwater port, railroading used to be Wilmington's major industry. In 1840 the Wilmington and Weldon Railroad, with 161 miles of continuous track, was the longest in the world. About 1900 it merged with several other rail lines to become the Atlantic Coast Line Railroad, with headquarters in Wilmington. But in 1960 the company moved the whole shebang to Jacksonville, Florida. Unlike enterprises that move away these days, though, Atlantic Coast Line did not leave its employees in the lurch but took all 1,000 of them, along with their families, to Florida.

The museum depicts the history not just of the Atlantic Coast Line but also of railroading in the Southeast, through a variety of exhibits. The red caboose in the children's corner is a draw for kids and can be booked for birthday parties. For more historical viewing, the museum also has a 1910 Baldwin steam engine; a Seaboard Coastline Railroad caboose; and a Richmond, Fredericksburg, and Potomac Railroad boxcar. Other displays include everything from railroaders' gear going back more than a hundred years to illustrations of ghost stories about train disasters. For the hobbyist, large layouts of Lionel and HO-gauge model railroads are enough to send you to the nearest model railroad store. The museum is open Monday through Saturday 10:00 a.m. to 5:00 p.m., Sunday from 1:00 to 5:00 p.m. April through September; the rest of the year, it's open Monday through Saturday 10:00 a.m. to 4:00 p.m. Admission is $6 for adults, $5 for senior citizens and military, $3 for children ages two to twelve. Children under two are free (910-763-2634; www.wilmington railroadmuseum.org).

One attraction locals know well and tourists often miss is the **Louise Wells Cameron Art Museum,** at the intersection of Independence Boulevard and the Seventeenth Street Extension. It's remarkable especially for an important collection of the original color prints of Mary Cassatt, the nineteenth-century American artist who worked with the Impressionists in France. This museum is community-supported and does not operate on government funds. Until recently the museum housing the collection, St. John's Museum of Art, comprised three historic buildings on Orange Street. But while the museum collections grew, the buildings wouldn't stretch any farther, and only about 11 percent of the museum's holdings could be displayed at once, so supporters raised funds for a new building, with a new name, in a new location. St. John's Museum of Art closed the last day of December 2001. The new Louise Wells Cameron Art Museum, designed by architect Charles Gwathmey, has 42,000 square feet, about triple the earlier space, and it sits on a campus of almost 10 acres.

Like St. John's, it is the only accredited art museum in the region and has, in addition to the Cassatt work, a permanent collection featuring 200 years of North Carolina art and temporary exhibitions that change regularly. The facilities include an extensive gift shop, a cafe, and a sculpture garden. A series of Confederate defensive mounds that were built near the end of the Civil War on the property provide a new dimension the old museum didn't have. The museum galleries open at 11:00 a.m. Wednesday through Sunday and close at 5:00 p.m., except on Friday when they're open until 9:00. Admission is $8 for adults, $5 for students, and $3 for children ages two to twelve (910-395-5999; www.cameronartmuseum.com).

You can walk to **Chandler's Wharf** and the **Cotton Exchange** on the Cape Fear River. These two complexes of restored historical warehouses and buildings now house a variety of specialty shops and restaurants rather than maritime activities. They are near where the River Walk meets the Cape Fear Bridge. Among the restaurants in this area, **Elijah's Oyster Bar** on Ann Street at the waterfront (910-343-1448; www.elijahs.com) and the **Pilot House,** also on the Ann Street waterfront (910-343-0200; www.pilothouserest.com) serve lunch and dinner. A more recent addition, **Le Catalan,** a wine bar, wine shop, and cafe at 224 South Water Street, across from the Chandler's Wharf shops (910-815-0200; www.lecatalan.com), features a wine bar, light meals, and desserts with a French accent.

From all these points along the river, you can see the **Battleship** **North Carolina,** a memorial to the 10,000 North Carolinians in the armed services who died during World War II. The ship, which was in service from 1941 to 1947, has been moored directly across the Cape Fear River from historic downtown Wilmington as a memorial since 1961. A self-guided tour through the crew's quarters, galley, sick bay, engine room, pilothouse, and other areas takes about two hours. Admission is $12 for adults, $10 for senior citizens and active or retired military people, and $6 for children ages six to eleven. The entrance—with parking, a visitor center, a gift shop, and a snack bar—is at the intersection of U.S. Highways 17/74/76/421. The ship is open daily from Memorial Day weekend to Labor Day 8:00 a.m. to 8:00 p.m., and closes at 5:00 p.m. other times (910-251-5797; www.battleshipnc.com).

To shift from history to contemporary attractions: If you're interested in the entertainment business, you can tour the **Screen Gems Studios,** 1223 North Twenty-third Street. Even people who live here don't seem to realize that North Carolina has become a big moviemaking state. This is a real, working studio, not a space gussied up for tourists. The walking tour takes about an hour and includes real works in process. As a tour guest, you must not get in the way of production, the actors, or the crew, and you may take pictures only in certain designated areas. They've shot not only such movies as *Day of the Jackal* and *Teenage Mutant Ninja Turtles* here, but also television series including *Matlock* and *Dawson's Creek,* as well as many television commercials. Tours are offered on weekends, and the tour schedule varies depending on the weather and whatever else is going on, so it's a good idea to call ahead (910-343-3433) if you plan to include the studios in your activities. Admission is $12 for adults, $10 for military, $8 for senior citizens, $5 for children ages five to twelve, while children younger than five are free (www.screengemsstudios.com).

The people of Wilmington love a party, and there's no better one than **Riverfest,** which celebrates the city's history and its location between the Cape

Fear River and the Intracoastal Waterway. Riverfest always happens the first weekend each October along Front Street and in the historic downtown district. The first Riverfest, in 1979, was the scheme of a group of Wilmingtonians looking for a way to revive Front Street and the downtown after retailers moved to a mall and shopping centers. That first party comprised a few concessions, trolley rides, and fireworks. People liked it so much the town did it again the following year and has continued ever since, adding new entertainment each year. You can expect to find more than 150 craft vendors, three stages of entertainment, a variety of races and contests, and exhibits, all set in the mood that comes with longtime, ongoing success (www.wilmingtonriverfest.com).

When it comes to places to stay, Wilmington has a healthy number of hotels and motels, as well as about twenty bed-and-breakfast facilities. Two of these stand out as special places, each with easy access to the historic district. *Front Street Inn,* 215 South Front Street, is a twelve-room hostelry in a beautifully restored brick building that used to house the Salvation Army of the Carolinas. When Richard and Polly Salinetti, the owners of the Front Street Inn, decided there should be more to retirement than golf, they set off in search of the perfect bed-and-breakfast inn. It took them six months to find Wilmington and five minutes to fall in love with the Front Street Inn. The inn was established more than a decade ago by a craftsman and a decorator who knew how to take advantage of the building's 14-foot-high ceilings, large window casings, and maple floors, creating an atmosphere of light, humor, and zest, with rooms so different from one another they almost defy description. The Georgia O'Keefe suite, for instance, is filled with art gathered from sources ranging from thrift shops to galleries. The Jacques Cousteau suite has an exotic fish tank. Some walls are painted by local artists. In the breakfast room, color and plants and big windows complement buffet offerings that feature seasonal ingredients and might include anything from smoked salmon to homemade granola and yogurt. From the Sol y Sombra (Sun and Shade) Bar you can choose from an assortment of beverages including wine, beer, and champagne. The place also has an exercise room and a game room. The inn is close to the historic district and good restaurants. For those who can't leave business behind, wireless, dial-up, and DSL Internet connections are available. The Salinettis bring the laid-back approach of maturity, along with a lively dose of humor, to their undertaking. "You can mention old," Richard says (914-762-6442 or 800-336-8184; www.frontstreetinn.com).

At 114 South Third Street, *Rosehill Inn Bed and Breakfast* is the kind of place other innkeepers visit for a night out. Built in 1848, the neoclassical revival house has a fireplace of Italian marble and rosewood and a beautifully refinished pulpit staircase. Throughout the house, especially in the six guest rooms, bright colors figure prominently in the decor (910-815-0250 or 800-815-0250; www.rosehill.com).

Land of Ferries and Forts

Just a few miles away from the historic port of Wilmington, you come to a series of beaches: Wrightsville, Carolina, Wilmington, and Kure. For folks seeking out-of-the-way places, the beaches don't offer much secluded charm, but they can be fun, with enough amusement and entertainment to please the kids without doing in Mom and Dad, especially if you avoid the peak summer season. A number of historical and marine attractions are especially important and interesting.

Wrightsville Beach is 12 miles east of Wilmington. It operates as a year-round island resort and has plenty of motels and some nice, casual, moderately priced seafood restaurants.

The **Wrightsville Beach Museum of History** (303 West Salisbury Street, 910-256-2569; www.wbmuseum.com) is one of those grassroots enterprises that reflects its own small area in unique detail and just makes you feel good with its honesty. The museum is in the fourth-oldest cottage on the island and does two things. First, it provides a good example of what beach cottages in the area used to be like, furnished just with odds and ends left over from permanent homes. And it houses a variety of permanent and changing exhibits that tell you about the history, geography, and culture of Wrightsville Beach.

For instance, the kitchen remains pretty much intact, with white ceramic tile, a white porcelain kitchen sink, and an assortment of cooking utensils typical of the early twentieth century. Photographs show how other rooms might have been furnished with stuff collected here and there. A 12-foot model of Wrightsville Beach in about 1910 shows the Lumina Pavilion, where couples danced to the music of Benny Goodman, a bathhouse for changing into beachwear, and a trolley, as well as sections of beach and the boardwalk. The model is still a work in process, and the museum solicits additions and contributions to it.

Changing exhibits may include anything from the history of surfing to a retrospective on lifeguards to photographs from the collection of a local news photographer. The museum gives attention to the history of the barrier islands, the beach, the Civil War, and Hurricane Hazel. An oral history video shows area residents recalling life as it used to be in Wrightsville Beach.

The museum is open from 10:00 a.m. to 4:00 p.m. Tuesday through Friday, noon to 5:00 p.m. Saturday, and 1:00 to 5:00 p.m. Sunday. Admission is $3.

Driving south from Wilmington on US 421 for a little less than 20 miles takes you to the beaches on *Pleasure Island.* This area is highly commercial and built up, but if you stick it out to Kure Beach, you'll find two attractions worth taking time to see if you're interested in the naval aspects of Civil War history and in marine life.

On US 421, 3 miles south of Kure Beach, is *Fort Fisher National Historic Site.* The fort stood up under heavy naval attack during the Civil War, and some of the 25-foot earthwork fortifications that protected the Cape Fear River and the port of Wilmington from Union forces remain. Reading about such parapets is one thing; looking at them and musing on how they must have been built before the days of bulldozers is a more vivid experience, intensified by such touches as a reconstruction of the gun emplacement and a history trail. There's also a museum that displays Civil War artifacts and offers an audio-visual show, models, and dioramas on the history of the fort. If you travel with a picnic cooler, you'll enjoy the picnic area on the site. Admission is free but donations are appreciated. Open April through October, 9:00 a.m. to 5:00 p.m. Monday through Saturday, 1:00 to 5:00 p.m. Sunday; November through March 10, 10:00 a.m. to 4:00 p.m. Tuesday through Saturday; closed on major holidays (910-458-5538; www.nchistoricsites.org/fisher).

When you get this far south on the island, you will have two choices: You can take the Fort Fisher Ferry to Southport, which brings you close to the Brunswick Islands, from whence you began driving, or you can backtrack up the island and take the bridge across to Wilmington, another starting point. At first glance the obvious way to avoid the dilemma of decision would be to begin by taking the ferry from Southport to Fort Fisher, then drive north on the island, and finally cross over to the delights of Wilmington. You may indeed decide to do it that way, especially if you're not traveling during the peak summer months. But you need to know that the ferry crossing takes an hour. For current schedule information when it's time to decide, phone (800) BY-FERRY or check the Web site: www.ncferry.org.

For a committed off-the-beaten-path traveler, a drive of about 75 miles up Interstate 40 from Wilmington to Duplin County is worth a day, or several days. This area is full of history, pretty country, and nice people. It's away from the inevitable development along the shore but still part of the coastal plain. Highway 24/50 takes you into Kenansville, a town of a little over 1,000 people graced with many restored antebellum houses as well as three antebellum churches. *Liberty Hall Plantation* (409 South Main Street; 910-296-2175; www.libertyhallnc.org/libhallmain.swf) is the restored nineteenth-century ancestral home of the Kenan family, who date back to the time of the Revolution. The Kenan family's influence and their philanthropic activities are still strong in the town. The plantation includes twelve support buildings, in addition to the mansion, and a visitor center and gift shop. It is open Tuesday through Saturday 10:00 a.m. to 4:00 p.m. and from 2:00 to 4:00 p.m. Sunday. Closed on major holidays. Admission is $5.00 for adults, $2.50 for children.

Next to Liberty Hall is *Cowan Museum,* the restored 1848 Kelly-Farrior House, a Greek Revival structure filled with more than 2,000 household and farming artifacts from this rural area. Other buildings on the property include a furnished log cabin and a one-room school. Open 10:00 a.m. to 4:00 p.m. Tuesday through Saturday and from 2:00 to 4:00 p.m. Sunday. Admission by donation (910-296-2149; www.cowanmuseum.com).

Directly across from the plantation and museum stands *The Murray House Country Inn,* 201 NC Highway 24/50 (910-296-1000; www.murray houseinn.com). Murray House Country Inn is a restored 1853 Greek Revival mansion listed on the National Register of Historic Places. Its six guest rooms, all with private entrances in a newer carriage house, are furnished with a mix of antiques and good reproductions and connected to the main house with formal gardens. The rooms have become popular with business travelers because they are quiet and comfortable. Breakfast is served in the main house, and rates include a tour of the home. Lynn and Joe Davis bought the house specifically to prevent its deterioration. "It took us a year to get the guy to sell," Lynn Davis recalls. They bought and restored the place in 1990 and opened as a bed-and-breakfast in 1994. "It just seemed like the right thing to do with the house," Lynn says. A visit here would be a rich experience for anyone interested in architecture and history. Lynn grew up in Kenansville and knows a lot about the town, its old families, and its architecture.

Another bed-and-breakfast across from the Cowan Museum and Liberty Hall Plantation is the *Graham House Inn,* 406 South Main Street (800-767-9397; www.grahamhouseinn.com). It's an Italianate-Revival home built in 1855, located in the National Register Historic District, with four guest rooms. Two have private baths, and two with a shared bath would provide good accommodation for friends or family members traveling together. Innkeepers Nick and Phyllis Halbrook have only three house rules: No smoking, lock the door, and make yourself at home. The guest rooms have fanciful names— Garden Bird, Rabbit, Seashore, Butterfly—and are decorated appropriately. The Butterfly Room has special significance because Phyllis has made a hobby of raising butterflies. She brings the eggs inside in early summer to watch the whole process of their development until butterflies emerge about the middle of July, when she turns them loose outside.

One of the best established restaurants in the area is *Country Squire Restaurant,* between Kenansville and Warsaw, a few miles to the north, at

748 NC Highway 24/50, (910) 296-1727. The restaurant serves lunch and dinner. The extensive menu ranges from soups, salads, and burgers to steaks and prime rib. The Squire has a standing offer to anyone who can consume a 72-ounce steak in an hour. The meal costs $85, but if you eat it in an hour, it's free. There are rules about what you must eat besides the meat, including tomato juice, celery sticks, salad, and side dishes. The restaurant has all ABC (liquor) permits and a big wine list, which may make either the **Vintage Inn Motel** or a country guest house appealing after dinner (910-296-1831; www .countrysquireinn.com).

A little to the south of Kenansville, in Beulaville, **Tarkil Branch Farm Homestead Museum** (1198 Fountaintown Road; 910-298-3804; www.tarkil farmsmuseum.com), in a restored 1830s homestead, shows you what early farm life would've been like for families living in rural North Carolina in the 1800s. The museum has period furnishings in the home, nine outbuildings, and old farm equipment. Wagon tours and a hiking trail are available. The museum is open Saturday from 9:00 a.m. to 5:00 p.m.

If you're interested in North Carolina wineries, you may want to schedule a trip on your way back to Wilmington to **Duplin Winery,** about an hour's drive from the coast. The winery is in Rose Hill, on U.S. Highway 117, about halfway between Wilmington and Goldsboro. The winery conducts tours and tastings and, of course, sells its wines. Duplin Winery (800-774-9634; www .duplinwinery.com) is especially well known for its Magnolia, a soft dry table wine; its Hatteras Red; and its scuppernong dessert wine.

The winery has added a bistro to its offerings. The winery is open Monday through Saturday 9:00 a.m. to 6:00 p.m. and Friday 9:00 a.m. to 9:00 p.m. Lunch is available from 11:30 a.m. to 2:00 p.m. Monday through Saturday, and dinner from 6:00 to 10:00 p.m. Friday.

From Wilmington the best way to head north is to drive on US 17 for a while. Stretches of it are annoyingly full of strip-city areas where traffic is heavy

Fly Away, Butterfly

Innkeeper Phyllis Halbrook describes the process of raising butterflies this way: "The butterflies lay the eggs. (I cannot tell you if they are butterfly eggs or caterpillar eggs.) They are about the size of the head of a pin. A little, tiny caterpillar will hatch from this egg. I actually bring the eggs in the house and watch them. I do not want to take the chance of a lizard or a bird finding the little caterpillars and eating them. The caterpillars will go into a chrysalis (cocoon) when they have eaten enough and grown large. They will stay in this stage until they are ready to come out as butterflies. When they emerge as butterflies, I turn them loose outside."

and slow. One interesting stop, right on the highway shortly after you leave Wilmington, is the **Poplar Grove Plantation** (910-686-9518; www.poplar grove.com). This is a nonprofit operation supported by the Poplar Grove Foundation. It has an unusual history in that it not only survived the Civil War, but also became economically successful again by growing peanuts. The original plantation operated in the tradition of the times, as a self-supporting agricultural community with more than sixty slaves. The manor house burned down in 1849 and was rebuilt the following year where it now stands. When you visit the plantation, guides in period costume lead you on a tour of the manor house—a three-floor Greek Revival building—and the outbuildings, describing what daily life on the plantation was like.

sweet, sweet

The word *scuppernong* is an Indian word meaning "sweet tree." Scuppernong is one of the oldest grapes in America, and a favorite among Carolinians, who like things sweet.

The outbuildings include a tenant house, smokehouse, herb cellar, kitchen (plantation kitchens were always in separate buildings), blacksmith shop, and turpentine and saltworks display. With or without a guide, looking at these buildings dramatically brings home some realities of history. A visitor looking at the small, roughly finished, uninsulated tenant house said, "It's hard to imagine that a whole family actually lived in here." Another visitor, seeing the mock hams, sausages, and bacons hanging in the smokehouse, wondered what the real thing would have been like in such hot weather and said, "It's a wonder everybody didn't die of food poisoning."

Open Monday through Saturday 9:00 a.m. to 5:00 p.m., Sunday noon to 5:00 p.m. Admission is $8 for adults, $7 for active military and for senior citizens, $5 for children ages six to fifteen. Last tour begins at 4:00 p.m. Closed Easter Sunday and Thanksgiving Day. Closed Christmas week and remains closed until first Monday in February.

Continuing north on US 17 takes you through some very local, untouristy areas, such as Holly Ridge. If you want more of a sense of the area, shortly after you pass Holly Ridge turn left on Verona Road, and following the signs, head toward Haws Run. You'll go by some pretty little houses with lovingly tended gardens, then an abandoned trailer park, and finally, many occupied mobile homes on the way back out to US 17. This detour of only a few miles gives a view of what many small North Carolina communities near the coast are like.

Then you're into the area around Jacksonville, which is shaped and colored by **Camp Lejeune Marine Base.** Traffic is fairly heavy, and the area bulges with the kind of commercial development that surrounds military bases: motels, restaurants, arcades, shopping centers, and the like. But even though driving through such a section isn't as relaxing as spinning along a country road, it's tremendously instructive and sometimes funny. Most of the people you see in the vehicles are heartbreakingly young men with perfect posture and haircuts so short you can almost see their scalps from the next automobile. Often they're in pairs or groups, and often they're towing boats or hauling bikes. The progression of the establishments and signs you pass along the road tells a story: Foxy Lady, New Ink Tattoo Shop, a motel sign that proclaims WELCOME MR. NUNNERY, Real Value Diamond Outlet, an assortment of churches, and the Maternity and Newborn Store.

Here's information of a more dignified nature. Camp Lejeune is one of the most complete training centers in the world and covers 110,000 acres. You may wish to stop at the Beirut Memorial, honoring those killed in Beirut and Grenada. It is outside the gate of Camp Johnson on Highway 24. You can't get onto the base without a pass, and you can't get a pass without a driver's license and registration certificate. The information center at the main gate on Highway 24 is open twenty-four hours a day (910-451-2197; www.lejeune .usmc.mil/mcb/index.asp).

From Jacksonville you could logically continue up US 17 to New Bern, or you could travel east on Highway 24 toward the ocean to check out the Bogue Banks and then go on to Morehead City, Beaufort, and Atlantic and ferry across to the Outer Banks. Better yet, if you're not hurrying, avoid this section of Highway 24, which runs along another edge of the marine base, and continue north about 15 miles more on US 17, where you pick up Highway 58. It runs southeast along the side of the Croatan National Forest and is a much more pleasant drive to the coast. **Cedar Point** is a nice place to stop for a picnic or a rest and perhaps a hike along the Cedar Point Tideland Trail. You'll find camping areas and picnic tables in the shade along the water. Nearby is Cape Carteret, a little town that's probably pretty much solved its crime problem by locating its liquor store right next to the police station and town hall.

Places to Stay in the Southern Coast and Islands

HOLDEN BEACH

Gray Gull Motel
At the bridge
Holden Beach
(910) 842-6775
www.graygullmotel.com

OCEAN ISLE BEACH

Ocean Isle Inn
37 West First Street
(800) 352-5988
www.oceanisleinn.com

The Winds
310 East First Street
(910) 579-6275
(800) 334-3581
www.thewinds.com

SOUTHPORT

Lois Jane's Riverview Inn
106 West Bay Street
(800) 457-1152
www.loisjanes.com

Riverside Motel
103 West Bay Street
(910) 457-6986

SUNSET BEACH

Sunset Inn
9 North Shore Drive
(910) 575-1000
(888) 575-1001
www.thesunsetinn.net

WILMINGTON

Front Street Inn
215 South Front Street
(910) 762-6442
(800) 336-8184
www.frontstreetinn.com

Rosehill Inn
114 South Third Street
(910) 815-0250
(800) 815-0250
www.rosehill.com

WRIGHTSVILLE BEACH

Harbor Inn
701 Causeway Drive
(910) 256-9402
(888) 507-9402
www.harborinn.com

Places to Eat in the Southern Coast and Islands

CALABASH

Captain Nance's Seafood Restaurant
Riverfront
(910) 579-2574

Ella's of Calabash
1148 River Road
(910) 579-6728

SOUTHPORT

Sandfiddler Seafood Restaurant
1643 North Howe Street
(910) 457-6588

Thai Peppers Restaurant
115 East Moore Street
(910) 457-0095

WILMINGTON

Elijah's
2 Ann Street
Chandler's Wharf
(910) 343-1448

Riverboat Landing
2 Market Street
Chandler's Wharf
(910) 763-7227

The Northern Coast and Islands

Peaceful Places

Your next major stop as you head north along the coast is **Morehead City,** a deep port where the Intracoastal Waterway joins the Atlantic Ocean. It is both a commercial fishing town and a summer resort area, appealing especially to sport fishers. The waterfront is more devoted to commerce than tourism, has more than 5,000 square feet of continuous wharf, and includes a lot of shipping storage space. That means the waterfront isn't really pretty; it's too commercial and busy, but the activity is authentic and interesting. As a traveler, if you aren't here to fish, you're probably here to eat fish. The area has plenty of moderately priced motels and more seafood restaurants than you could patronize in two weeks' hard eating. If you ask people where to go, they'll most often make the unlikely sounding recommendation of the ***Sanitary Fish Market Restaurant*** (252-247-3111; www.sanitaryfishmarket.com). It's just a block from U.S. Highway 70, on Bogue Sound. Some reviewers have speculated that the name was intended to reassure customers that this place is sanitary, even though some seafood restaurants are not, but that's not quite accurate. The

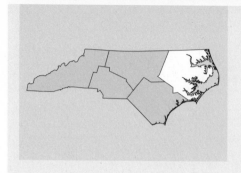

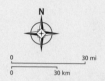

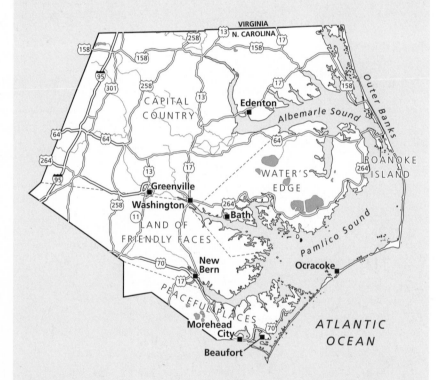

name was originally coined to signify an understanding between the man who rented out the first small market building and the partners who started their fresh seafood market there, that they'd sell no beer or wine and they would keep the place clean and neat. When the market also became a restaurant, it was with twelve stools at a counter and a two-burner kerosene stove. People liked the fresh seafood, and the market and restaurant kept growing. Now it's a big, casual, family-oriented place that seats more than 600 people and serves all kinds of seafood. Although sweet tea remains the beverage of choice for many customers, you can order wine or beer now.

At the other end of the spectrum, *Café Zito,* 105 South 11th Street (252-726-6676; www.cafezito.com) seats about forty people inside, with room for sixteen more on the porch. It is open for dinner Wednesday through Monday, with Sunday and Monday being tapas nights and Wednesday, Thursday, Friday, and Saturday regular dinner nights. The fare is fresh Mediterranean with some local favorites included. The wine list is varied. Exhibits of work by local artists and photographers hang on the walls, and the cafe is right across the street from The History Place.

The History Place, 1008 Arendell Street, is the kind of place that makes you feel good about people, just regular folks, and what they can accomplish when they set their minds to it. The Carteret County Historical and Genealogical Society owns and operates the museum almost entirely on volunteer help and donated funds. The museum opened in 1988 in a building that had served at various times as a school and a church, but in 2001 the museum moved to its new, greatly expanded space on Arendell Street. For tourists the displays

ANNUAL EVENTS IN THE NORTHERN COAST AND ISLANDS

Kill Devil Hills
Annual Artful Gala
(late February)
(252) 473-5558

Manteo
Virginia Dare's Birthday Celebration
August 18
(252) 473-2127

National Aviation Day–Orville Wright Birthday
August 19
(252) 441-7430

Morehead City
Annual N.C. Seafood Festival
Waterfront
(mid-October)
(252) 726-6273

Outer Banks
Annual Stunt
Kite Competition
Jockey's Ridge State Park
(mid-October)
(252) 441-4124
or (800) 334-4777

oddburials

People in Beaufort like to tell stories. Unquestionably their favorites are those about the Old Burying Ground. The oldest date you can make out on a grave marker is 1756, but the cemetery was deeded to the town in 1731. One story is about the English soldier who was buried standing up because he swore he would never lie down on foreign soil.

And then there's the little girl buried in a barrel of rum. Seems that before her father took her off to England on a ship, he promised her mother that he would bring the child back again. Unfortunately, she died aboard the ship, and embalming her in rum was the only way he could think of to keep his promise.

of county artifacts, including Native American items, pieces from the Civil War and World War II, a fully furnished Victorian parlor, and clothing from the 1800s, is probably the most interesting aspect of the museum. But the facilities for historical research and genealogical study are also widely used and richly detailed. The museum is open Tuesday through Saturday 10:00 a.m. to 4:00 p.m. Admission is free (252-247-7533; www .thehistoryplace.org).

From Morehead City it's just a short drive over the Paul Graydon Bridge to **Beaufort.** The first step to having fun in Beaufort is learning to say it properly— *BOW-ford.* This separates it from that place in South Carolina spelled the same way but pronounced to rhyme with "phew." People in Beaufort, North Carolina, care and respond accordingly.

This was once a fishing village, settled by French Huguenots and English sailors more than 275 years ago. The port was active during three wars: the American Revolution, the War of 1812, and the Civil War. Today Beaufort is a laid-back vacation area in which historic preservation and restoration have been impressive. Much of the downtown has been designated a National Historic Landmark, and the Beaufort Historical Association has restored a number of early buildings that are open to the public.

Local art is offered in the **Mattie King Davis Art Gallery** on the grounds of the Old Town Beaufort Restoration Complex, where local artists and craftspeople display their pottery, weaving, oil paintings, watercolors, and other original art. It's open Monday through Saturday from 10:00 a.m. to 4:00 p.m. No admission fee.

The **North Carolina Maritime Museum,** 315 Front Street, contains artifacts ranging from fish and fossils to ships, including a model-ship collection and a collection of 5,000 seashells from all over the world. Serious boat people visit here to watch wooden boats being built and restored. Open Monday through Friday from 9:00 a.m. to 5:00 p.m., Saturday from 10:00 a.m. to 5:00 p.m., Sunday from 1:00 to 5:00 p.m. (252-728-7317). For a schedule of special events, write the museum at 315 Front Street, Beaufort 28516, or check the Web site: www.ah.dcr.state.nc.us. No admission fee.

One way to see the sights and learn a lot about local lore is by taking one of the **Beaufort Historic Site Tours** operated by the historical association. All tours leave from the welcome center at 130 Turner Street. Call ahead for all tour arrangements (252-728-5225 or 800-575-7483; www.historicbeaufort.com). Tours run Monday through Saturday from 9:30 a.m. to 5:00 p.m. March through November, 10:00 a.m. to 4:00 p.m. in winter.

The home tour includes not only old homes but also the jail, courthouse, and apothecary shop. Admission is $6 for adults, $4 for children.

From April 11 through October, the narrated English double-decker bus tours cover the downtown district and go out past a house that is reputed to have been a hangout for Blackbeard and his pirates in the late 1600s. The tour narrator gives a lively mix of fact and folklore. These tours run Monday, Wednesday, Friday, and Saturday and cost $8 per seat for adults, $4 for children ages seven to twelve.

Narrated tours of the Old Burying Ground at Ann Street, where stones date back to 1709 and possibly earlier, are offered Tuesday through Thursday in summer and fall. The narrator tells colorful stories about unusual circumstances through which people came to be buried here. Admission is $8 for adults, $4 for children seven to twelve. You may walk around the grounds anytime for free.

A nice place to stay in Beaufort is the **Pecan Tree Inn,** 116 Queen Street (252-728-6733 or toll-free 800-728-7871; www.pecantree.com). The owners, Dave and Allison DuBuisson, emphasize luxuries. Pecan Tree Inn is the kind of place you stay for a special getaway in surroundings nothing like home. The 1860s Victorian inn was originally built to serve as a Masonic lodge. Now it is furnished with period antiques and bed styles ranging from romantic canopies to brass, iron, and wicker. It has seven rooms, two of them with two-person

AUTHOR'S FAVORITE PLACES IN THE NORTHERN COAST AND ISLANDS

Beaufort	Wanchese
North Carolina Maritime Museum	Hope Plantation
Portsmouth Island	Somerset Place
Aurora Fossil Museum	
Mattamuskeet National Wildlife Refuge	

Shiver Me Timbers!

Most of the coastal towns and islands in the area lay some claim to Blackbeard, the notorious pirate who built a fleet of captured ships and terrorized the seas in the 1700s. He captured a French Guinea ship in 1717, renamed it *Queen Anne's Revenge,* and put forty huge guns, called blunderbusses, aboard. Later he deliberately ran the sailing vessel aground near Beaufort, which was known as Fishtown in those early days, as part of a plan to dump his fleet and crew, while escaping with his loot and getting a pardon from England. In 1997 salvage crews found what they believe to be the remains of *Queen Anne's Revenge* in about 20 feet of water at Beaufort Inlet. They found a blunderbuss barrel, a ship's bell, and a cannon ball. All these items now belong to the state of North Carolina.

Jacuzzis. Each of the rooms has cable TV, and wireless Internet connection is available throughout the inn. On the second floor, one of the inn's two suites has a private entrance with stairs to the brick courtyard and gardens below, so that lavish blooms complement the lavishly decorated room inside. This inn anchors 5,000 square feet of perennial gardens, paths, and water features. No matter the time of year, you'll always find something pretty in these gardens.

You'll find yet another kind of lodging at **Beaufort Inn,** 101 Ann Street, (252-728-2600 or toll-free 800-726-0312; www.beaufort-inn.com). This is a small-scale hotel that the owners, Bruce and Katie Ethridge, like to say combines the privacy of a hotel with the ambience of a bed-and-breakfast. The inn, which has three stories and forty-four rooms, each with private bath, telephone, and TV, is an attractive, well-settled place, with nice furnishings, a dining room with a fireplace, and an outdoor hot tub. The Ethridges have had the inn for more than twenty years and are definitely not impersonal absentee owners—they're there. In addition to a full breakfast served in the dining room anytime between 7:00 and 10:00 a.m., they offer refreshments on weekends from 3:00 to 6:00 p.m.

Beaufort has a number of restaurants, all within walking distance of the town's lodgings. Two of them have what one innkeeper calls "best kept secret allure."

Blue Moon Bistro, 119 Queen Street (www.bluemoonbistro.biz), serves dinner Tuesday through Saturday. Call (252) 728-5800 for reservations. The atmosphere here is deliberately funky, the menu sophisticated, the wine list extensive. Appetizers range from steamed pork dumplings to pan-seared scallops au poivre. The entrees can be as simple as grilled Angus steak and as exotic as a risotto of white beans, sun-dried tomatoes, and chèvre over grilled eggplant.

Aqua, 114 Middle Lane (252-728-7777; www.aquaexperience.com), is a Spanish tapas-style restaurant, with the slogan "Small plates, big wines." Everything comes to you in small portions, so you can order several to make a meal or pass around the table. The idea is to sample lots of different appetizers, and these can be paired with appropriate wines by the staff, or you can make your own choices. Artful arrangement of the food on each plate is an important part of the presentation. You might order something like lump crab cake on citrus fennel slaw with a chipotle glaze or a cheese plate with assorted condiments. Foods in season influence the menu. The wines are not off the grocery store shelf, either. Aqua has a sort of hidden feel, as it is located on Middle Lane just west of and next door to the Back Street Pub. The restaurant serves Tuesday through Saturday.

One could stay in Beaufort a long time just wandering around, eating seafood, and sitting on the porch reading trashy novels. But you can find more adventure if you want it, too. On the waterfront, near the North Carolina Maritime Museum on Front Street, you'll find **Outer Banks Ferry Service** (252-728-4129), which will take you to **Shackleford Banks,** an island populated only with wild horses; **Carrot Island,** a good place for shelling, as well as Bird Shoals and Sand Dollar Islands; and on **Cape Lookout,** tours to visit the lighthouse and keepers' quarters and a jeep ride to the cape point. These are great activities in good weather but miserable places on cold, stormy days—assuming you could even get a ferry to take you over then—so it's better to arrange a trip once you see how the weather is going to be.

Wet Adventure

I paddled my first sea kayak in Beaufort. This is not something you start out doing gracefully. Getting into a life vest and wet suit takes some squirming. Crawling into the small open area of the kayak becomes an exercise in humility. And sitting with your legs stretched straight out in front of you seems an impossibility.

But then somebody gives you a shove off the sloped ramp and into the water, and after a few tentative strokes, paddling this thing across the waterway to an island seems doable.

It takes a while to remember which rudder to push and even longer to get really proficient at paddling so the boat goes where you want it to. Then it all comes together, and the kayak moves silently and efficiently across the water, and except for avoiding other boats and catching glimpses of the wild ponies and the birds on the islands, nothing else matters.

Be warned: Sea kayaking is addictive.

Assuming you are ready, eventually, to leave Beaufort, you should push on north almost to the end of US 70 East, to the little town of *Atlantic* (not to be confused with Atlantic Beach), where you can catch the ferry to the Outer Banks. Looking at your map, you will see that the Outer Banks is a long series of islands off the North Carolina coast. Some of them are fully developed resort areas; others have no concessions or services at all.

In particular, visit *Portsmouth Island.* It's uninhabited now, but 635 people once lived on the 30-mile-long island in the village of Portsmouth. Ultimately, they couldn't survive the weather, especially hurricanes. A particularly bad one in 1846 opened Hatteras and Oregon Inlets and changed shipping patterns, which cut off future economic development for the village. Gradually the people left, first the young and then the old. According to Joel Arrington, writing in the magazine *Wildlife in North Carolina,* only fourteen people remained on the island in 1950; the last male resident died in 1971, after which the remaining two women gave up and moved to the mainland. The buildings of the village remain a little beat-up but intact, maintained by the National Park Service.

Your difficulty in seeing the village will be that, even after you've ferried across to the island, if you want to cover any distance, you'll need a four-wheel-drive or all-terrain vehicle to travel the 18 miles up the beach from the ferry landing to the village, because there are no roads. In addition to ferry services, two reliable companies offer tours and transportation.

One of the most lovingly cared for buildings is the Portsmouth Village Methodist Church. Indeed, the sight of half a dozen or so men in fishing clothes, sitting quietly on the benches inside the old church when they're supposed to be at water's edge fishing, may be as special an experience as visiting the village. For information about ferry hours, call Morris Marina (252-225-4261; www.portsmouthislandfishing.com). For information about land transportation, contact Portsmouth Island ATV Excursions (252-982-4484; www.portsmouth islandatvs.com). These tours leave from Ocracoke Island.

A simpler way to visit the village, though less colorful and a bit more on the beaten (or should it be rowed, in this case?) path, is to take a boat tour

Dance Wherever You May Be

The folks devoted to preserving Ocracoke Island and its history say it's not about the buildings so much as it's about the people. One oft-mentioned example is Sam Tolson, who earned his living as a waterman, but was loved for his dancing. He entertained at most celebrations on the island and is reputed to have been able to dance for hours while balancing a glass of water on his head.

The Human Touch

When I called the Core Sound Waterfowl Museum and Heritage Center, a real person answered—no recorded greeting, no telephone tree, but a real person. She said her name was Sheila and she told me her last name as well, because there are two Sheilas working there. I got the basic information about hours and activities, as well as an enthusiastic update on the progress of the museum property's development. My dog was barking most of the time. "Do you want a big old dog?" I joked.

"I already have a big old dog," Sheila said. "Her name is Miss Maggie." And for several minutes we commiserated about our dogs' infirmities and the sadness of watching them get very old and how we hoped their lives would end peacefully. I've been thinking ever since that we need more places where you can still interact with people you don't know on such a personal, human level.

beginning at Ocracoke Island. Contact Austin Boat Tours (252-928-4361 or 252-928-5431; www.austinboattours.com). If you're not sure how to manage the trip and would like more information and advice, call the ranger station (252-728-2250) for enthusiastic, knowledgeable help. They have a list of all the ferrying services and can put you in touch with the one that will work best for you.

Harkers Island is another "people place" that doesn't attract a lot of tourists. Here some people still remember when hunting waterfowl for food was a natural part of daily existence, not a recreational sport. They remember carving decoys because they needed them to attract ducks, not to set up on the mantel as decorator items. The ***Core Sound Waterfowl Museum and Heritage Center*** honors that Down East heritage and provides a place for carvers to practice the old art and younger people to learn it, or at least see it in action. Most days you'll find two or three local wood-carvers at work on the porch, telling stories about the days when waterfowl were so plentiful their clusters looked like islands out in the sound. When decoys got lost or drifted away, it wasn't a big deal. They just carved more as part of the daily routine. Nothing fancy about it. The early decoys didn't have to fool anybody but the flocks of birds high overhead.

The museum is actively working on all kinds of other historical projects, with an emphasis on teaching and preserving the old ways. This includes quilting bees. A finished quilt is raffled off to raise money for work on the museum. A new, much larger museum is in the works—on 16 acres at Shell Point, next to the National Park Service's Cape Lookout National Seashore headquarters near the tip of the island. It's a community effort, the money being raised by local people, with such attractions as a viewing platform on

Willow Pond built by volunteers with donated materials. Whatever state the place is in when you get to Harkers, it's a heartwarming stop. The museum is open year-round, 10:00 a.m. to 5:00 p.m. Monday through Saturday and 2:00 to 5:00 p.m. Sunday. Admission is free. For more information call (252) 728-1500; www.coresound.com.

Portsmouth Island and Harkers Island are part of the 56-mile-long *Cape Lookout National Seashore* (252-728-2250; www.nps.gov/calo), which comprises North Core Banks, South Core Banks, and Shackleford Banks. A good place to sort out all the possibilities is at the visitor center at the end of Harkers Island, in a house that used to be the keepers' quarters near the Cape Lookout Lighthouse, at the end of the island. The lighthouse itself is not open for visitors, but it's a great subject for photographs and sketching. The center is open 9:00 a.m. to 5:00 p.m. seven days a week. Closed Christmas and New Year's Day. A variety of tours and camping arrangements are available, but before you sign up for anything, remember that the undeveloped islands don't have roads, bathrooms, or water, so you must be able to climb in and out of boats and walk a reasonable distance to spend time on them. You also need to carry in your own drinking water. As one park ranger says, "It's really a backcountry experience." It doesn't hurt to take along a good insect repellent, either. One reliable concessionaire affiliated with the National Park Service providing ferry, tour, and camping options is Morris Marina Kabin Kamps Ferry Service, Inc. (252-225-4261) on North Core. Since the companies providing such services change, check the National Seashore Web site for current information.

Land of Friendly Faces

The entire area along the northern coast, the barrier islands, and the Outer Banks is a maze of toll ferries, free ferries, private ferries, and bridges. The way you organize your trips here depends on everything from the weather to how much time you want to spend driving or being ferried. Remember that a ferry is not a fast way to travel. In planning trips in this area, it sometimes works better to find a pleasant base to which you return after each foray in a new direction. Try *New Bern* as a slightly inland base from which, one way or another, you can get to a wonderful variety of places to spend a day or so. Everyone in New Bern will have ideas for you, which will certainly include Oriental.

Oriental is about 25 miles east of New Bern on Highway 55. It has won a reputation as the sailing capital of the East Coast and almost always has a sailing school or camp in progress. Except for some antiques shops, a modest motel or two, and some restaurants, there's not much here except nice people. If you want to spend a night at a bed-and-breakfast here, the ***Inn at Oriental,*** at 508 Church Street (252-249-1078 or toll-free 800-485-7174; www.innatoriental.com), has twelve rooms with private baths, king- and queen-size beds, and facilities for the handicapped. The inn was built at the turn of the twentieth century and has been restored to duplicate the feel of an English country inn—with contemporary amenities. The innkeepers serve a big breakfast.

For a fascinating glimpse of this town's activities and people, check the Web site, www.towndock.com, for information about recent news and events. From this site, HarborCam has new pictures every ten minutes. Local people leave it on to see who is arriving at or leaving The Bean, a coffee shop near the water, where many of them hang out.

crossingthewater

The North Carolina ferry system links many coastal and island communities that would otherwise take hours to reach by road or be completely inaccessible except by private boat. The system, which has been running since the mid-1940s, is operated by the North Carolina Department of Transportation. It is one of the largest ferry systems in the nation.

Crossing times range from twenty minutes to get from Cherry Branch to Minnesot to two and a half hours for the trip from Ocracoke to Swan Quarter. Schedules vary with the seasons. For full details call (800) BY-FERRY or check the Web site: www.ncferry.org.

Then again, once you're in New Bern, you may not want to go anywhere else at all—not just because there's so much to see and do but also because this is one of the friendliest towns anywhere. To give you an idea, a couple staying at a bed-and-breakfast inn in the historic district was walking to a nearby restaurant where they had dinner reservations when they stopped to admire an especially nicely restored house. The owners, who happened to be on the porch, invited the couple in for a drink and showed them around. They spent so much time chatting that the couple never did make it to the restaurant.

On the outside chance that you might not be so generously befriended by strangers, stop in the tourist center at the Chamber of Commerce about 2 blocks from US 70, near the Trent River at the end of Middle Street, when you get to town. Signs point the way from all major entrances. Everyone here is extraordinarily friendly, too. If you're an antiquer, be sure to get a copy of the brochure, "Antiques Shops of New Bern," which gives particulars on more than a dozen antiques shops, complete with a map and an explanation of American furniture styles from Queen Anne (1725–1750) through the arts and crafts and mission styles of the early 1900s.

Tryon Palace, New Bern

You'll also be able to pick up full details on Tryon Palace Restorations and Garden Complex, where first a royal government and then an independent state government were housed. In colonial times **Tryon Palace,** at 610 Pollack Street, was known as the most beautiful building in America. The elaborate formal gardens as well as the elegant buildings and furnishings have been restored.

Tours conducted by guides in costume lead you through the rooms; give you a look at demonstrations of candle making, cloth making, cooking, and other period activities; and fill you in on specific facts about the buildings and their earlier, illustrious occupants. If you just want to walk around in the gardens, you can take a self-guided tour. The complex (252-514-4900 or 800-767-1560; www.tryonpalace.org) is open year-round, Monday through Saturday from 9:00 a.m. to 5:00 p.m. and Sunday from 1:00 to 4:30 p.m. Closed Thanksgiving Day, December 24–26, and January 1. Admission is $15 for adults, $6 for students with identification. Write Tryon Palace, Box 1007, New Bern 28560.

Much less well known than the Tryon Palace are these two small museums, each within walking distance of the other.

The **New Bern Firemen's Museum,** across the corner at 408 Hancock Street, houses a collection of memorabilia of North Carolina's earliest fire company, from 1845, and of the Button Company, a rival volunteer company. The New Bern Firemen's Museum claims the title of "oldest volunteer fire company in North Carolina." The museum guide himself has been a volunteer fireman for many years. The displays include early steamers and pump wagons, large photographs, and the mounted head of an old fire horse named Fred, who, at least according to publicists, died in harness answering a false alarm in 1925. No information is offered about what happened to the rest of the horse. Open Monday through Saturday from 10:00 a.m. to 4:00 p.m. Closed Thanksgiving, Christmas, and New Year's Day. Admission is $5.00 for adults, $2.50 for children (252-636-4087; www.newbernmuseums.com).

At ***Bank of the Arts,*** 317 Middle Street (252-638-2577; www.cravenarts .net), about a block away, you'll find artists' exhibits in sculpture, oil, watercolor, pottery, and photography. The exhibits change every month. Originally a neoclassical bank building, it is now home to the Craven Arts Council and Gallery. The gallery has 30-foot-high ceilings with ornate colored plaster in the Beaux Arts style. Sometimes afternoon concerts, storytellers, and folksingers are featured. Open Tuesday through Saturday 10:00 a.m. to 6:00 p.m.

The ***New Bern Trolley Cars*** (252-637-7316 or 800-849-7316; www.new berntours.com) combine the fun of motion with the expertise of tour guides who know the history of New Bern and tell it well. The trolley tours, which run through the historic downtown district, last ninety minutes. Tour hours vary with the seasons, so you'll do better by calling to find out what's happening during your visit to the area. Tickets are available where the trolley begins its route, next to Tryon Palace: $15 for adults, $8 for children up to age twelve.

In a town as historically significant as New Bern, you could easily get overwhelmed by more historical data than you really want on a vacation, but to enjoy the area you should know at least a few basic facts. The community was first settled in 1710 by Swiss and German immigrants, who named it for Bern, Switzerland. It was capital of the colonies from 1766 to 1776 and then state capital. Economically, the area flourished mostly because of its port at the time of the Revolution, slumped during the Civil War, then recovered fairly quickly. From about the time of World War II, it has gradually restored its historical spots and become a comfortably established, low-key attraction.

Irrelevant but fun to know: Pepsi-Cola was invented here, but the inventor went bankrupt during a sugar scarcity. Caleb Bradham created a drink in 1898 at his pharmacy that he said did not contain the "impurities" found in bottled health tonics and other drinks, referring to the alcohol and narcotics some of them contained. People liked it and started calling it "Brad's drink." Bradham's photograph shows a good-looking man with dark hair, a long face, high arching eyebrows, and a quirky smile under a narrow mustache. He looks like the drink made him happy. He made the stuff in the cramped basement of his store, bottling the syrup for his fountain and other pharmacies in the area. In a few years he was doing enough business to realize he was on to something, and incorporated as Pepsi-Cola on December 24, 1902. Today the ***Birthplace of Pepsi-Cola,*** 256 Middle Street, is a memorabilia gift shop in the same location, owned by the Pepsi-Cola Bottling Company. You can buy a fountain Pepsi and drink it sitting at a table surrounded by Pepsi memorabilia—signs and shirts and lamps and key rings and magnets and limited-edition displays. A video narrated by Walter Cronkite telling the Pepsi-Cola story is available to watch while you're in the store. The store is open Monday through Saturday 10:00 a.m. to 6:00 p.m. (252-636-5898; www.pepsistore.com).

An interesting and historical, yet cheery and comfortable, place to stay in New Bern is ***Harmony House Inn,*** 215 Pollock Street (252-636-3810 or 800-636-3113; www.harmonyhouseinn.com). Sooki and Ed Kirkpatrick, the proprietors, bring to innkeeping the kind of personable warmth that makes business travelers who stay there regularly feel free to stop in unannounced, use the phone in the inn's office, and then hurry out to the car, saying they'll be back to spend the night on the way through tomorrow.

The story of the house is complex. It began as a four-room, two-story home with Greek Revival styling. As the family grew, the house was enlarged. Around the turn of the twentieth century, when the children grew older, two sons wanted the house, so it was sawed in half, and one side was moved 9 feet away from the other. A huge hallway and another set of stairs were put in to join the building yet divide it into two separate dwellings. Now the two hallways, front doors, and sitting areas are all part of the inn. It's furnished with antiques and reproductions created by local craftspeople, and in the parlor is an 1875 organ in perfect working order. Breakfast is always an extravaganza, including eggs, cheese, meat, cereal, and fruit.

After a day of touring, you can rest a while and then walk to dinner. ***Henderson House,*** right across the street at 216 Pollock (252-637-4784), has been serving fine meals for more than twenty years. The atmosphere is

Showing the Colors

During the summer and into autumn in New Bern, you'll notice the streets are lined with trees blooming in a range of colors from palest pink to bright red to dark purple. *Lagerstroemia indicia,* commonly known as crape myrtle, is the official shrub of New Bern. Originally native to China and tropical and subtropical countries, crape myrtle is popular throughout the South and not hardy north of Baltimore. Hybridizers have created dwarf versions of the plant for smaller gardens. The bark on *Lagerstroemia* flakes away from the wood in patches, showing a lighter color underneath that attracts the eye in winter after the tree has shed its leaves and branches.

BETTER-KNOWN ATTRACTIONS IN
THE NORTHERN COAST AND ISLANDS

New Bern
Tryon Palace
(800) 767-1560
www.tryonpalace.org

Manteo
Lost Colony Outdoor Drama
(252) 473-2127
(800) 488-5012
www.thelostcolony.org

Roanoke Island
North Carolina Aquarium
(252) 473-3493
www.ncaquariums.com

Nags Head
Jockey's Ridge State Park
(252) 441-7132
www.jockeysridgestatepark.com

Kill Devil Hills
Wright Brothers National Memorial
(252) 441-7430
www.nps.gov/wrbr

elegant. Dining specialties include a hot soup and a cold fruit soup, as well as seafood, beef, and chicken entrees. All spirits are available. As you'd expect, all the desserts are homemade. Everything is delicious, the kind of dining that guests at the bed-and-breakfasts talk about over breakfast the next morning. The restaurant is open for dinner Wednesday through Sunday.

Water's Edge

One interesting trip from New Bern is the drive north on US 17 to Washington, where you pick up U.S. Highway 264 to Bath, Belhaven, and Swan Quarter. The trip winds through mostly rural areas.

You'll find a lot of local color just before you come to Washington, at *Chocowinity,* billed as "Home of the Indians," where the high school boasts various athletic triumphs each year. Chocowinity is a crossroads community, not set up to lure or serve tourists, so don't count on it as a place to stop, fuel up, eat, and so on. Look at it as an absolutely honest glimpse of small-town coastal North Carolina.

From here you can drive on through Washington to Bath or get to Bath by crossing the Pamlico River on the ferry, which you approach by following Highway 33 East from Chocowinity through corn and tobacco country, past a brick house with a stonework chimney that's bigger than the house, past Possum Track Road, and on to Aurora—a drive of about 33 miles. This route actually backtracks some, and you could get to Aurora faster by taking Highway

1003 from US 17 just outside New Bern, but then you'd miss Chocowinity. It all depends on how much exploring you want to do.

Twin Lakes Resort, 1618 Memory Lane (252-946-5700; www.twinlakesnc .com) in Chocowinity, offers swanky camping. You have a choice of trailer sites (some shaded), tent sites, and pull-throughs, supplying water and electricity. Also on the grounds are hot showers, campfires, laundry facilities, pay phones, ice, firewood, church services, a boat ramp, a fishing pier, waterskiing, a playground, recreational facilities, a camp store, and a picnic area. People sometimes bring big tents, refrigerators, and small television sets—everything they need to stay for a long time. Call to check rates and make reservations.

Close to the juncture of Highways 33 and 306, the little town of Aurora—population about 500—is home to the *Aurora Fossil Museum,* on Main Street. This museum is great for kids who are turned on by hunting for artifacts and equally rewarding for anyone looking for a better understanding of the geological history of eastern North Carolina, from the birth of the Atlantic Ocean to the present.

Millions of years ago this part of the state lay under the ocean. Fossils anywhere from five to twenty-two million years old are on display in the museum, along with a variety of murals and an eighteen-minute video explaining the history of the region. The fossils include giant teeth from 40-foot sharks, bones from extinct birds, and skeletons of dolphins that had necks. Some scientists speculate that the existence of the neck proves dolphins once lived on land and evolved to adapt to the sea.

The museum gets its artifacts from a large phosphate mine a few miles north of town. An exhibit in the museum shows a mock phosphate pit to illustrate how phosphate is mined and where the fossils come from. And outside the museum stands a huge pile of coarse phosphate materials through which visitors may sift for fossils. What you're most likely to find here are prehistoric shark's teeth.

The museum is about more than fossils and prehistoric times and now includes such exhibits as a collection of Native American artifacts. The museum is open 9:00 a.m. to 4:30 p.m. Monday through Saturday, Sunday 1:00 to 4:30 p.m. Closed on holidays. Admission is free (252-322-4238; www.aurorafossil museum.com).

From Aurora, Highway 306 North runs to the Pamlico River Ferry. The ferry is free. The crossing takes about twenty-five minutes. From the ferry landing, go left on Highway 92 into historic *Bath,* where you come first to the visitor center.

Bath is the kind of place you fantasize about when you dream of leaving the rat race for a simpler way of life. The town, with a population not much

Whitfield's Curse

Bath opened the first public library in the American colonies in the early 1700s, started the first shipyard in the state in 1701, and was the state's first capital in 1744. So why did such a forward-looking town never grow the way some other seaport towns did?

Local legend has it that the townspeople rejected Methodist evangelist George Whitfield when he came in 1774 to save their souls. They didn't want to hear his preaching, and they wouldn't give him a place to stay in town. Whitfield got back at them by placing a curse on the village: ". . . you shall remain, now and forever, forgotten by men and nations. . . . "

After that the town burned three times, and even today the population stays at about 200 souls, which may or may not be saved.

over 200, only 3 blocks long and 2 blocks wide, is friendly and without guile; people cutting their grass or working in their gardens wave as you walk or drive by. They're proud of their history but see it with enough humor to name the state liquor store "Ye Olde ABC Package Store."

The folks in the **Historic Bath Visitors Center** at 207 Carteret Street encourage you to see the twenty-five-minute orientation film, "A Town Called Bath," before you begin a self-guided walking tour or take one of the guided tours. These tours are given on the hour, with the last tour leaving an hour before closing time. Hours are 9:00 a.m. to 5:00 p.m. Monday through Saturday and from 1:00 to 5:00 p.m. Sunday, from April through October 31. Winter hours are 10:00 a.m. to 4:00 p.m. Tuesday through Saturday, 1:00 to 4:00 p.m. Sunday. Tours take about an hour and a half. Modest admission is charged (252-923-3971; www.pamlico.com/bath).

You can approach the history a couple of different ways. Bath was the home of Blackbeard, the pirate, and some of his loot is still supposed to be buried somewhere in the area. It's also the oldest incorporated town in North Carolina. The Palmer-Marsh House, from the colonial period, dates back to about 1740. The St. Thomas Church, which was begun in 1734, is the oldest church in the state. It has been restored and is still used by the Episcopal Diocese as an active place of worship, although visitors are allowed to come in anytime for a self-guided tour. The St. Thomas parish had a collection in the early 1700s of more than 1,000 books and pamphlets from England, and that collection became the first public library in North Carolina.

From Bath, it's a pretty drive of 11 miles on Highway 99 to Belhaven. Here you can visit **Belhaven Memorial Museum,** in Old City Hall (211 East Main Street; 252-943-6817; www.beaufort-county.com/Belhaven/museum/Belhaven

misseva's coughsyrup

2 tablespoons castor oil

1 tablespoon lemon juice

2 tablespoons paregoric

1 cup brown sugar

Mix all ingredients well.

Seems like this needs more liquid, but maybe just the threat of having to take it was enough to stop a cough.

.htm). The collection represents the idiosyncratic personal interests of Eva Blount Way in collections she began about 1900, when she would have been about thirty years old. She began with buttons, ending up with about 30,000 of them. This won't make much sense if you're so young you've seen only standard plastic buttons found on most clothing today. But before plastic, buttons were made from all kinds of materials: precious metals, gemstones, wood, shells. They were often highly ornate, hand produced, and beautiful. In Eva's day, practically all women had jars full of buttons or kept buttons on long strings. Eva's collection just got a little out of hand. She also got interested in old coins, early American kitchenware, coffee grinders, antique dolls, and toys. The displays now include Civil War items, military memorabilia from two world wars, farming tools, and so on. One quirky addition is an X-ray machine from the 1920s that looks like something from a Flash Gordon serial. According to the museum's advertising, "It's like spending a day in your grandmother's attic." Belhaven Memorial Museum is open every day but Wednesday 1:00 to 5:00 p.m. Admission is free; donations are appreciated.

At Belhaven pick up US 264 East, crossing the Intracoastal Waterway to Swan Quarter—a nature lover's paradise—filled with water, woods, and wild-life, where people so far have made only the lightest noticeable mark. Most of this distance is lovely, although you'll probably see a lot of heavy equipment in some areas. In early summer hibiscus bushes bloom along the road, red and yellow cannas adorn the lawns of farmhouses and mobile homes, and apple trees bear so heavily that the fruit seems to be dripping from the laden and drooping branches.

At Swan Quarter you can either take the ferry to Ocracoke, probably the best known of the barrier islands, or you can continue driving up the coast along US 264 to Manns Harbor, where you cross the bridge to Roanoke Island and continue on over the **Outer Banks** islands. If you plan to take the ferry, a two-and-one-half-hour ride, call the Ocracoke Visitors Center (252-928-4531) ahead of time to check on current schedules and weather conditions.

Ocracoke, an old fishing village, is fun if you're willing to take a couple of days and just hang out; if all you do is drive through, you'll miss most of what it has to offer. Of course there's history. As early as 1715, Ocracoke was a port of the North Carolina colony, where Blackbeard, the pirate, buried his treasure and lost his head. The head got carried off to Bath; presumably the treasure's still somewhere on the island. These days, fishing, bicycling (you can rent bicycles here), and bird hunting are bigger attractions than treasure hunting. But mostly Ocracoke is a place to escape the chrome-and-plastic world of commercial tourism. For full information about the island, ferries, and marina, contact the Ocracoke Visitors Center (252-928-4531). ***Ocracoke Island Lighthouse*** (888-493-3826; www.ocracoke-nc.com/light), on Point Road, is the oldest lighthouse still in use in North Carolina. It was built in 1823. The tower is 75 feet tall, built of brick and concrete, with 5-foot-thick base walls. The white tower serves as an entrance beacon to Ocracoke Inlet. The tower is not open to the public, but you may tour the grounds. Admission is free.

> ## "ibegtodiffer . . ."
>
> Another North Carolina travel writer who was on a panel with me told the audience that she was "underwhelmed" by Ocracoke and advised them not to bother going there. For sure, she said, there was nothing for her twelve-year-old son to do there. The moral is that if you or the people traveling with you want specifically organized "things to do," skip Ocracoke. The fact that the writer quoted is still alive and in good health says a lot for my self-control and restraint.

Fair warning here—Ocracoke gains in popularity as a tourist destination every year, and to enjoy it as a slower-paced place, you need to plan a trip that doesn't land you on the island at the peak of the summer season in July and August. Although you can still enjoy the island's 16 miles of clean, unspoiled beaches without crowding or concessions then, you'll find the area around the harbor full of people wandering about, gaping, and filling the restaurants. Not that there's anything wrong with that. Ocracoke, after all, has set itself up to serve tourists. But you'll get a much better sense of the place and its people during the slower times.

A good example of this is ***Edwards of Ocracoke,*** 226 Back Road, a place to stay in the village. This is one of the long-established lodgings, with motel rooms and efficiencies, cottage apartments, and a couple of private cottages all clustered around a tree-shaded yard with lawn chairs, grills, and a place to clean fish. The accommodations are relatively inexpensive and quite plain, but comfortable. It's a place with no affectations, run by Wayne, Trudy, and Bert Clark, all of whom came to the place after leaving more high-powered jobs and education. It's friendly and homey. But in the busiest times, such as mid-July, it's also full of people, so you definitely won't have any sense of privacy and silence on a tiny island (800-254-1359; www.edwardsofocracoke.com).

Virtually everyone who visits the island ends up having at least one meal at *Howard's Pub and Raw Bar Restaurant,* on Highway 12 at the north end of the village. This is a big, clattering place with a menu that has everything from thick, hand-shaped burgers to oysters on the half shell. Portions are generous, service is friendly, and the atmosphere is casual. People seem to be having a good time, especially those seated on the screened porch. In addition to a wine list, Howard's has a huge line-up of beers, more than 200 of them, from domestic Coors and Rolling Rock to microbrewery organic beers such as Butte Creek Pale Ale to regional microbrewery specialties. Also, Howard's has a line of T-shirts, hats, sweatshirts, mugs, magnets, and the like emblazoned with its logo. For all the commotion, you don't get the feeling of being churned through a corporate eating place here, and especially in the off-season, it's fun. The restaurant is open every day of the year, beginning at 11:00 a.m. (252-928-4441; www.howardspub.com).

Another popular restaurant on the island is *Captain Ben's Restaurant,* on Highway 12, just north of the ferry terminal. The restaurant specializes in seafood; its signature dishes are shrimp scampi and Maryland crab cakes. You can enjoy wine or beer here, in a casual atmosphere. The restaurant is open April through October, from 11:30 a.m. to 9:00 p.m., serving lunch and dinner (252-928-4741; www.ocracokeguide.com/captainbens).

No matter how much you like it, sooner or later you'll have to leave Ocracoke. A free ferry will take you from Ocracoke to Cape Hatteras. Hatteras is pretty well built up and can have heavy traffic on its main highway, but you should plan on a visit to the *Pea Island National Wildlife Refuge,* south of the Oregon Inlet, where you can see more birds than you even knew existed— more than 250 different species. Serious bird-watchers spend days here. You need a good insect repellent, a shirt with long sleeves, a hat with a brim, suntan lotion, and drinking water to make the experience comfortable. Binoculars help, too. Some observation decks let you see not only the ocean and wildlife but also shipwrecks on the shore. The refuge is open every day from dawn to dusk. The information office is open daily 9:00 a.m. to 4:00 p.m., from April through October, and admission is free (252-987-2394 or 252-473-1131; www.fws.gov/peaisland).

Next, still along the Outer Banks, at Frisco, you'll find the *Native American Museum and Natural History Center* (53536 Highway 12; 252-995-4440; www.nativeamericanmuseum.org). The museum has a nationally recognized but too-seldom-seen collection of Native American artifacts and exhibits. In the natural history center, you'll find educational displays, special films, live exhibits, and a nature trail winding through the maritime forest. The people who work here say it's impossible to tell what the most popular exhibits are because favorites vary with each individual, but the stone artifacts attract a lot of attention, the Hopi wishing drum really does work, and people who commune with nature in the maritime forest claim some unusual experiences. The gift shop is popular, too, because it sells genuine Native American crafts. The museum is open Tuesday through Sunday 11:00 a.m. to 5:00 p.m. To request information by mail, write the museum at Box 399, Frisco 27936. Modest admission is charged.

It's possible to drive on up the Outer Banks, but it's monotonous in some undeveloped areas, full of traffic elsewhere, and generally just not as interesting as you'd expect it to be. You might do better to ferry back across to Swan Quarter and from there drive north on US 264, toward Manns Harbor, where the bridge takes you across to Manteo on Roanoke Island. This trip takes you into the ***Mattamuskeet National Wildlife Refuge,*** a breathtaking wilderness of 50,000 acres comprising Lake Mattamuskeet, marshland, timber, and cropland. The lake is 18 miles long and about 6 miles wide, the largest natural lake in North Carolina.

In parts of the acreage, water levels are controlled mechanically to allow local farmers to plant corn and soybeans and to allow for overseeding some acres to provide food for the wildlife. The wooded areas along the boundaries of the refuge contain pine and mixed hardwoods. Some commercial logging and controlled burning are used to keep the woodlands healthy.

Headquarters for the refuge (252-926-4021; www.hydecounty.org) is off Highway 94, 1.5 miles north of US 264, between Swan Quarter and Englehard. Stopping in is a good way to learn all the possibilities of the place. At various points you can crab, fish in fresh- or saltwater, and hunt. The area begs for bird-watching, photographing, and painting. Depending on the time of year, you might spot swans, Canada geese, song- and marsh birds, and even bald eagles, as well as deer, bobcats, and river otters. Some hunting of swans, ducks, coots, and occasionally deer is allowed.

But this is a refuge administered by the U.S. Fish and Wildlife Service of the Department of the Interior and operates by its rules. You can't camp, swim, or collect exotic plants here. There are restrictions on firearms. The refuge is open for daylight use daily. For full details on how to enjoy the place and lists of lodgings available nearby, write Refuge Manager, Mattamuskeet National Wildlife Refuge, Route 1, Box N-2, Swan Quarter 27885.

Mattamuskeet Lodge on the property is no longer open for visitors inside because of structural problems, but it's still an interesting place to take pictures of from the outside, and the story of the lodge stands as proof that people have been messing with the environment to make money for a long time. Beginning in 1911, three different investors tried to drain Lake Mattamuskeet to build a community they wanted to call New Holland and farm what would be rich soil once the water was gone. They built a pumping station in 1915, where four coal-fueled steam pumps moved 2,000 gallons of water per second. This was the largest pumping station in the world. But the whole enterprise was so expensive that each of the investors ultimately gave up on the idea and the U.S. government took over the land in 1934, establishing a waterfowl sanctuary. The Civilian Conservation Corps turned the pumping plant into a lodge, with an observation deck in the tower that had been a smokestack. The lodge has been empty since 1974, but local volunteer groups, the nonprofit group Partnership for the Sounds, and the U.S. Fish and Wildlife Service are raising money to restore the lodge so it can be used for research and education about migratory waterfowl. The first weekend in December, the *Swan Days Festival,* with local craft and food vendors, guided tours of the refuge areas, and workshops, focuses attention on the lodge and the refuge. The refuge office and lodge Web site (www.albemarle-nc.com/mattamuskeet/refuge/) provide details.

When you're in the area, it's fun to gas up at the *Mattamuskeet Sportsman's Center* (252-926-5411) on US 264, where the proprietor will dispense information, advice, directions, and such necessities as fishing and hunting equipment, bait shrimp, worms, ice, candy, beer, and soda. Oh, yes, and food.

From Mattamuskeet Lake, US 264 continues through lonely marsh and woodland up to Manns Harbor and across to Roanoke Island. The main community here, Manteo, used to be a small resort area. It's growing now, not excessively, but too much to suit the longtime residents, who remember when the road through town didn't turn into bumper-to-bumper ribbons of automobiles during rush hour.

Roanoke Island

You'll remember from your grade-school history lessons that *Roanoke Island* is where the English first tried to establish a colony in the New World in 1585, encouraged by Queen Elizabeth I and led by Sir Walter Raleigh. They named it for Raleigh but couldn't keep it going. A year later those who had survived

Rain Time

The weather was cold and blustery the first time I saw a performance of *The Lost Colony*. As I was getting ready to sit down, a young man's hat blew off and landed at my feet. I retrieved it and ended up sitting next to him.

Shortly into the performance, I realized he was saying every performer's lines along with the actors—and he had it all down perfectly. He saw me notice and explained that he used to be in the show. It was common for the actors to learn each other's lines, he said, in case one of them couldn't perform and needed a stand-in.

By this time the rain was coming down pretty hard. The young man said the Indian dancers had two dance tempos—regular time and rain time. When the weather was bad, they danced faster to get the whole show finished so they wouldn't have to give back money to a rained-out audience.

This night, although the crowd sat willingly under umbrellas watching the show, the dancers just couldn't go fast enough. Pouring rain brought everything to a halt, and as we left, theater staff handed us tickets for another performance.

returned to England. In 1587 Raleigh tried again, this time including women and children in the group led by John White. Virginia Dare was born here. Then Sir Walter went sailing away for supplies. By the time he got back, three years later, the colony had vanished, leaving no signs of what might have happened to it. The *Fort Raleigh National Historic Site* (www.thelostcolony .org) memorializes the lost colony with a restoration of the old fort and a granite marker commemorating Virginia Dare's birth as the first English child born here. From June through August, the drama *The Lost Colony,* performed outdoors at the Waterford Theatre on the site, tells the story. (Long before he appeared as Andy Taylor in the Mayberry television shows, Andy Griffith played Sir Walter Raleigh in this production.) Everything about this outdoor drama happens on a grand scale, on a stage in front of the bay so the water almost seems to be a backdrop. Many of the effects are marvels of engineering. For instance, three ships "sail" in front of the stage, moved by a combination of ropes and human energy. Moderate admission is charged. Phone (800) 488-5012 for exact schedules. Be sure to ask what the current policy is regarding bad weather.

Next to the theater, the *Elizabethan Gardens* (252-473-3234; www .elizabethangardens.org), created by the Garden Club of North Carolina as a memorial to the lost colonists, bloom from spring until fall, with roses, crape myrtle, lilies, hydrangeas, and summer annuals. The gardens feature an extensive collection of old garden ornaments, some dating back to the time of the first Queen Elizabeth, as well as a sunken garden, a wildflower garden, an herb garden, and camellias and azaleas in season. Open April and May 9:00 a.m. to 6:00 p.m.; June, July, and August to 7:00 p.m.; September and October to 6:00 p.m.; November to 5:00 p.m.; December, January, and February to 4:00 p.m.; March to 5:00 p.m. Admission is $8 for adults, $7 for senior citizens, $5 for children ages six to eighteen; children under five are admitted free.

Complete your history lesson by visiting the **Elizabeth II** *State Historic Site,* across the bridge and opposite the Manteo waterfront. The museum (252-473-1144; www.roanokeisland.com) contains exhibits depicting life in the sixteenth century, including a reproduction of a sailing vessel similar to what would have been used to bring the first colonists to Roanoke in 1585. A twenty-minute multimedia program gives you the feel of those early voyages and what it would have been like to live on the ship. In the summer costumed actors portray early mariners and colonists. After seeing the film, you may tour the ship. Operating hours vary seasonally. Moderate admission is charged.

In downtown ***Manteo*** (named for an Indian of Roanoke who went back to England with the early sailors) on U.S. Highways 64/264, you can pick up a bit of local family history by staying at ***Scarborough Inn*** (524 US 64; 252-473-3979; www.scarborough-inn.com), run by longtime residents of the island. Six rooms in the inn and four in the annex are furnished with comfortable old furniture that has been in the family, or at least in the community, for generations. It's not fancy stuff but the kind of things you remember from visiting old Aunt Lizzie or Great-Grandma. Nearly every piece has a story that Rebecca

Elizabeth II

and Fields Scarborough, who love to talk, will tell you gladly. The rooms are simple but comfortable. Two units over the barn are outfitted with king-size beds. Each room has a private bath, a small refrigerator, and a coffeemaker with coffee provided. No breakfast is served, but Rebecca leaves a couple of packs of doughnuts by the coffeemaker. Rates include the use of bicycles for exploring the island.

drinkup

Before Prohibition, North Carolina produced more wine than any other state in the country. Settlers cultivated scuppernong grapes more than 400 years ago in the settlement of Sir Walter Raleigh, The Lost Colony.

For a special occasion, you might try the *Tranquil House Inn.* Located on the Shallowbag Bay waterfront in downtown Manteo, the inn whispers "luxury" when you enter. The building is a reproduction of a typical nineteenth-century Outer Banks inn, with added contemporary conveniences a nineteenth-century traveler wouldn't even have dreamed about. Because of the pale cypress woodwork, glass, and stained glass throughout, the inn's interior seems almost as bright and sunny as the docks outside. The inn has an upscale gourmet restaurant with a fine wine list. In the guest rooms you'll find not only the expected amenities such as television and telephone, but also Oriental carpets, fine furnishings, and hand-tiled bathrooms. Rates, commensurate with the luxurious atmosphere, vary seasonally and include a buffet breakfast (405 Queen Elizabeth Avenue; 252-473-1404 or 800-458-7069; www.tranquilinn.com).

The distinctly local *Endless Possibilities,* 105 Budleigh Street (252-473-5121; www.ragweavers.com), a charity-based organization to raise funds for the Outer Banks Hotline Crisis Intervention and Prevention Center, is also a source of inspiration, education, and woven pieces for visitors. Endless Possibilities opened in 2002, selling fiber art to raise money for the hotline and also teaching volunteers to weave. Many of the weavers have come from difficult relationships and homes and find their work here part of rebuilding their lives. Visitors are invited to sit at a loom and try it themselves. A volunteer will help take the weaving off the loom and tie the knots to finish it. Other woven pieces, handbags, rugs, wall hangings, and scarves are for sale as well.

The other community on Roanoke Island, *Wanchese* (named for another Indian who took off for England), doesn't seem to know it is surrounded by tourists. Most of the people of Wanchese fish for a living. Driving on Highway 345 South to the village, you pass modest homes—many with a boat in the yard—battered vans, worn pickups, and lots of churches, flowers, and pets. Signs in some of the yards invite you to buy hand-carved duck decoys, driftwood, wood crafts, and nursery plants. All the people you see in the community will talk to you pleasantly and seem to enjoy your watching them work on the docks. At least one family maintains a "shedder" operation for harvesting soft-shell crabs as they shed their shells.

Fisherman's Wharf Restaurant (252-473-5205), a large, unpretentious restaurant on the wharf, surrounded by pilings, wild stands of Queen Anne's lace, and rolls of chicken wire, specializes in broiled and fried seafood and Wanchese crab cakes at modest prices. From your table you can watch the same fishing fleets that probably caught what you're eating. Sometimes broadcasts from a religious radio station drift through a speaker at the door. Serves lunch and dinner Monday through Saturday from noon to 9:00 p.m., from mid-April through October or later, depending on the weather. Closed Sunday.

From Manteo, a short drive across the bridge on US 64/264 takes you to Bodie Island (which isn't really an island anymore but a location along the northern section of the Outer Banks), where it's worth stopping to see the Bodie Island Lighthouse, operating since 1872. Aside from Coquina Beach, a good beach for swimming and fishing, you won't find many attractions here. A turn to the south, however, takes you to Hatteras Island, home of the tallest lighthouse in America, the *Cape Hatteras Lighthouse.* When the Cape Hatteras Lighthouse was built in 1870, it stood thousands of feet from the Atlantic Ocean. But erosion gradually brought the sea closer and closer.

Cape Hatteras Lighthouse

Experts said the lighthouse would fall into the ocean if it were not somehow protected. After lengthy controversy about what to do and how to do it, Congress authorized nearly $12 million to move the lighthouse away from the shoreline, preserving it as a historic structure.

In June 1999 the old lighthouse was moved 1,300 feet inland, barely an inch at a time, while North Carolinians watched reports of the progress on the Internet and on nightly television news.

Now the lighthouse stands 3,000 feet from the ocean at high tide, about the same distance as when it was first built, and is open for visitors. If you're up for climbing more than 260 steps, you can stand on a balcony at the top to survey the area.

What used to be the lighthouse keeper's home is now a visitor center where you can check out exhibits about local history and pick up a map for a self-guiding nature trail that begins nearby.

In the summer season the lighthouse is open every day from 10:00 a.m. to 4:00 p.m. In the off-season it closes earlier. The visitor center is open from 9:00 a.m. to 5:00 p.m. daily. Admission is free. This area is undeveloped because the protected Cape Hatteras National Seashore comprises Hatteras, some of the southern end of Bodie, and Ocracoke. Here you can see natural beaches and their attendant wildlife, seashells as they wash ashore and accumulate, and vegetation dwarfed and gnarled by salt and wind but not threatened by macadam. For more information on the area, write the Superintendent, Cape Hatteras National Seashore, Route 1, Box 675, Manteo 27954, or call (252) 473-2111; www.hatteras-nc.com/light/.

It's a different story turning north from Bodie Island. You drive through the kind of beach-strip conglomeration of motels, restaurants, gas stations, fast-food chains, and beach shops that typifies most popular beach areas. As a follower of unbeaten paths, you might choose to skip it, unless you're interested in seeing the ***Wright Brothers National Memorial*** at ***Kill Devil Hills,*** which marks the spot where Wilbur and Orville Wright first got off the ground in powered flight on December 7, 1903. The visitor center here has full-size copies of the brothers' glider and their first plane. The brothers' workshop and living quarters have been re-created, too. Open daily from 9:00 a.m. to 6:00 p.m. in summer, to 5:00 p.m. the rest of the year. Admission is $4 per person, children ages fifteen and younger free (252-441-7430; www.nps.gov/wrbr).

Just south of Kill Devil Hills, on the U.S. Highway 158 Bypass in Nag's Head, ***Jockey's Ridge State Park*** (252-441-7132; www.jockeysridgestatepark .com) makes a good place to stop, play in the sand, and get some exercise. This is the highest sand dune on the East Coast, where prevailing winds generally range from 10 to 15 miles an hour. Kite flying here is just about perfect.

Hang gliding is popular, too. The park has a picnic area and a shelter, as well as swimming and fishing on the sound.

Enjoy a more rural setting at **Nags Head Woods Preserve** (701 West Ocean Acres Drive; 252-441-2525). This is a 1,400-acre maritime forest with more than 5 miles of hiking trails. It also has a visitor center and a gift shop, and you can arrange kayak field trips in the summer. The preserve is open from 10:00 a.m. to 3:00 p.m. Monday through Friday, also on Saturday in the summer. Closed on major holidays.

Once you get this far north on the Outer Banks, it makes more sense to keep driving north on US 158 across the bridge onto the mainland than it does to backtrack. Following US 158, you can pick up U.S. Highway 17 South at Elizabeth City. **Elizabeth City** merits at least a brief stop, if only because it is at the site of a canal dug in 1790 with the unlikely name of Dismal Swamp Canal. A Coast Guard installation nearby and the local shipyard make this clearly a working, rather than a vacationing, area. The town, however, has a number of interesting historical buildings that are easy to check by taking a walking tour (Elizabeth City Area CVB, 400 South Water Street; 866-324-8948; www.discoverec.org).

The **Museum of the Albemarle** (252-335-1453; www.museumofthe albemarle.com), about 3 miles south of town on US 17, provides information on what is known as the Historic Albemarle Area, along with displays of artifacts and exhibits related to local history. (Colonists first revolted openly against the English monarchy here.) The exhibits tell the story of the area's people from the time of its Native Americans. Open Tuesday through Saturday from 9:00 a.m. to 5:00 p.m. and Sunday from 2:00 to 5:00 p.m. Closed Monday and major holidays. Admission is free.

Another interesting spot in Elizabeth City is the **Historic Main Street District,** one of four National Register Historic Districts in Elizabeth City. It has the largest number of brick antebellum commercial buildings in the state. The early nineteenth- and twentieth-century storefronts are now home to specialty shops, restaurants, art galleries, and antiques shops. Free brochures for a self-guided tour of the district are available at the Museum of the Albemarle.

And you don't have to have a boat to enjoy the **Mariner's Wharf** (252-335-4365) on the Intracoastal Waterway waterfront, where boats are offered free dockage for forty-eight hours. The "Rose Buddies" greet each boat with a rose and a welcome to Elizabeth City. These are not town workers, just local people who like to be friendly and helpful.

The next community along US 17, Hertford, the Perquimans County seat (population only about 2,000), is on the Perquimans River, which feeds into Albemarle Sound. It's worth a stop to visit the **Newbold-White House,** a colonial Quaker homestead, believed to be the oldest house in North Carolina, probably built about 1730. The house has been restored, preserving much of the original handwork of the brick chimneys and walls and some of the woodwork. Though not the original, the furnishings are authentic period pieces. Open from March to Thanksgiving, Tuesday through Saturday 10:00 a.m. to 4:00 p.m., Sunday 2:00 to 5:00 p.m., other times by appointment. Admission is $3; students with ID, $1 (151 Newbold White Road; 252-426-7567; www.newboldwhitehouse.com).

returninghome

Dorothy Spruill Redford, a descendant of the Somerset slave families, published a book entitled *Somerset Homecoming: Recovering a Lost Heritage* (Doubleday, 1988). In it she details the research it took to identify and find descendants of the Somerset families; describes contacting them; and tells about the huge, emotional reunion or, more accurately, first union, they held on the plantation. Redford includes much plantation history in her book as well.

You can learn a lot about the character of the area by taking two tours here, the **Historic Hertford Walking Tour** (252-426-5657), Hall of Fame Square, Church Street, and a self-guided driving tour of the **Old Neck Rural Historic District** (252-426-7567; www.perquimans.com).

The walking tour takes you by old waterfront homes and the 1828 Perquimans County Courthouse and into a district of antiques stores and cafes. The Historic Hertford District is listed on the National Register of Historic Places. You can also get a free map for the driving tour of Old Neck Rural Historic District, New Hope Road, and Old Neck Road. The driving tour runs through a National Register Historic District and into the countryside, past old plantation homes.

As an alternative plan if you are pressed for time, you may decide to skip the northern Outer Banks and go back from Roanoke Island on US 64, which takes you across the Alligator River and through the **Alligator River Refuge** (it's not clear whether the refuge protects people from alligators or the other way around), where you'll find lots of wildlife, picnic areas, and boating access. Either way, make your next stop Edenton, the first capital of colonial North Carolina. From US 64, take Highway 32 North. On US 17, keep going about 15 miles west from Hertford.

Capital Country

Although **Edenton** is in no way backward, it has managed to retain the calm and slower pace that we associate with earlier times and has done an outstanding job of preserving its historical sites and promulgating the facts.

Blackbeard lived here, even though he hung out in Bath and maybe left his treasure there. This would have been good pirate country. It was a busy port town in the eighteenth and early nineteenth centuries. During the Revolutionary War, supplies were shipped from here to Washington's army farther north.

Edenton had some of the earliest female political activists, too. In 1774 fifty-one women gathered in the courthouse square to sign a declaration vowing not to drink English tea or wear English clothing.

To steep yourself in colonial and Revolutionary War history, you have a choice of a guided or self-guided walking tour or a trolley tour. Pick up a walking-tour map or join a guided tour for a modest fee at the **Historic Edenton Visitors Center,** 108 North Broad Street (252-482-2637; www .edenton.com). A free audiovisual presentation gives you some orientation in the area's history. The Barker House (ca. 1782) was the home of Thomas Barker, a colonial agent in England, and his wife, Penelope, one of those ladies who boycotted English tea and clothing.

Call the visitor center also to arrange a guided walking tour of Historic Edenton. It takes a couple of hours. The tour includes four interesting buildings: Chowan County Courthouse, one of the oldest in the country, built in 1767; the Cupola House, noted for its elaborate Georgian woodwork inside; the James Iredell House State Historic Site, built in 1773, home of the first attorney general of North Carolina; and St. Paul's Episcopal Church, built in 1736. You may also purchase tickets to go into individual buildings apart from the tours.

In addition to the walking tours, you can take a guided trolley tour, which goes into the outskirts of town as well as through the downtown. Walking tours leave several times a day. They include time inside some of the homes. The cost of tours is moderate and varies according to their length and the number of homes visited. The visitor center is open from 9:00 a.m. to 5:00 p.m. Monday through Saturday, 1:00 to 5:00 p.m. Sunday, with shorter hours in the winter (www.edenton.nchistoricsites.org). You'll know you're at the visitor center when you see the flag with a teapot flying in the doorway.

Because it's so pleasant, full of flowers, friendly people, and lovely waterfront vistas, spending the night in Edenton rests and relaxes you.

The **Lords Proprietors' Inn** (888-394-6622; www.edentoninn.com), at 300 North Broad Street, has earned a reputation as one of the most elegant and gracious inns in the state. The inn comprises three separate restored homes in the historic district, grouped around a lawn and gardens and the Whedbee House, on a brick patio. The inn, which has sixteen rooms and two suites with all conveniences, has grown gradually since Arch and Jane Edwards moved to Edenton from Washington, D.C., and bought the first house to begin the inn in 1982. The dining room offers upscale gourmet cuisine.

All the guest rooms are light and airy. The common rooms have lots of open space, beautifully refinished old floors, and many whimsical decorating touches.

As for casual places to eat when you're in town, you're in for a true off-the-beaten-path experience at *Lane's Bar-B-Que* (252-482-4008) on Highway 32 south of town. For the most fun, sit at one of the five tables in the front rather than in the larger dining room in back. Up front you can enjoy the company and comments of the local workers, such as the men from nearby Edenton Utilities, as they have lunch and swap wisecracks. "Boy, did it rain or did it rain?" "It was so bad I had to get up in the trees and swing to the truck."

The restaurant serves burgers and a variety of home-cooked platters, but the barbecue deserves first place on your list of choices. Open from 11:00 a.m. to 8:30 p.m. every day.

When you study North Carolina history, much of it seems to be about war campaigns, documents, and declarations. Two plantation tours in the area give you a more personal look at history on the day-to-day level.

Hope Plantation, about 20 miles west, in Windsor on Highway 308, 4 miles west of the highway bypass, re-creates rural domestic life in northeastern North Carolina during the colonial and Federal periods. The plantation belonged to Governor David Stone, who also served in the state House of Commons and later as a U.S. senator. Stone owned more than 5,000 acres, planted mostly in wheat and corn. The plantation had all the mills, shops, and work areas necessary to be self-sufficient.

The two homes on the plantation, one dating from 1763, the other from about 1803, are examples of architecture that combines medieval English, Georgian, and neoclassical traits, reflecting the changing needs and knowledge of North Carolina colonists. Touring them, you see examples of how they might have been furnished, based on research about the plantation. The project continues to develop, with a reconstruction of the kitchen on its original foundation, restored outbuildings, and historically authentic vegetable and flower gardens. Moderate admission charged. Open Monday through Saturday from 10:00 a.m. to 5:00 p.m. and Sunday from 2:00 to 5:00 p.m. Closed at 4:00 p.m. in winter. Also closed Thanksgiving and Christmas Day. For full information, write to the plantation at 32 Hope House Road, Windsor 27983, or call (252) 794-3140; www.hopeplantation.org.

The second plantation also deserves much wider attention. *Somerset Place,* a nineteenth-century coastal plantation near Creswell, belonged to Josiah Collins, a successful merchant who came to Edenton from England in 1774. He and other investors formed the Lake Company, which acquired more than 100,000 acres of land next to Lake Phelps. They dug (or, more accurately, had slaves dig) a 6-mile-long canal through an area known as the

Great Alligator Dismal, to join the lake to the Scuppernong River and drain the swamps. When things were going well, gristmills and sawmills produced rice and lumber to ship down the canal in flatboats. But the flooding it takes to grow rice bred mosquitoes that made the slaves sick, so eventually the plantation grew corn and wheat instead.

Collins bought out his partners in 1816, and at his death passed the property on to his son. Later, Josiah Collins III took over. He turned Somerset Place into one of the state's largest plantations, working more than 300 slaves by 1860. Most North Carolinians didn't own slaves; Collins was one of only four planters in the state with more than 300.

The great fascination in visiting Somerset Place lies in the uncommonly detailed records the Collins family kept, especially about the black people on the plantation. The records detailed not only births, deaths, and marriages but also jobs and skills. Thus today we know that the cook was Grace and that one slave, Luke Davis, had only one job, cleaning carpets. We know that two sons of Collins III were playing with two slave boys one winter when all four boys drowned in the canal.

Additional information comes from the accounts of Dr. John Kooner, a physician who used to stay at the plantation for several weeks at a time, treating the slaves and the Collins family. He described an elaborate African dance that slaves Collins had imported directly from Africa apparently taught to the rest of the slave community. They performed it every year at Christmas, beginning at the great house, snaking to the overseer's house, and ending up at the slave quarters. Everyone on the plantation participated, either as a slave dancer or a spectator.

One of the most interesting and important aspects of research at Somerset Plantation is the ongoing archaeological study and excavation there, aimed at learning more about how the early African-American slaves lived and struggled to preserve their own culture and beliefs. In the absence of written records, such artifacts as pottery suggest that the slaves kept up their West African crafts and that later a Creole culture developed on the plantation.

Archaeological exploration has turned up the remains of slave houses, a hospital and chapel, and the plantation's formal garden, as well as the original brick boundary walls.

This kind of priceless information continues to come to light at Somerset Place, where personable and knowledgeable guides work hard to pass it on. You won't experience a routinized, canned tour here.

Ultimately, the Civil War did in the plantation. The Collins family died elsewhere, and today the site is run by the state.

Somerset (252-797-4560; www.somersetplace.nchistoricsites.org) is open April 1 through October 31, Monday through Saturday from 9:00 a.m. to 5:00

p.m., Sunday from 1:00 to 5:00 p.m.; November 1 through March 31, Tuesday through Saturday from 10:00 a.m. to 4:00 p.m., Sunday from 1:00 to 4:00 p.m. Closed Monday during winter when hours are shorter. All hours may vary, so call ahead. Admission is free. At Creswell, the turn for the plantation is marked with a sign. The address is 2572 Lake Shore Road, Creswell.

It's a quick drive from here to the office and main parking lot of ***Pettigrew State Park*** (2252 Lake Shore Road; 252-797-4475), bordering on Lake Phelps. Actually, Somerset Place State Historic Site lies within the park, too. And a hiking trail from the parking lot takes you to the Somerset Place buildings in about five minutes. The trail continues to the Pettigrew cemetery. Another part of the trail, known as the "Carriage Trail" because the Collins family used to like taking carriage rides along the route, leads to an overlook from which you can tread a boardwalk through the cypress woods. Some families like to settle in a picnic area in the park, then walk over to the historic site, rather than starting out at Somerset Place.

A park entrance and parking lot are 9 miles south of Creswell, off US 64 on Highway 1166. One of the park's main draws is fishing—largemouth bass, yellow perch, and panfish are plentiful. The lake is also good for shallow-draft sailboats, canoeing, and windsurfing. The park forest has a variety of deciduous trees, along with wildflowers and lower shrubs, all in enough variety to keep nature travelers with botanical interests happy. As for wildlife, a variety of waterfowl, owls and other birds of prey, and lots of woodland animals, including deer, frequent the area. Pettigrew has a few campsites but no hookups.

Finally, you can inspect some displays of prehistoric Indian culture, including dugout canoes, that will help give you a sense of the area's history over a long period of time. The park is open from about dawn to nightfall, varying with the season. Call ahead to check hours for your visit. Admission is free.

Places to Stay in the Northern Coast and Islands

BEAUFORT

Beaufort Inn
101 Ann Street
(252) 728-2600
(800) 726-0312
www.beaufort-inn.com

Inlet Inn
Corner Queen and Front Streets
(252) 728-3600
(800) 554-5466
www.inlet-inn.com

Pecan Tree Inn
116 Queen Street
(252) 728-6733
(800) 728-7871
www.pecantree.com

KILL DEVIL HILLS

Best Western Ocean Reef Suites
107 Virginia Dare Trail
(252) 441-1482
(800) 937-8376
www.bestwestern.com

KITTY HAWK

Beach Haven
4104 Virginia Dare Trail
(252) 261-4785
(888) 559-0506
www.beachhavenmotel.com

MANTEO

Tranquil House Inn
405 Queen Elizabeth Street
(252) 473-1404
www.tranquilinn.com

MOREHEAD CITY

Comfort Inn
3100 Arendell Street
(252) 247-3434
(800) 422-5404
www.moreheadhotels.com

Hampton Inn
4035 Arendell Street
(252) 240-2300
(800) 467-9375
www.hampton-inn.com/hi/
moreheadcity

NEW BERN

Aerie Inn
509 Pollock Street
(252) 636-5553
www.aeriebedandbreakfast
.com

Comfort Suites
218 East Front Street
(252) 636-0022
www.comfortsuites
newbern.com

Places to Eat in the Northern Coast and Islands

BEAUFORT

Net House
133 Turner Street
(252) 728-2002

The Spouter
218 Front Street
(252) 728-5190

KILL DEVIL HILLS

Flying Fish Café
2003 Croatan Highway
(252) 441-6894

Port-O-Call Restaurant
504 South Virginia
Dare Trail
(252) 441-7484

MANTEO

1587 Restaurant
405 Queen Elizabeth Street
(252) 473-1587

MOREHEAD CITY

Mrs. Willis' Restaurant
3004 Bridges Street
(252) 726-3741

Sanitary Fish Market and Restaurant
501 Evans Street
(252) 247-3111

NEW BERN

Henderson House
216 Pollock Street
(252) 637-4784

Pollock Street Delicatessen
208 Pollock Street
(252) 637-2480

THE NORTHERN COAST AND ISLANDS WEB SITES

Kitty Hawk Kites, hang gliding
www.kittyhawk.com

New Bern
www.newbern.com

Outer Banks
www.outerbanks.org

Shelling
www.nps.gov/calo/seashells.htm

The Upper Piedmont and Sandhills

Sir Walter's Country

You should probably get here soon if you want to enjoy the Raleigh area. Although the population hovers around a few thousand less than 280,000, depending on your source, the entire area is developing or at least spreading out rapidly, especially in the direction of Durham. But the area is so rich in history, culture, and amenities that it would be a shame to skip it.

Raleigh, the state capital, named for Sir Walter Raleigh, offers a variety of historical sites, museums, and fine old architecture in addition to the government buildings downtown.

Plan on stopping at **Historic Oakwood,** at North Person Street between Jones and Boundary, if you're interested in Victorian homes. This historic district of more than 400 homes, many restored, is considered one of the best examples of an unspoiled Victorian neighborhood in the country.

The **Oakwood Inn,** 411 North Bloodworth Street, offers you an opportunity to spend the night in an 1871 Victorian home in the heart of the historic district. The proprietors, Doris and Gary Jurkiewicz, know a lot about the area and keep maps with lots of information about the old houses on hand. The inn

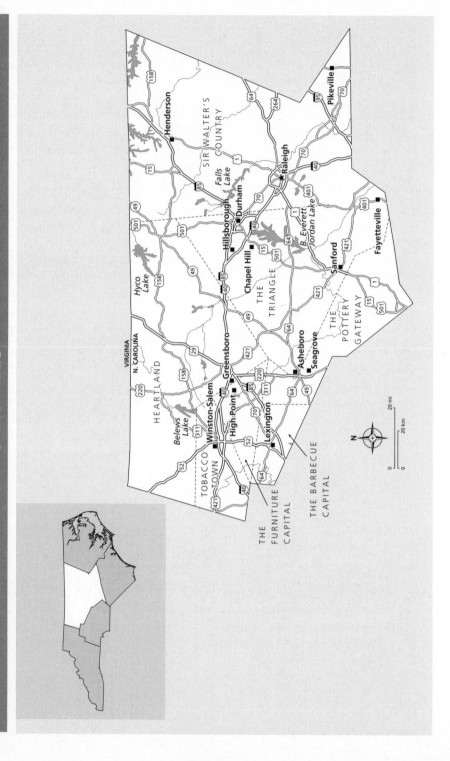

VIRGINIA

N. CAROLINA

HEARTLAND

Belews Lake

TOBACCO TOWN

Hyco Lake

SIR WALTER'S COUNTRY

Falls Lake

Henderson

Winston-Salem

High-Point

Lexington

THE FURNITURE CAPITAL

THE BARBECUE CAPITAL

Greensboro

Asheboro

Seagrove

Hillsborough

Chapel Hill

THE TRIANGLE

Durham

Raleigh

Pikeville

B. Everett Jordan Lake

Sanford

THE POTTERY GATEWAY

Fayetteville

SANDHILLS

20 mi

20 km

N

offers telephones, cable television, and high-speed wireless Internet in guest rooms, and gas log fireplaces add coziness to every room. Oakwood breakfasts fall in the gourmet category and are included in the rates (919-832-9712 or 800-267-9712; www.oakwoodinn.bb.com).

Several museums deserve your attention. *The North Carolina Museum of History,* 5 East Edenton Street, concentrates on exhibits, artifacts, and dioramas related to state history, transportation, and, of course, the Revolutionary and Civil Wars. It also has good exhibits about women in North Carolina. The museum is open Tuesday through Saturday from 9:00 a.m. to 5:00 p.m. and Sunday from noon to 5:00 p.m. Closed major holidays, and admission is free (www.ncmuseumofhistory.org).

The *North Carolina Museum of Natural Sciences* is between Jones Street and Edenton on North Salisbury Street (919-733-7450 or 877-462-8724; www.naturalsciences.org). Here you divide your attention between stuffed and skeletal remains of what once was, and living specimens of what still is, from across the state. In the whale hall a 50-foot whale skeleton hung from the ceiling dominates the exhibits. Another highlight is "Willo," the first dinosaur discovered with a fossilized heart. The living conservatory here is filled with live monarch butterflies and ruby-throated hummingbirds, in a re-creation of a dry tropical forest that also has cacti, heliconias, and orchids. Museum hours are the same as those at the museum of history. Admission is free.

Black history is beginning to receive organized, formal recognition in this area. The *African-American Cultural Complex,* 119 Sunnybrook Road, displays a large collection of items created by African Americans in three houses along a nature trail. They include innovations in science, art, business, medicine, politics, and sports. Hours by appointment (919-250-9336; www.aaccmuseum.org).

The *Martin Luther King Jr. Memorial Gardens* (919-834-6264; www.king-raleigh.org), 1500 Martin Luther King Jr. Boulevard, features a life-size statue of Dr. King and a twelve-ton granite water monument honoring twenty-five pioneers in civil rights and education in a setting of more than 8,000 flowers. The park is open twenty-four hours a day. Admission is free.

ANNUAL EVENTS IN THE UPPER PIEDMONT

Old Salem Reenactment of original Fourth of July held in 1783 July 4 (336) 721-7300	Winston-Salem Annual Piedmont Crafts Fair (mid-November) (336) 725-1516 www.piedmontcraftsmen.org

For insight into life in Raleigh's early days for both plantation owners and their slaves, visit **Mordecai Historic Park** (919-857-4364; www.raleigh-nc .org/mordecai), at the juncture of Wake Forest Road and Mimosa Street, on Person Street, just a mile from the state Capitol and downtown Raleigh. With several thousand acres, this was one of the largest plantations in Wake County before the Civil War, growing corn, wheat, cotton, and food for the people on the plantation. To give you an idea of its size, the area now known as Historic Oakwood stands on what used to be Mordecai property. Five generations of the same family lived in **Mordecai House,** and their eighteenth- and nineteenth-century furnishings, art, and books still fill the place.

Slaves did all the labor on the plantation. Records show that some of them grew their own rice and practiced traditional African farming, crafts, cooking, and music there. The park includes a re-created kitchen garden of vegetables, herbs, fruits, and flowers typical of the mid-nineteenth century. An 1842 kitchen from Anson County has been set up next to the garden where the original kitchen probably stood.

Open Tuesday through Saturday 10:00 a.m. to 4:00 p.m., Sunday 1:00 to 4:00 p.m. Tours begin on the hour. Admission is $5 for adults, $3 for children ages seven to seventeen, free for children six and under.

Also allow time for the **North Carolina Museum of Art,** at 2110 Blue Ridge Avenue (take the Wade Avenue exit off Interstate 40). The building, designed by the architect Edward Durrell Stone, who designed the John F. Kennedy Center in Washington, D.C., and the original Museum of Modern Art in New York, is important; so are the eight major collections. Arranged in chronological order, they cover 5,000 years of art, displaying work by artists from Botticelli to Monet to Andrew Wyeth. You'll also find exhibits of Jewish ceremonial art along with Greek and Roman sculpture. Tours are available at 1:30 p.m. A cafe and gift shop operate during museum hours.

A True Story

Each year in July, the African-American Cultural Complex presents the outdoor drama, *Amistad,* the story about a mutiny on a slave ship that resulted in what is now considered the first civil rights case in America. It is the only outdoor drama in the United States written, produced, and directed by African Americans. In song, dance, and speeches, performers dramatize how the Africans were taken from their native land, were imprisoned on the ship, revolted at sea, and went to trial in America.

The drama's producers say the episode stands as an early example of people of different cultures, races, genders, and faiths uniting in a democratic action. Call (919) 250-9336.

The museum (919-839-6262, extension 2154; www.ncartmuseum.org) is open Tuesday through Saturday from 9:00 a.m. to 5:00 p.m. (until 9:00 p.m. Friday) and Sunday from 10:00 a.m. to 5:00 p.m. Closed Monday and major holidays. Admission is free, except for some special exhibits.

Another approach to art is *Artspace,* 201 East Davie Street (919-821-2787; www.artspacenc.org), a nonprofit visual arts center in downtown Raleigh where you can watch artists at work and also visit shows in two galleries. Artists sell work out of their studios as well as from the galleries and in the gift shop. Artspace is open from 10:00 a.m. to 6:00 p.m. Tuesday through Saturday. The first Friday of every month, Artspace is open until 10:00 p.m. Admission is free.

The *Raleigh City Museum,* 220 Fayetteville Street Mall, gives you an intensely local, idiosyncratic look at the people and history of the town. This is one of those places that came into being because of the determination of people who live here. Beth Crabtree, a local historian, determined that the city needed a special home to honor its history and collect its artifacts before they became scattered, and in the early 1990s she began working to make it happen. After her death, another local woman, Mary Cates, picked up the torch and marshaled even more support. The resulting museum, with both changing exhibits and displays of artifacts, is housed in the ground and first floors of the old Briggs Hardware Store, a building dating from about 1890–1900. The private, nonprofit museum collects artifacts through the effective device of asking for them: "Share your artifact and its historical story." The results range from eighteenth-century tools and portraits to photographs and household items, and the collection continues to grow. The museum is open Tuesday through Friday 10:00 a.m. to 4:00 p.m., Saturday 1:00 to 4:00 p.m. Admission is free. Fayetteville Street Mall is between Salisbury and Wilmington Streets, a block from the Capitol (919-832-3775; www.raleighcitymuseum.org).

An unusual restaurant for a Southern town is the *Irregardless Cafe,* at 901 West Morgan Street (www.irregardless.com). When they describe it, people tend to call it the "vegetarian restaurant," but it does serve chicken, steaks, and duck as well as the vegetarian entrees. Don't be fooled by the sprouts in the salads. These aren't old hippies or young health-food nuts; they're folks who've figured out how to get the best flavor out of fresh ingredients with the least amount of doctoring. The menu changes daily to take advantage of fresh vegetables and meats. To dispel the notion that you're doing something that's good for you, you can order anything you like from the full bar. The homemade desserts will keep you on the sinful side, too. Open for lunch Tuesday through Friday from 11:30 a.m. to 2:30 p.m.; dinner Tuesday through Thursday from 5:30 to 9:30 p.m., Friday and Saturday to 10:00 p.m. Dancing until midnight Saturday. Sunday brunch 10:00 a.m. to 2:00 p.m. Call (919) 833-8898 to make reservations.

If you like gardens and plants and farmers, you'll want to add several more stops to your itinerary—the **Raleigh Farmers Market** and the **J. C. Raulston Arboretum** at North Carolina State University. The Farmers Market, 1201 Agriculture Drive in the warehouse section of town, draws crowds of locals with fresh produce sold by local truck farmers. Even if you're traveling and don't want to haul a lot of carrots across the state, it's fun to wander around watching the people and sampling the wares. Depending on your taste in fresh fruits and vegetables, it might be a little more fun to visit here during spring strawberry season or summer peach time than, say, for fall turnips or winter squash, but the market is open year-round from 5:00 a.m. to 6:00 p.m., Sunday 8:00 a.m. to 6:00 p.m. (919-733-7417; www.ncdamarketing.org). The arboretum at North Carolina State University, 4301 Beryl Road (take the Hillsborough Street exit off the beltline; 919-515-3132; www.ncsu.edu/jcraulstonarboretum), grows thousands of plants from around the world. In addition to special interest areas, such as the silver-and-white garden and a Japanese garden, a long perennial garden shows what it's possible to grow outside in North Carolina every month. Open daily from 8:00 a.m. to dusk. Admission is free.

Two more gardens appeal to horticulture enthusiasts: **Joel Lane House Gardens,** at the corner of St. Mary's and West Hargett Streets, and the **Raleigh Municipal Rose Garden,** at 301 Pogue Street, in a residential neighborhood near North Carolina State University. The Joel Lane House Gardens are authentic colonial Revival style, with espaliered fruit trees, pomegranate trees, a grape arbor, and, in the herb garden, medicinal and culinary herbs. The gardens are open daily from sunrise to sunset, with tours available March to the first of December, Tuesday through Friday from 10:00 a.m. to 2:00 p.m. and 1:00 to 4:00 p.m. Saturday. Admission is free. Phone (919) 833-3431 for details. The Raleigh Municipal Rose Garden, which has an amphitheater for concerts and stage productions, contains sixty different varieties of roses, about 1,200 plants, with something in bloom from late May until fall. Seasonal flowers, trees, and shrubs are included in the garden. Open daily, sunrise to sunset. Admission is free (919-821-4579; www.raleigh-nc.org/parks&rec/).

AUTHOR'S FAVORITE PLACES IN THE UPPER PIEDMONT

North Carolina State University Arboretum

Cedar Creek Gallery

Hillsborough

Seagrove

Old Salem

Selma

Nahunta Pork Center

Ava Gardner Museum

For a nice break from the city, head north, either on U.S. Highway 1 or on U.S. Highway 401 and Highway 39, to Henderson, not far from the Virginia border. The *Kerr Lake State Recreational Area,* 269 Glasshouse Road (252-438-7791; www.kerrlake-nc.com), is a 50,000-acre lake that stretches from North Carolina into Virginia, with 800 miles of shoreline. You'll find everything from picnic areas to camping facilities and hiking trails. The area has 700 campsites, twenty-one boat ramps, fourteen picnic shelters, and three community buildings. Admission to the park is free, but there is a fee for camping: $20 for electrical and water or $15 for nonelectrical, just water, for both tents and recreational vehicles. The Vance County Tourism organization sponsors July 4 fireworks and a Labor Day Parade of Lights flotilla.

While you're in the area, treat yourself to the *Cedar Creek Gallery,* 1150 Fleming Road, a workplace and sales outlet for top-quality craftspeople. Their brochure says, "Expect to be overwhelmed," and that's not hype. The gallery displays are spread through many rooms. Much of the work is pottery, but you'll also find fine glass, handmade stereopticons, stringed instruments, jewelry, and toys that are too splendid to put into the hands of kids. The quality is so outstanding that people tend to walk along talking in hushed tones, though that's not at all the demeanor of the artisans themselves. In the rear of the gallery, the *Museum of American Pottery* displays the entire range of local pottery, from the old folk pottery of places such as Cole and Jugtown to the works of contemporary studio potters. The exhibits include information about basic potting procedures and such things as salt glazes, too. From Henderson go south on Interstate 85, take the second Butner exit (186), turn left on U.S. Highway 15 North, turn right at the first crossroads, and left on Fleming Road to the gallery. Open daily from 10:00 a.m. to 6:00 p.m. (919- 528-1041; www.cedarcreekgallery.com).

From Raleigh, driving southeast on U.S. Highway 70, toward Goldsboro, takes you to *Selma, Pikeville,* and *Smithfield,* three small towns that you can easily visit on the same day. But if you are an antiques lover, you may decide to devote a full day to the town of Selma. As you head in this direction, the landscape gradually flattens out.

Signs from US 70 (as well as from Interstate 95 and Interstate 40) will direct you to Selma, a town that has pulled itself from the doldrums of empty old buildings to become an antiques mecca. The story begins in 1997, when Bruce Radford, town manager, was trying to figure out a way to restore the town to its earlier vibrancy. The town needed a theme, he thought. And it came to him during a golf game. He swung at the ball and got an inspiration, more or less at the same time. The golf ball went into the woods, but his idea was so good it flourishes even now that he has moved on. Using some financial incentives, promise of advertising support, and a lot of local enthusiasm, the town of Selma has seen its downtown buildings restored as antiques malls and shops, many with living quarters upstairs, artisans' studios, and shops for such antiques-related activities as upholstering.

In this same area, the **Nahunta Pork Center,** 200 Bertie Pierce Road, Pikeville, is a family operation that has grown from early slaughterhouse days, when they supplied hogs to barbecue houses, into a plant that includes a retail store where you can buy pork products so fresh that you can almost still hear the squeal. The difference in flavor between this and grocery-store meat that has spent several days in storage, transit, and case-life is obvious after a single bite. The sausage is made from an old family recipe, as is the barbecue sauce the store sells.

When Nahunta Pork Center went retail, a lot of people predicted the center wouldn't make it because there weren't enough customers in the area. They were wrong. In 1984 it claimed to be America's largest retail pork store, with forty employees processing about one hundred hogs a day. Today the center claims to be the largest all-pork retail displayer in the eastern United States.

Part of the beauty of the place is that it's oriented to small farmers, not agri-industry producers. The Nahunta Pork Center is especially known for its hand-rubbed country hams. The center is open from 8:00 a.m. to 5:30 p.m. Monday through Friday, 8:00 a.m. to 3:00 p.m. Saturday (919-242-4735; www .nahuntapork.com).

When you're through here, hop back on US 70 and follow the signs a few miles to Smithfield and the **Ava Gardner Museum.** Ava Gardner was born in this area, lived here when she was young, and is buried here. The museum was started by Tom Banks, who met Ava while she waited for rides near the campus of Atlantic Christian College, which he was attending, in the little town of Wilson.

Oink

Larry Pierce, manager of Nahunta Pork Center, wearing the white smock and hat that is standard dress for anyone going into any of the buildings where pork is handled, is headed into the ham house. As he opens the door, he turns slightly and says, "You ever hear about the chicken and the pig planning what each will contribute to an important breakfast?

"The pig says, 'I'm contributing bacon.'

"The chicken says, 'I'm contributing eggs.'

"The pig says, 'You're making a commitment. I'm making a sacrifice.'"

And grinning at his own pork humor, Pierce goes on into the chilly building.

It Started with a Kiss

According to local lore, Tom Banks would speed past Ava on his bicycle and yell, "Hey, girlfriend!" One day, she ran after him, pulled him off the bike, and kissed his cheek. Banks was smitten permanently.

Later he became a publicist on one of her movies, *My Forbidden Past*. No matter what else he did in a career that took him from New York to Florida, he kept up with what was happening to Ava, making scrapbooks of newspaper clippings about her. He also collected photographs, posters, audio- and videocassettes from her movies, and anything else he could find. In the 1970s he visited her in London and told her he was going to donate everything to start a museum in her honor.

In 1981 he bought the teacherage in Smithfield where she had lived when her mother taught school. He moved his collection there and opened the museum in 1982.

Since then the museum's had a few different locations, and the collection has continued to grow with donations of costumes, Ava's good china from her years in London, even her collection of Frank Sinatra records. The museum now has more than 100,000 items, and is finally housed in a permanent location at 325 East Market Street, in what used to be a Belk's Department Store.

The museum is open Monday through Saturday 9:00 a.m. to 5:00 p.m., Sunday 2:00 to 5:00 p.m. Admission is $6 for adults, $5 for senior citizens sixty-five and older and teens thirteen to sixteen, $4 for children ages six to twelve. Children under six admitted free (919-934-5830; www.avagardner.org).

The Triangle

In a sense, **Durham** is closer to Raleigh than it used to be. With both communities expanding laterally, it's not hard as you drive between the two places to imagine that they'll soon run together. And when people speak of "The Triangle," they're typically including Raleigh. But the increasing development has brought more traffic, which slows driving between Raleigh and Durham, so Chapel Hill and Durham more often package themselves as a tourist unit not necessarily including Raleigh. Durham is a tobacco town; Duke University was endowed by and named for the Duke family, which made Durham a tobacco center.

Although tobacco is not as important in the area as it once was, criticizing smokers is not a good way to make friends here. The Duke family pioneered in marketing cigarettes in America. You can understand something of the mystique

Duke Homestead Festivals

The Duke Homestead holds four major festivals a year: the Herb, Garden, and Craft Festival in June; the Tobacco Harvest Festival in September; an Evening at the Homestead, for children, in October; and Christmas by Candlelight in December.

and importance of tobacco by visiting the *Duke Homestead State Historic Site and Tobacco Museum,* established on the Duke family farm. Take the Guess Road exit off I-85 to 2828 Duke Homestead Road. Depending on when you're here, you'll see tobacco being planted, cultivated, harvested, or prepared for market and have the opportunity to participate in part of the processing.

On the property, the old family house, two tobacco factories, a curing barn, and a packhouse show you how it used to be. In the visitor center, tobacco-related exhibits include advertising, signs, machinery, and an old cigar store Indian. Open Tuesday through Saturday 10:00 a.m. to 4:00 p.m. Hours change, so it's a good idea to call ahead (919-477-5498; www.dukehomestead .nchistoricsites.org).

Duke money also created a dominant institution in this area, *Duke University.* In 1924 a $6 million gift from the family made it possible to expand what was then Trinity College. A large endowment and subsequent grants followed. The result is Duke University's two large campuses spread west and east of Durham, with great stone buildings and acres of grass and woods seeming to be enough for a huge student population. In fact, everything is large except the student body. Enrollment is in the neighborhood of 10,000 students, most of whom have to walk a lot to cover the large distances. The campuses are called, appropriately enough, East Campus and West Campus. You get to East Campus by following the signs from U.S. 15/501 Bypass to Highway 751 onto Duke University Road. The Georgian buildings of the original college are here.

To get to West Campus, take the Hillsborough Road exit from I-85 and go east on Main Street. On the West Campus the massive Gothic *Duke University Chapel* dominates (919-684-2572; www.chapel.duke.edu). James Duke, founder of the university, planned it that way. In March 1925, when he was walking the woods that have become West Campus, he designated the highest ground as the chapel site, saying that he wanted the central building of the campus to be "a great towering church" so dominating that it would have a spiritual influence on the young students who studied there. This edifice is worth a visit.

Horace Trumbauer of Philadelphia, who designed Duke's mansion on Fifth Avenue in New York, was the architect. The chief designer was Julian

Duke University Chapel

Able, the first black architect graduated from the department of architecture at the University of Pennsylvania.

Duke chose to have the church built of gray stone from a quarry in nearby Hillsborough. The result is a Gothic church patterned after the original Canterbury Cathedral. A 210-foot tower soars skyward, housing a fifty-bell carillon. A 5,000-pipe organ was built into the rear of the nave several decades after the chapel's construction.

The organ, designed by Dirk Andries Flentrop of Holland, is based on an eighteenth-century organ of classical design, constructed of solid wood and using no electricity except to power the blower. It was built in Holland, where it was played to ensure its quality. It was then totally dismantled, with each pipe wrapped separately, and shipped to Duke University. After the organ's first official use at Christmas 1976, one critic wrote that the organ "breathes music." In daylight the red, green, and gold trim on its mahogany seems to combine with the glow of its 5,000 long slender pipes.

Sunlight streams through seventy-seven stained-glass windows. These and the ornamental lead and gold symbols in the doors of the building were designed and created by G. Owen and Bonawit, Inc., of New York.

Instead of kings and saints at the portals, the chapel memorializes Protestant heroes such as Luther, John Wesley, Thomas Jefferson, and Robert E. Lee.

James Duke, his brother Benjamin, and their father Washington are entombed in a small memorial chapel. Statues, showing all three men lying comfortably pillowed and gracefully draped, are carved in marble atop their tombs beneath the windows. The chapel is open daily from 8:00 a.m. to 5:00 p.m. Interdenominational worship services are at 11:00 a.m. on Sunday.

Also on the West Campus, the **Sarah P. Duke Memorial Gardens** (418 Anderson Street; 800-367-3853; www.hr.duke.edu/dukegardens/dukegardens .html) have lots of open grass for kids to romp on and paths through wooded areas, as well as all kinds of seasonal flowers, a gazebo, and a lily pond. The 55 acres feature more than 2,000 kinds of plants, including the Blomquist Garden of Native Plants and the Asiatic Arboretum. Admission is free.

Another stop to feed your fascination with natural science is the **Museum of Life and Science & Magic Wings Butterfly House,** 433 Murray Avenue. Spread over 78 acres, the museum has a variety of science and nature displays, including a mock-up of the *Apollo 15* and a nature center with native animals. A train ride through the outdoor park gives you a chance to see everything from bears and wolves to farm animals. And the tropical butterfly house, the largest museum butterfly house east of the Mississippi, features species from Asia, Africa, and Central and South America. Open from 10:00 a.m. to 5:00 p.m. Monday through Saturday, noon to 5:00 p.m. Sunday. Closed New Year's Day, Thanksgiving, and Christmas. Admission is $9.50 for adults, $8.50 for senior citizens, and $7.50 for children ages three to twelve. Miniature train ride is $2.00 extra (919-220-5429; www.ncmls.org).

Two attractions in Durham pay homage to the role of African Americans in the region. **Hayti Heritage Center,** 804 Old Fayetteville Street, features works and artifacts of African Americans, visual arts galleries, and dance and community meeting spaces. Both contemporary and traditional art, by local, regional, and national African-American artists, is on display. Hayti was once a focal African-American marketplace with thriving neighborhoods. The center is downtown, easy to find by taking Expressway 147 to exit 12. It is open from 10:00 a.m. to 5:00 p.m. Monday through Friday, 10:00 a.m. to 3:00 p.m. Saturday. Weekend hours may vary depending on special events and activities. For details call (919) 683-1709; www.hayti.org.

St. Joseph's AME Church, at 804 Old Fayetteville Street, was one of the first autonomous African-American churches in America. The church was originally the sanctuary for St. Joseph's AME Church, which was begun in 1869. Phone and Web site are the same as Hayti Heritage Center.

BETTER-KNOWN ATTRACTIONS IN THE UPPER PIEDMONT

Raleigh
North Carolina State Capitol
(919) 733-4994

Winston-Salem
Old Salem
(336) 721-7300
(888) 653-7253

Historic Stagville, 5825 Old Oxford Highway, is a center for African-American studies and a place to learn about African-American plantation life, culture, and society before the Civil War. Historic Stagville has an eighteenth-century plantation house, part of which contains offices, with the rest open to the public. Four slave houses and an 1860 barn are on the property as well. Displays and research here emphasize the various cultures from which the slaves came, forming a new African-American culture in which self-reliance flourished. The barn, for instance, was built by master-craftsmen carpenters: slaves. Research here also demonstrates that there was more to the lives of the slaves than working all day for the master, although they certainly did that. But in their own community and homes, they also cultivated vegetable gardens, participated in athletic events, and took part in community affairs. Artifacts found on the property suggest that slaves brought from various parts of Africa kept some of their traditions and secret religious practices, which they used to create a new African-American culture. Historic Stagville is open from 10:00 a.m. to 4:00 p.m. Tuesday through Saturday. Admission is free (919-620-0120; www.historicstagvillefoundation.org).

While you're in the Triangle, take a picnic to the *B. Everett Jordan Lake,* a 47,000-acre lake created by the U.S. Army Corps of Engineers for flood control. All water recreation is available at some part of the lake—boating, swimming, and fishing—as well as hiking and camping. As you drive around in the area, you'll probably notice several different roads, all marked with signs, leading into access areas. One is U.S. Highway 64 at Highway 51, which leads to several recreation areas. Another is off US 64 going north on US 15/501, a point southwest of Durham, which takes you from Pittsboro, through Bynum and into Chapel Hill, home of the *University of North Carolina at Chapel Hill.* Chapel Hill and Durham are so close together that residents frequently live in one community and work in the other. The area south of Chapel Hill is still fairly rural and is a popular living area for university people with an itch to rusticate.

About 8 miles south of Chapel Hill, on US 15/501, just outside the community of *Pittsboro,* you'll find one of the most unusual examples of gentrified rural living imaginable. *Fearrington Village,* built around what used to be a barn, silo, farmhouse, and a few outbuildings, now comprises an inn with thirty-three rooms, a restaurant, a market and cafe, a series of shops, a residential area with town houses and freestanding homes, and such services as a pharmacy, bank, and beauty shop. It really is a village—an upscale one—in the middle of perennial gardens and fields dotted with cows. Not just any cows, of course: Scottish Belted Galloway cows, black at both ends and white in the middle, like walking Oreo cookies. Nobody milks these cows or eats them. They're pets. Or stage setting.

More than twenty-five years ago, R. B. and Jenny Fitch bought the Fearrington family dairy farm and started work on a planned community here. They didn't tear down existing buildings, and they built new ones to fit in unobtrusively. For instance, the granary became the market, deli, and cafe. The old milking barn houses a home-and-garden shop. The Potting Shed, in the old corncrib, sells plants propagated from the Fearrington gardens.

Living here isn't for anybody with shaky finances, and neither is staying at *Fearrington House Inn,* with rates running to several hundred dollars a night. The prices at the *Fearrington House Restaurant* or the *Fearrington Market Cafe,* however, are comparable to those in restaurants anywhere.

Activities such as touring the gardens, which are wonderful, are free. And you can browse in McIntire's, a good independent bookstore, shop for wine and gourmet treats, pick up handmade pottery and jewelry, and perhaps attend a reading by a well-known author in the renovated barn.

For more information about food, lodging, and activities in Fearrington Village, call (800) 316-3829; www.fearringtonvillage.com.

The town of Pittsboro is worth wandering through, too. It has lots of antiques shops and the kinds of stores that cater to people fixing up old houses, as well as a natural foods store and several restaurants. This is the kind of place where "real" farmers still mix on the sidewalks with men in Bermuda shorts and Birkenstocks.

The earliest settlers of this area were families who moved from the plantations on the coast to get away from the humid summer heat and the illnesses that came with it. The town of Pittsboro was formed in 1787. The early buildings were modest frame structures, but the new courthouse in 1843 was the first brick building. For a small town, Pittsboro had a lot of activity. Crowds gathered to see a Confederate statue unveiled, a murderer hanged, and President Theodore Roosevelt coming through. When electricity came in 1922, people danced in the street. This and a good bit more about the town's history is detailed in an outstanding little brochure, "Pittsboro Historic District," which includes a map of local structures and short paragraphs about their history. Most of the stores and restaurants in town have copies.

Another brochure, "Chatham County," also free in the stores, suggests a self-guided walking tour that begins at the present courthouse. The courthouse is at the center of a highway circle typical of many small Southern towns, with shops and restaurants lining the circle as well as streets radiating out from the curve.

A brochure called "Historic Pittsboro Antiques Walk" maps antiques, collectibles, and memorabilia shops within easy walking distance.

A potter, Lyn Morrow, has a shop and studio just 5 miles north of Pittsboro on US 15/501 that is a "must stop" if you enjoy places that are offbeat but still deal in quality. **Lyn Morrow Pottery** is located inside a house she's painted in cobalt blues and turquoise. Assorted metal sculptures stand around the front yard. Lyn says people sometimes wonder why she painted her house in such psychedelic colors, but when you see her pottery, you understand. It's not remotely psychedelic, but blue and turquoise are her predominant colors, and in that way her pottery stands out from that of the seventy or so other potters whose work she sells. She's been a potter for more than thirty years and not only knows her craft but also knows all the potters in a wide region as well. Lyn Morrow Pottery is open Tuesday through Saturday 10:00 a.m. to 5:00 p.m., Sunday noon to 5:00 p.m. (919-545-9078; www.lynmorrowpottery.com).

Just a mile or so north of Lyn, still on US 15/501, Joyce Bynum's **Stone Crow Pottery** has become an established studio and shop over more than twenty-five years, in an old log cabin. The stairs to the second floor of the display area bear a sign warning visitors to limit the number of people on the second floor at one time to ten. The showroom atmosphere is rustic. Joyce's work includes some unusual platters, mugs, and bowls decorated with three-dimensional figures such as fish and animal faces. She also works a lot with slip trail decorating. Her pieces tend toward whimsy and humor, and she likes the concept of functional art. Stone Crow Pottery is open Wednesday through Saturday 10:00 a.m. to 5:00 p.m., Sunday 1:00 to 5:00 p.m. (919-542-4708; www.stone-crowpottery.com).

Also on US 15/501, shortly after you pass the access roads to the lake between Bynum and Pittsboro, two more women practice their craft in a ramshackle building beside the road. Neolia and Celia Cole make pottery in the North Carolina production tradition, specializing in spongeware, a soft brownish glaze called "butterware," and a shocking red glaze. The pots at **Cole's Pottery,** 3410 Hawkins Avenue, Sanford, are not the sleek stylish pieces of studio potters but the made-for-use mugs, bowls, pitchers, and teapots of the kind that served local people for daily use in earlier days. The sisters also make a variety of miniature tea sets and vases. They sign each piece with a comment like, "Love, Neolia Cole," and "Let me go home with you." Kenneth

George works with the Coles now. "Neolia's my grandma," he says, in the softest Southern accent imaginable. They all continue working in the styles they've always done and enjoy the tradition. "We're still old-school," Kenneth says. Their stock, like that of most North Carolina potters, fluctuates with demand. Sometimes they can hardly keep up, and the shelves will be sparsely filled; other times pots crowd every available inch. Nobody gets upset if you stop in, look around, and leave without having bought anything. Open Monday through Friday from 8:00 a.m. to 5:30 p.m. and Saturday from 8:00 a.m. to 3:30 p.m. (919-776-9558).

The attractions and people of this Pittsboro area reflect its proximity to Chapel Hill and the influence it has on the area.

Chapel Hill, almost the geographical center of North Carolina, is recognizably a college town, the kind in which the campus and the town meet at a wall running along the campus green, where students sit on the wall to see and be seen, and where the businesses across the street are mostly campus-oriented. Visitors actually tour the campus, less because of its history than because it is so Norman Rockwellish, sort of an artist's conceptualization of a campus, with trees and grass and historic buildings—even some ivy here and there.

Franklin Street, running along the edge of the university campus and bordering the town, is where town and gown come together. Local people pride themselves on having prevented the street from turning into nothing more than a row of souvenir shops, as has happened in many college towns. Lindsay Chappell, writing for *Images Magazine,* said, "If you could stand at one end of Franklin Street and see all the way to the other, you'd pretty much be glimpsing the soul of Chapel Hill." Along this street you find art galleries, coffeehouses, restaurants, beer spots, and shops. *Crook's Corner,* 610 West Franklin Street, seems to serve townspeople, students, and visitors in about equal numbers. The restaurant's signature dish is shrimp and grits. The restaurant offers a huge variety of beers. Crook's Corner is such an institution in town that people plan to go there for celebrations of all kinds, from family reunions to graduations to winning prizes in contests. The chef, for more than a decade, has been Bill Smith, who looks as though he enjoys food but does not appear particularly cheflike, even in costume, so perhaps it was inevitable that he publish *Seasoned in the South: Recipes from Crook's Corner and from Home.* It's a compilation of his recollections about people in Chapel Hill, famous people who've visited the restaurant, advice on cooking, and recipes. This is the kind of book one can enjoy reading, whether intending to cook or not. And if you eat at Crook's, it's good to know that the spectacular banana pudding gets some of its glory from a large amount of butter (919-929-7643; www.crookscorner.com).

A couple of blocks away, **_Carolina Brewery_** claims the title of Chapel Hill's first microbrewery and serves contemporary American fare, including many dishes made with beer. Carolina Brewery was named "best brew pub in the Southeast" one year. It features live blues on Thursday nights. Carolina Brewery is open Monday through Thursday 11:30 a.m. to midnight, Friday and Saturday to 1:00 a.m., Sunday 11:00 a.m. to 11:00 p.m. (919-942-1800; www .carolinabrewery.com).

Chapel Hill is known for the quantity and quality of its arts and crafts, not just in the retail arena but also in its programs at the University of North Carolina and in the university's **_Ackland Art Museum,_** at the corner of Columbia and Franklin Streets. The museum claims its collection of Asian art is the most significant in North Carolina. Other exhibits in the museum show collections of Indian and Western art, as well as pottery and wood carvings, two areas especially intrinsic to the state. The entire collection totals some 15,000 pieces, including a broad representation of the history of European painting and sculpture, with works by Rubens, Delacroix, Degas, and Pissarro. African and Asian art are also well represented. The museum is open Wednesday through Saturday 10:00 a.m. to 5:00 p.m., Sunday 1:00 to 5:00 p.m. Admission is free (919-966-5736; www.ackland.org).

Right next door to the Ackland, students, faculty, and visiting artists in the university's art program exhibit their work in **_Hanes Art Center._** Admission is free. Call (919) 962-2015 for hours.

The Only True, Authentic, Genuine Cornbread

This is wisdom from true, authentic, genuine Southerners: If it's sweet, it isn't cornbread. If it's fluffy, it isn't cornbread. If it wasn't baked in an iron skillet, it isn't cornbread. And if it's made with yellow, rather than white, cornmeal, it probably isn't cornbread.

Recipes for Southern cornbread vary little. They call for cornmeal (preferably white), egg, buttermilk, or sour milk, and baking powder and baking soda mixed together; this is poured into a hot skillet where a generous portion of fat has melted, and it is baked in a hot oven. Lard used to be the fat of choice; these days it's butter. This produces a round of cornbread that is crisp on the outside and moist inside. One of the best ways to eat it is with a bowl of pinto beans, a slice of raw sweet onion, and a glass of sweet tea.

As for that soft stuff that has flour and sugar mixed in with the other ingredients, Scott Lewis, one of the authors of _The Gift of Southern Cooking,_ says, "That's a Yankee thing."

More art in the **Morehead Galleries** of the university's Morehead Planetarium deserves attention. The walnut walls below the rotunda are hung with a variety of American and Old Master paintings, including portraits of the Morehead family, which was prominent in the state's history. In the North Gallery you can view the huge Bruxelles Tapestry, reaching to the ceiling. The galleries are open Monday through Friday 10:00 a.m. to 5:00 p.m., Sunday 12:30 to 5:00 p.m. Also open evenings Thursday, Friday, and Saturday. Gallery admission is free. Phone (919) 962-1236. Call for planetarium show details or check the Web site: www.moreheadplanetarium.org.

The **North Carolina Botanical Garden,** on Old Mason Farm Road, off US 15/501 Bypass, is one of the largest natural botanical gardens in the Southeast, with 600 acres of land that includes nature trails, aquatic plants, herbs, and a surreal-looking collection of carnivorous plants, some of which make the Venus fly trap look mundane. Collections of regional plants are arranged in settings to simulate their natural habitat. The gardens are open weekdays from 8:00 a.m. to 5:00 p.m., Saturday 9:00 a.m. to 5:00 p.m., Sunday 1:00 to 5:00 p.m. During daylight savings time months, the gardens are open an hour later. Admission is free (919-962-0522; www.ncbg.unc.edu).

Make a quick 12-mile side trip north on Highway 86 to **Hillsborough,** where a lot of history is condensed in a small area. Hillsborough was a capital of colonial and revolutionary North Carolina and a center of politics. During the Revolution Cornwallis's troops grouped for deployment here. The state convention to ratify the federal Constitution met here in 1788; in 1865 the Confederate general who signed the surrender in the Civil War headquartered here. Colonial, antebellum, and Victorian architecture mingle comfortably along the streets. The Hillsborough Historical Society likes to say that the town is a living, not a reconstructed, community.

As you drive toward the town, no matter which way you take, your first reaction is going to be that this guidebook has made some kind of mistake,

They Won't Eat People

Several of North Carolina's botanical gardens grow a variety of carnivorous plants. The more you see of them, the more fascinating they become in their shapes and colors and growth patterns. The common Venus fly trap you find mixed in with houseplants in retail stores doesn't begin to suggest the differences of these exotic plants. If you get interested in them as you tour gardens, North Carolina horticulturists sometimes suggest the book, *The Savage Garden* (Ten Speed Press, 1998), by Peter D'Amato. It is packed with pictures and information about the different species, where to get them, how to grow them, and (if you really get hooked) how to propagate them.

Everybody Celebrates

The first Sunday in December, the community celebrates the **Christmas Candlelight Tour,** which begins at the Dickson House. People of all ages help get ready for it. A volunteer inside the Dickson House jokes about being almost as old as the building. Outside, volunteers have lined the walkway with luminaria, and a little boy who can't be more than a year or two old is carefully inserting a candle into each holder, while his parents and their friends watch and help.

because you'll be driving past all the standard convenience stores, fast-food restaurants, and grocery chains that ring most communities these days. But keep going, because moving on into town is kind of like discovering Brigadoon.

The town has become more aggressive about advertising to attract tourists in the past few years. One of the town's ads says it is "an easy day trip from just about anywhere." This is true, but Hillsborough is also rather removed from other attractions in the area, sitting, as it does, almost at the Virginia border.

To pick up a map for a walking tour, stop at the **Orange County Visitor Center,** 150 East King Street. You can also get information about shops, museums, and restaurants in the area.

The visitor center is in the **Alexander Dickson House,** an eighteenth-century farmhouse with marvelous woodwork. The small rooms remind you that people lived in this area without grandiose mansions. One room has a fireplace of brick and slate, the floors are pine, and the walls are painted in subdued blue and cream shades. Because you're in the South, you're inevitably going to get a bit of Confederate lore here. The Dickson House was the last headquarters of the commander of the largest Confederate armies to surrender to the Union. The house does not stand in its original location, which was at the southwest intersection of what are now I-85 and Highway 86. The Hillsborough Preservation Fund bought the house and the outbuilding General Wade Hampton had used as an office and moved them a mile and a quarter to the center of town.

Part of the charm of the house and the town is that the preservation and activities seem to be family affairs, with people of all ages involved in taking care of the area, planning tours and special events, and greeting tourists. In Hillsborough, historic preservation doesn't feel like a stuffy look back so much as an ongoing community activity.

A good example of this is the garden and courtyard outside the Dickson House, maintained by volunteers. **Helen's Garden** was dedicated in 1990 in the name of Helen Blake Watkins and her late husband, who moved to Hillsborough in 1956 and contributed to local landscaping and preservation projects. After her husband died, Helen donated land she owned as the new site for the Dickson House. A Chapel Hill landscaper designed the garden to show plants that were typically used for food and medicine, with something growing almost all year long. Even in December a few blue flowers bloom, Carolina jessamine climbs across the roof of the outbuilding, and rosemary grows as high as a tall man. Crows circle lazily overhead as though they are watching over the garden. The garden is free and open to the public every day. Visitor center hours are Monday through Saturday 10:00 a.m. to 4:00 p.m., Sunday 1:00 to 4:00 p.m. Admission is free (919-732-7741; www.historic hillsborough.org).

Montrose Gardens (320 St. Mary's Road; 919-732-7787) is a nationally known complex of gardens that Governor William Alexander Graham and his wife, Susan Washington Graham, began in the mid-nineteenth century. In addition to gardens for sun-loving plants, you'll find a rock garden and a woodland garden.

Another interesting site in Hillsborough is the *Burwell School Historic Site,* 319 North Churton Street. The house and outbuildings were built about 1821 and served as a school for women—they called it a "female school" back then. The house includes furnishings from the days when the Reverend and Mrs. Burwell lived in and ran the school there. The property has a nice formal garden as well. Call (919) 732-7741 for details (www.historichillsborough.org). Admission is free.

The Hillsborough Garden Club founded the *Orange County Historical Museum,* at the corner of Churchton and Tryon Streets, in the Confederate Memorial Building, to show how people lived in Orange County from the days of the Indians to the end of 1865. Mostly the museum contains local pieces, including a display of old dental instruments, a 160-year-old working loom, and an old hand-pumped organ from the local Presbyterian Church. The museum is open every day but Monday 1:00 to 4:00 p.m. in January and February; 11:00 a.m. to 4:00 p.m. Tuesday through Saturday and 1:00 to 4:00 p.m. Sunday the rest of the year. Admission is free (919-732-2201; www.historic hillsborough.org).

Find more history at *Occaneechi Indian Village,* downtown on South Cameron Avenue by the Eno River, a reconstructed village with huts, a cooking area, and a sweat lodge that appear as they would have from the late 1600s up to about 1710.

The reconstruction is a cooperative effort by the Occaneechi Band of the Saponi Nation, the town of Hillsborough, Orange County, and the University of North Carolina. Although the village attracts tourists, it is also a tool the tribe uses to teach the history and customs of the Occaneechi people. They lived in

North Carolina in the early 1700s but moved with other small tribes to Virginia by 1710. By the 1780s, the Indian people began moving back to the Piedmont area, settling near Hillsborough to farm, hunt, and fish. The tribe reorganized in 1984 and has been working to educate its own people and their neighbors about their practices. This includes holding powwows and festivals and making presentations in schools. For more information about their activities, call (919) 304-3723; www.occaneechi-saponi.org.

After your Hillsborough side trip, you can follow US 64 west from Pittsboro to Asheboro. This little community of something more than 16,000 is home to the ***American Classic Motorcycle Company and Museum*** (336-629-9564; www.american-classic-motorcycle.com), a meeting spot for Harley-Davidson enthusiasts at 1170 U.S. Highway 64. Ed Rich, proprietor, distinguishes between enthusiasts and bikers. "The bikers, they're more the party types. The enthusiasts are into history and restoration."

Rich started collecting old Harley-Davidsons in 1971 and has been building the collection ever since, opening the museum in 1980. His is one of the largest privately owned collections in the country. The collection of more than forty bikes fills the second floor of his store. One of his treasures is a red 1936 model El61 knucklehead, one of only two known to exist in original condition. It has the original paint and 17,000 miles on the odometer.

You don't have to know anything about Harleys to enjoy this place. It's enough to enjoy the enthusiasm of others. Rich is like a missionary when it comes to teaching people about the world of Harleys. "A lot of heritage and history go with it," Rich says.

Going in every direction from Asheboro, you have wonderful possibilities.

The Pottery Gateway

Although the area bustles with activity, don't look for anything special in the way of food or lodging. Steakhouses and a few motels are about all you'll find, but these are pleasant and entirely acceptable when you just need a meal and a night's sleep, not an experience.

For an experience, go to the south side of Asheboro on U.S. Highway 220, where signs and arrows direct you to the ***North Carolina Zoological Park.*** The zoo (800-488-0444; www.nczoo.org) is big, set on more than 1,000 acres, though not all are being used yet. It's famous, and it's certainly not far off the beaten path. Go anyway. It got to be big and famous because they're doing such a good job with the concept of keeping the animals in natural environments without bars. Sometimes a natural gulf separates the people from the animals, sometimes a clear barrier. For instance, the aviary, under a glass dome, houses hundreds of exotic birds along with thousands of tropical plants. In other sections you can watch elephants, herds of antelope, and even crocodiles, all apparently blissfully unaware of an audience or confinement.

If you are traveling with an eye to understanding the state of North Carolina, the North Carolina Streamside exhibit is special. It depicts the wild-life and habitat from the mountains to the coast in a series of displays with everything from fish and snakes to otters splashing in a pool. Seeing everything involves walking a couple of miles or more, but for a modest fee you can ride in a tram that follows the same route as the footpaths. There is also a modest admission fee to the park itself. Open daily from 9:00 a.m. to 5:00 p.m. Closed an hour earlier in winter.

Pisgah Covered Bridge, one of only two left in North Carolina, spans a branch of the Little River. Located on US 220 in the little community of Pisgah, the area also has hiking trails, picnic tables, and parking. The bridge itself was damaged in 2003 but has been renovated. It is open daily 8:00 a.m. to 5:00 p.m. (800-626-2672; www.visitrandolph.org).

From the natural to something near the ultimate in machinery, the *Richard Petty Museum* displays race cars, trophies, and films of famous races on the grounds of Petty's garages. Most of the awards belong to Richard, but some belong to Lee Petty, his father. Sometimes the garages are open for tours. Showcases commemorate Petty's 200th win and his 1,000th start. If you know about NASCAR racing fans, are aware of the intense partying that goes along with any race day for some of them, and have seen the huge banners advertising Goody's Headache Powders that go up at convenience stores on big race weekends, you may find humor in the Goody's Mini-Theater and Photos. Among the displays are a Chrysler Hemi engine and several race cars, all number 43. (Every car Richard Petty drove was number 43.)

Racing is so important in North Carolina that the results of all races in which local drivers participate are broadcast on local television sports news. Petty is a much-loved North Carolina hero. He has received honorary degrees from North Carolina colleges. It would be a mistake, however, to suppose this is a uniquely North Carolina phenomenon. Among Petty's artifacts are letters of congratulations from Presidents Ford, Reagan, and Bush.

Petty's racing days have ended, but his reputation as the king of racing remains intact. Even if you're unaware that Petty is the king of racing and don't care a fig for the sport, you might find spending some time among people who do a fascinating cultural experience. Signs off US 220 near the zoo south of Asheboro at the Level Cross exit direct you to the museum. Modest admission fee; children under twelve free. Open Monday through Saturday from 9:00 a.m. to 5:00 p.m. (336-495-1143; www.pettyracing.com).

You could spend all day at the zoo; the Richard Petty Museum needs only an hour or so; the next attraction, *Seagrove* and the potteries, could take a week.

The Asheboro area has at least half a dozen motels from which you could make an easy jog to Seagrove. Or you could stay right in the Seagrove community.

The *Duck Smith House Bed and Breakfast,* 465 North Broad Street, is a fully restored turn-of-the-twentieth-century hostelry with a fireplace, furnished with antiques and original artwork. It has four guest rooms and serves breakfast as part of the rate (336-873-7099 or 888-869-9018; www.ducksmithhouse.com).

Restaurants are in such short supply in pottery country that several potteries have picnic tables for shoppers who bring their own lunch. A good restaurant in Seagrove, on US 220, is the *Jugtown Cafe* (336-873-8292). The food ranges from subs, croissant sandwiches, and burgers to country-cooking plate specials with several vegetables. The food is good and prices are moderate. The cafe is open Monday through Wednesday from 6:00 a.m. to 2:00 p.m., Thursday through Saturday from 6:00 a.m. to 8:00 p.m., Sunday from 7:00 a.m. to 2:00 p.m.

Also on US 220 in Seagrove, *Seagrove Family Restaurant* serves breakfast, sandwiches, salads, and such dinner items as hamburger steak with cheese and grilled onions, baked ham, and fried chicken. Open Monday through Thursday 5:00 a.m. to 3:00 p.m., Friday 5:00 a.m. to 8:00 p.m., Saturday 5:00 a.m. to 2:00 p.m. (336-873-7789).

Before you start, accept the fact that it's physically impossible to stop at every pottery in one day. It was impossible a few years ago when they numbered in the thirties; now that there are approximately ninety, your only alternatives are to choose your stops selectively or to plan several trips. New places open regularly, so don't limit your stops to those mentioned here.

The people whose job it is to promote tourism in the area have all but thrown up their hands in despair over keeping up with the growing number of potteries or with trying to tell you when they are open. As a representative for Randolph County Tourism puts it, "If somebody decides to go to the beach for a week, they just close down and go."

This is not true of all the potteries; many run thoroughly professional businesses with enough staff to keep things going even during vacations. But as Dan Triece of DirtWorks Pottery explains, potters in the area these days fall into roughly three groups: those open seven days a week, those open five days a week (usually Tuesday through Saturday), and those that operate on weekends. The weekend potters generally have other jobs and throw pots as a hobby.

Two stops at the beginning of your excursion into pottery country can help you decide which potteries you want to visit. The **Museum of North Carolina Traditional Pottery,** 122 Main Street, provides information, maps, and brochures about potteries in the area. A collection of work by various potters in the window will give you an idea what kind of work each does, so you can seek out those that appeal to you the most. For hours of operation, call (336) 873-7887, or visit www.tourseagrove.com. Admission is free.

Barely a fast walk away, the **North Carolina Pottery Center,** at the junction of US 220 and Highway 705, has exhibits that trace the history and development of North Carolina pottery from the prehistoric Native Americans to the present, with more than 200 items on display. One large display behind glass shows the current work of more than ninety potters in the area. Brochures and maps are also available here. The center is open 10:00 a.m. to 4:00 p.m. Tuesday through Saturday. Admission is $2, high school students $1, younger children free (336-873-8430; www.ncpotterycenter.com).

Seagrove's best-known annual event is the **Seagrove Pottery Festival,** sponsored as a fund-raiser by the Museum of North Carolina Traditional Pottery. Each year on a Saturday and Sunday in mid-November, the festival includes an auction of signed and dated limited-edition pottery by local potteries, as well as booths by local potters and other traditional crafters, who demonstrate, display, and sell their wares. In true Tar Heel tradition, the festival provides lots of pork barbecue and chicken, too. For exact dates, phone (336) 873-7887.

A second big event is the annual **Seagrove Winterfest,** in mid-February. This is when most pottery shops have taken a rest after the Christmas rush and have their shelves restocked. Then potteries often introduce their new shapes, glazes, and colors. For more information, call (336) 873-7887.

Originally this part of the country attracted production potters who made the storage jugs, pitchers, crocks, and bean pots farmers used every day, because both the heavy red clay for potting and the timber stands for fueling the kilns were right here. No doubt local moonshine was one of the products that got stored in the jugs. A rich culture developed around potting, complete with family traditions in design and glazing. As other materials came along for making utensils to cook and store food, the potters turned more to producing items for tourists. But the actual potting stayed basically the same. Over three and four generations, feuds and disagreements came up, and sometimes a member of a famous potting family would splinter off to start an independent pottery.

The old families continue making the same kinds of pottery today. Tourists and gift shop owners buy it up faster than the wheels can turn.

Newcomers fill out the scene with more artistic studio pottery, which is usually more elaborately shaped, decorated, and glazed. These pieces take longer to make.

Some of the new potters are local young people who have studied in the well-respected program at Troy Technical College nearby. Others, transplants from elsewhere, have been attracted by the concentration of potters that draws customers and ensures support. It would be wrong to say that all new potters make studio pottery and all old-timers practice production pottery, however. You'll find a good bit of crossover. The best thing to do is simply look at the work, talk to the potters, and make your choices.

upclose

The North Carolina mystery writer Margaret Maron wrote *Uncommon Clay,* a mystery novel set in Seagrove that gives you a good idea of how the people of the community relate to each other and their work. She spent a lot of time here to learn about the potting world, and although her story is fiction, the kinds of rivalries and friendships she describes really do exist.

Many of the materials these days are shipped in from elsewhere rather than dug from local ground, and some kilns are fired by oil, gas, or electricity rather than wood. But the atmosphere is still that of a unique culture engrossed in a hands-on kind of work.

Wherever you stop, talk to the people. They're used to it, they like it, and it's an integral part of the experience. As you do, you can't help noticing the arthritic hands of some of the old potters. As a younger artisan explained it, "My pots will never be quite as good as theirs, because you need to keep wetting the clay with cold water for the very best results, and I use warm water. I've seen what twenty and thirty years of cold water and clay does to your hands. I'm afraid I'm not quite that dedicated."

The largest concentration of potteries begins on Highway 705, off US 220. The state road numbers are clearly marked, so it is easy to follow the map through the countryside, traveling from one pottery to another. No two are alike, nor are their wares. Part of the fun is in the discovery and surprise; you don't need full information ahead of time about each place, but the following are a few guaranteed to be special. They are all marked on the free maps available at every pottery. The following listing is far from complete but gives you an idea of the various kinds of work done by some of the established potters.

Phil Morgan Pottery (336-873-7304; www.seagrovepotteries.com) features Phil's elegant crystalline glazes on porcelain and his wife's more traditional earthenware, much of it in pleasing muted rose and blue tones and decorated with flowers.

Potts Pottery (336-879-4295; www.pottspotteryinseagrove.com) is a newer endeavor by Jeff and Linda Potts. Linda's grandmother was a Cole—the Potts say they represent the ninth generation of Coles, famous traditional folk potters. They use local clay and produce traditional earthenware tableware and serving pieces. Some of the glazes, especially the blue, resemble those of the old Cole pottery, but you will see differences in sheen.

Ben Owen Pottery (336-879-2262 or 910-464-2261; www.benowenpottery .com) displays the work of Ben Owen III, who was recognized as a boy for having superior talent, on a par with that of his grandfather. Young Ben works as an artist, producing shapes and designs inspired by Egyptian and Japanese work. His pots are on display in museums around the country. The Owen family has been famous for its bright red glazes.

At ***Westmoore Pottery*** (910-464-3700; www.westmoorepottery.com), open since 1977, Mary and David Farrell make reproductions of the earthenware and salt-glazed stoneware typical of the eighteenth and early nineteenth centuries. They also make stunning reproductions of Moravian pottery as well as create new designs in the old traditions. The couple and the pottery have received national attention in more than one country-oriented magazine for their work. It is especially popular with people involved in authentic historic restoration and representation.

The people at ***Cady Clay Works*** (910-464-5661), John Mellage and his wife, Beth Gore, produce wood-fired pieces with vibrant colors and contem-

Potting in North Carolina

porary designs. They usually have some spectacular, extra-large bowls that are surprisingly lightweight for their size.

DirtWorks Pottery (336-873-8979) is the permanent showroom of Dan Triece. Triece has won awards in the Southeast, especially for his copper luster raku. The shop carries woodcrafts, basketry, jewelry, and other North Carolina crafts as well as work by other regional potters.

Turn and Burn (336-873-7381; www.turnandburnpottery.com) produces a variety of pots, including horsehair and shino, a glaze from Japan notable for having a high feldspar content and being unpredictable in the kiln. David Garner, who says he grew up so surrounded by the craft he can't remember the first time he saw a pot made, has been potting for more than twenty years.

Milly McCanless started *Dover Pottery* (910-464-3586; www.doverpots .com) early in the 1980s. She is a first-generation potter who got into it because she had a dollhouse and wanted to make dishes for her miniature dining table. Then she discovered she was good at throwing big pots, too, and realized there was a much better market for them than for miniatures.

The Poole family owns and operates *Rockhouse Pottery* (336-879-2053), specializing in hand-carved pottery, Tar Heel (North Carolina) themes, stoneware, saltware, and large and small planters.

Holly Hill (336-873-7300) produces traditional, hand-turned, functional stoneware in the tradition of J. B. Cole, from one of the earliest potting families around.

At *Whynot Pottery* (336-873-9276; www.whynotpottery.com) you'll find stoneware in a variety of contemporary shapes and glazes, pieces that are especially well balanced.

Jugtown (910-464-3266; www.jugtownware.com) operates somewhat more commercially than the other potteries, including handwoven rugs and placemats, handmade toys, and other North Carolina folk crafts in its retail stock. Jugtown has been operating since 1920. The Jugtown stoneware is uniform enough in appearance to look nice beside the more regular, mass-produced commercial dinnerware and seems practically indestructible. There is a bathroom here, too. That may seem like a small thing, in the abstract, but after you've spent some time driving these country roads where you don't find pit stops every few miles, it's something to appreciate.

The hours of the various potters may vary by a half-hour or so in opening and closing, but most are open from 8:30 a.m. to 4:30 p.m. Tuesday through Saturday. Many are closed all day Sunday, though some open Sunday afternoon. The best time to go is Friday afternoon, after most of the kilns are opened on Thursday to bring out the new pots. Saturday morning is a good time, too, but by afternoon the wares will already be thinning out.

Although some early glazes contained lead, today's are lead-free and safe for table use. If you have any concerns about lead, ask in the pottery.

For a broad overview of potteries in the area, check www.visitrandolph county.com.

Heartland

Another possible trip from Asheboro is the short hop up US 220 to **Greensboro,** a pleasant city with a historic downtown and lots of surprises. There's some Revolutionary War history here, in a strange sort of way. Cornwallis won a battle against General Nathanael Greene's American troops, but in the process he lost so many men that he ultimately had to surrender at Yorktown. The **Guilford Courthouse National Military Park,** 6 miles north of Greensboro on US 220, commemorates the loss and the win with exhibits on the battlefield and displays and films in the visitor center (336-288-1776; www.nps.gov/guco). Hours vary seasonally. Admission is free.

Drawing on more recent events, Greensboro holds special significance for blacks. In 1960 black students from **North Carolina A & T State University** (originally the Agricultural and Mechanical College for the Colored Race) began the first sit-ins at Woolworth's segregated lunch counter. A & T is Jesse Jackson's alma mater. On the campus of North Carolina A & T State University, the **Mattye Reed African Heritage Center** displays African masks, paintings, black history books, and art objects. Open Tuesday through Friday 10:00 a.m. to 5:00 p.m., Saturday 1:00 to 5:00 p.m. Closed on University holidays (336-334-3209; www.ncat.edu/~museum). Admission is free.

Less than 10 miles east of Greensboro, the **Charlotte Hawkins Brown Memorial State Historic Site** (336-449-4846; www.ah.dcr.state.nc.us) honors Dr. Brown's fifty years as head of another school for blacks, Palmer Memorial Institute. The buildings are gradually being restored, and plans are to make the memorial a center for contributions of North Carolina blacks, including a research center with collection and computer facilities devoted to North Carolina black history. The complex includes cottages and dormitories, outdoor exhibits and trails, a visitor center in the old teacher's cottage, and a picnic area. Dr. Brown's house has been restored, and some of her original furniture reupholstered. Open Monday through Saturday from 9:00 a.m. to 5:00 p.m. Closed for major holidays. Admission is free.

Local history from the time of the early Indians to date shapes the displays at the **Greensboro Historical Museum,** 130 Summit Avenue, Greensboro, in what used to be the First Presbyterian Church. In a re-creation of nineteenth-century Greensboro, the museum displays a general store, the drugstore where

William Sydney Porter (O. Henry) once worked, a post office, a law office, a firehouse, a cobbler's, and a blacksmith's.

Other exhibits include room settings from historical homes, an exhibit of household items and clothing of Dolley Madison (a Greensboro native before she became First Lady), and a collection of antique automobiles. Open Tuesday through Saturday from 10:00 a.m. to 5:00 p.m. and Sunday from 2:00 to 5:00 p.m. Closed holidays. Admission is free (336-373-2043; www.greens borohistory.org).

If you're traveling with kids (or even if you're not, come to think of it), don't miss the **Natural Science Center,** 4301 Lawndale Drive (336-288-3769; www.natsci.org), where you can easily spend a day immersing yourself in the sights and sounds of everything from dinosaurs to star systems. This is a "participation museum," where you don't have to tell the kids "look, don't touch." For instance, you can put your hand into a real dinosaur footprint, pet and feed animals in the zoo, observe sunspots in the live solar observatory, and turn your imagination loose in the planetarium. The transparent anatomical mannequin, which you might want to save until after lunch, lets you study what goes on inside the skin of the human body. The museum is open Monday through Saturday from 9:00 a.m. to 5:00 p.m. and Sunday from 12:30 to 5:00 p.m. The zoo is open Monday through Saturday from 10:00 a.m. to 4:30 p.m. and Sunday from 12:30 to 4:00 p.m. A moderate admission fee covers the museum and zoo. Planetarium shows daily at 2:00, 3:00, and 4:00 p.m. are $2 extra.

When you've had enough of indoor attractions, Greensboro has three gardens worth some attention, collectively known as the **Greensboro Gardens.** The Greensboro Arboretum, Bog Garden, and Bicentennial Garden feature most of the plants native to the Piedmont region. The arboretum is on West Market Street at Lindley Park. It has nine labeled collections of indigenous species. The Bog Garden is at the corner of Hobbs Road and Starmount Farms Drive and features a variety of plants that thrive in wet areas. The Bicentennial Garden is at the corner of Cornwallis Drive and Hobbs Road. It emphasizes mass plantings of bulbs, annuals, and perennials, along with flowering trees and shrubs. Admission to the gardens is free. Call (336) 373-2199 or (800) 344-2282 for more information; www.greensborobeautiful.org.

In a more formal setting on the campus of University of North Carolina-Greensboro, the **Weatherspoon Art Museum** is located at Spring Garden and Tate Streets (336-334-5770; www.weatherspoon.uncg.edu). The museum, which has six galleries and a sculpture courtyard, is nationally known for its collections of modern and contemporary art, 6,000 objects mostly created after World War II. The permanent collection includes Matisse prints and bronzes, the Dillard Collection of Art on Paper, with 500 items, and 600 Japanese wood-block prints from the eighteenth through the twentieth centuries. The museum is open Tuesday through Friday from 10:00 a.m. to 5:00 p.m., Thursday 10:00 a.m. to 9:00 p.m., Saturday and Sunday 1:00 to 5:00 p.m. Admission is free. The museum's Web site offers an excellent overview of museum holdings and samplings of work from various collections. It also details changing exhibits.

The **Greenwood Bed and Breakfast,** 205 North Park Drive (336-274-6350 or 800-535-9363; www.greenwoodbb.com), built in the early 1900s, has been well renovated. Old oaks and the neighborhood park surround the home with greenery and shield the backyard swimming pool from the curious. The innkeepers serve a generous breakfast with fruit and homemade breads, which is included in the rates. The inn has five guest rooms, all with private baths.

Tobacco Town

From Greensboro you're looking at a drive of only about 20 miles west on I-40 to **Winston-Salem,** the tobacco town. It would be hard to overstate the influence of the R. J. Reynolds Tobacco Company. While Richard Joshua Reynolds was directing a rapidly growing business and hiring increasing thousands of people in the tobacco factories, his wife, Katharine, set about a long series of community improvement activities for the benefit of those same families. With Reynolds money and Moravian artistic influence, the area developed into a cultural center that still ranks high in the country today.

Perhaps the most audacious Reynolds act in later years was the lock-stock-and-barrel move of Wake Forest University from Wake County to Winston-Salem in 1950. President Truman came to wield the shovel in the groundbreaking ceremony. The **Museum of Anthropology,** on the campus, is billed as the only museum devoted to the study of world cultures, covering Africa, Asia, Oceania, and the Americas. Open Tuesday through Saturday 10:00 a.m. to 4:30 p.m. (336-758-5282; www.wfu.edu).

After studying the impact of Reynolds and tobacco, turn your attention to the Moravians. Moravians came from Pennsylvania to settle the area in 1753. They built Salem as a totally planned, church-governed community in 1766. Winston wasn't founded until 1849. In Salem, arts and crafts flourished; in Winston, it was tobacco and textiles. By the early 1900s the two towns had grown together and consolidated. It would be hard to say whether tobacco or the Moravians left the greater mark on the area, nor is it really pertinent; in the early days tobacco wasn't a dirty word, and nobody saw anything wrong with a strong relationship between church and chew.

If you see only one attraction here, it certainly should be **Old Salem,** a Moravian town restored so carefully that when you walk the streets and go into the buildings, you feel as though you've entered a time warp. To give you an idea of the pains staff people take with getting it right, people responsible for demonstrations of cooking and household activities take turns preparing research papers and consulting old diaries, journals, and letters to discover exactly how the households might have run. Unlike traditional historians who mainly study battles, politics, and industrial development, these re-creators also try, as well, to piece together the elements of day-to-day life. This isn't the only historic site where such activities are going on, but it's hard to imagine one where they're being treated any more earnestly or where the subject matter is any more fascinating. This attention to detail extends even to the food cooked from old Moravian recipes. The original gingerbread recipe used fresh gingerroot, but recipes in later years have shifted to powdered ginger because it's easier to find and keep. The Old Salem recipe still specifies fresh, grated ginger. At the **Winkler Bakery,** costumed bakers make cookies and bread in a wood-fired brick oven. The baked goods are for sale.

Costumed guides in the old kitchen cook in the huge fireplace and iron with flatirons heated there, all the while sweating genuine sweat—a fascinating reminder in this age of air-conditioning that just getting from one day to the next once took a lot of energy. Among the demonstrations offered in Old Salem are music from an organ built in 1797, potting, baking, and spinning.

Not all the buildings in the historic district are restored as tour buildings. Some are private homes. The presence of automobiles and real people living real lives doesn't seem to detract from the atmosphere; indeed it simply makes it feel more alive. Whatever tours you take, start at the visitor center (336-721-7300 or 888-653-7253; www.oldsalem.org). Moderate to high admission fees, depending on how many features you wish to tour. Get tickets for all Old

Old Salem

Salem tour attractions at the visitor center, open from 8:30 a.m. to 5:00 p.m. Monday through Saturday and from 12:30 to 5:00 p.m. on Sunday. All hours for attractions at Old Salem may vary. Call the visitor center or check the Web site for specifics.

Old Salem Gardens are reputed to be the best-documented, restored community gardens in America. Their authenticity is possible because the Moravians kept meticulous records. Many of the gardens have been re-created on their original sites and produce the same varieties of vegetables, flowers, and herbs described in old records. The attention to horticultural detail goes beyond the garden squares to include old cultivars of fruit trees in orchards, flowering vines on fences, and native trees in the landscape.

Having toured Old Salem, you'll need to eat at the *Old Salem Tavern Dining Rooms,* at 736 South Main Street in the district (336-748-8585). Continuing the sense of reenactment, costumed staff serve Moravian-style cooking by candlelight. Specialties include game and gingerbread from the old recipes. For the faint of palate, standard beef and chops entrees are also available. All spirits are served. The restaurant is open for lunch every day and for dinner every day but Sunday.

Also in Old Salem, the *Museum of Early Southern Decorative Arts* (336-721-7300 or 888-258-1205; www.mesda.org/mesda.html) gives you a close look at the results of extensive research into the regional decorative arts of the early South. The exhibits include furniture, paintings, textiles, ceramics, silver, and other metalware. You can't just wander in here. Guides take you through the building in small groups. You may buy tickets at the Old Salem Visitors Center. Museum hours are Monday through Saturday from 9:30 a.m. to 4:30 p.m. and Sunday from 1:00 to 5:00 p.m.

You might end a day in this historic manufacturing and artistic town at *Brookstown Inn,* a restored 1837 textile mill at 200 Brookstown Avenue (336-725-1120 or 800-845-4262; www.brookstowninn.com). The history of the inn matches that of the city for interest. Moravians opened the Salem Cotton Manufacturing Company and later sold it, and the buildings were subsequently

Sweet Stuff

Southerners have a notorious sweet tooth. The tea-drinking habits of North Carolinians are a good example. We drink tea iced—year-round, not just in summer. We put sugar in it and call it "sweet tea"; if you want it any other way, you have to say so by ordering "unsweet tea." Even then, if you don't want a mouthful of sugar, taste just a little sip when the tea comes, because the request for unsweet tea is so rare, servers may well bring you the sweet kind out of habit.

used as a flour mill and then as a moving-company storage house. The conversion to an inn created large guest rooms with odd nooks and crannies and high ceilings. An upstairs wall is covered with the graffiti (protected by an acrylic plastic sheet) of the young factory girls who boarded there. The decor is early American, with many handmade quilts and country accents. Rates include wine and cheese in the parlor, homemade cookies and milk, and continental breakfast in the dining room.

While you are in the Winston-Salem area, take a few minutes to drive to the old ***Shell gas station*** at the corner of Sprague and Peachtree Streets. You'll know you're there when you come to a huge orange and red structure shaped like a seashell, with two old gas pumps standing in front. This old gas station sold Quality Oil products in the 1930s and then fell into disuse and disrepair. It had a big crack sealed with a strip of black tar, and vandals had broken windows and fixtures and littered the ground.

Sarah Woodard, who wasn't even born when the station was in its glory days, oversaw the renovation, which was completed in 1997. Almost any time you stop in, some old-timers who remember when the station was operating are apt to be standing around reminiscing about earlier times. One of them says he always thought the Shell was the prettiest thing in town—and he still does.

The Barbecue Capital

On U.S. Highway 52, about 20 miles south of Winston-Salem, the town of ***Lexington*** is a must-stop for barbecue freaks. More than a dozen restaurants in this little town serve pork barbecue (if it's made with anything but pork it isn't really barbecue!) "Lexington style." The town has at least twenty barbecue restaurants, mostly, maybe even entirely, run by people whose families have been involved with barbecue for several generations. The first barbecue restaurant was in a tent in the middle of town, opened by Sid Weaver in 1919. Lexington barbecue is generally called "western style," though you need to be careful about what you say, because a slip of the tongue regarding barbecue in North Carolina is grounds for deportation to another country—preferably vegetarian. Authentic Lexington barbecue is made by cooking pork shoulders slowly over hickory wood fires until the meat is falling-apart tender, basting it with a "dip" of vinegar, ketchup, water, salt, and pepper. Some barbecuers may add a few other ingredients such as red pepper. As the drippings from the meat fall into the hot coals, the smoke rises to flavor the meat. Then the pork is chopped by hand to be served in sandwiches or on plates accompanied by red slaw and hush puppies. Bits of tomato make the slaw red.

Each year in the fall, the Lexington Barbecue Festival attracts in the neighborhood of 100,000 visitors. It's held in eight roped-off blocks of uptown Lexington and goes on with a variety of events besides eating. Check www .barbecuefestival.com for all kinds of details about Lexington barbecue, including current dates.

Eastern barbecue, typical on the coast and for some distance inland, uses the whole hog. After roasting, not necessarily over a wood fire, the meat is pulled from the bones by hand and chopped. The baste contains no tomato, and the barbecue comes with white or yellow slaw.

Complications arise in the disagreement about which is where and which is better because, inevitably, some places began blending techniques, and it's possible to come across eastern barbecue in the western part of the state and vice versa. "Real" North Carolinians can get testy on the subject. You can plunge into huge discussions on the subject, as well as participants' recommendations for their favorite barbecue spots, simply by typing "eastern nc barbecue" and "western nc barbecue" into a Web browser.

The Furniture Capital

High Point is mostly about manufacturing and selling furniture. The town, already active in the lumber business, first got into furniture building in the early 1880s, when a local lumber salesman noticed the big difference between the price of wood as it left the sawmill and the price it brought once it had been shipped away and turned into furniture. Sensibly, he and two local merchants risked all they had to start a furniture company close to the source of the wood. It was the right idea in the right place at the right time. Sales took off, and the future was set. Today High Point has 125 furniture manufacturing companies.

Unless you are professionally involved in the furniture business, avoid High Point in April and October, when for the better part of two weeks in both months the town hosts the *Southern Furniture Market,* usually referred to simply as

Talking the Talk

When you order barbecue at any of the twenty or so barbecue restaurants in Lexington, you'll be asked if you want it chopped or sliced. The sliced barbecue, obviously, comes in bigger pieces; the chopped usually has more of the crispy crust that formed on the outside of the shoulder as it roasted. Then you must choose whether you want a sandwich, plate, or tray. A sandwich comes on a soft, white roll, with barbecue and slaw. A plate includes barbecue, slaw, french fries, and rolls or hush puppies. A tray is a small container with barbecue and slaw. All barbecue is served with "dip" on the side as additional seasoning for the meat.

How the Experts Rate
North Carolina Barbecue

Blind Taste Judging

Judge No._____

Code No. _____

	Poor	Fair	Good	Very Good	Excellent
Appearance	2 4 6 8	10 12 14 16	18 20 22 24	26 28 30 32	34 36 38 40
Tenderness	2 4 6 8	10 12 14 16	18 20 22 24	26 28 30 32	34 36 38 40
Taste	4 8 12 16	20 24 28 32	36 40 44 48	52 56 60 64	68 72 76 80

Total

Score:_____

Key:
Appearance: Texture, color, fat to lean ratio, burnt meat.
Tenderness: Moist and tender vs. dry and tough.
Taste: Sauce too hot, too mild, or excessive vs. a pleasing blend of sauce and meat.

"market." Said to be the largest furniture show in the world (it fills 150 buildings totaling between five and six million square feet), this trade show attracts interior decorators and furniture retailers—in other words, buyers—from all over the world. More than 1,500 furniture company exhibitors show up for each market show. Multiply that by the staff each company brings to work the booths and add all the buyers who come looking for the latest goodies, and you get an image of a town, normal population on the shy side of 70,000, so overloaded that if it were a ship it would sink. Finding a place to stay or to eat is a challenge.

A valuable museum in the area is the **Springfield Museum of Old Domestic Life,** established in 1935 in the third meetinghouse of the Springfield Meeting, 555 East Springfield Road (336-882-3054). Museums, like history books, tend to focus on extraordinary events, wars, and politics and not on the commonplaces of day-to-day life. This museum is an exception. Here you can inspect the artifacts of daily life that have been used in the neighborhood for 200 years or more—spinning equipment, utensils, farm items, clothing, pictures from homes, toys, and a slew of fascinating odds and ends. The curator says, "Most of what we have has been donated by local Quakers."

She likes to emphasize the items that were commonplace in their day, objects crudely made to fill an immediate need. If you didn't know the way in which many of them had been used, you probably never could figure out what they were for. Such artifacts simply cannot be replaced.

One example is the log lifter. It looks like a crutch for a giant. Log lifters were devices created to get logs from the ground to high points in the walls when building log cabins. One man stood at each end of the log with a lifter and heaved.

Another example is a homemade Noah's Ark, with all the animals, two by two. This was a Sunday toy, made during the time when children in the community weren't allowed to play on Sundays with their regular toys, or do much else. It was carved about one hundred years ago by Yardley Warner for his twins, probably because he sympathized with the children's restlessness and wanted to make them a religious toy to keep them occupied on Sundays.

Another uncommon exhibit is the 4-foot-long tin horn the coachman blew at each stop of the stagecoach along the Old Plank Road. The number of blasts blown told people at upcoming stops, such as Nathan Hunt Tavern, what passengers would be wanting when they got there. Old Plank Road was built between Fayetteville and Winston-Salem by laying down boards next to one another to form a firm-surfaced highway. Part of the old road is now Main Street. A plank from the road and a notched mile marker are also in the display. A traveler in the dark could stop at the marker and feel the number of notches on it to know how far it was to Nathan Hunt Tavern. A model shows a stage-coach on a plank road with markers to give you an idea how it all worked.

Visiting here is more like going into an attic than a museum. "There's so much stuff, and you can handle it. You don't get the feeling of things resting on velvet that you can't touch," the curator says. The museum is open by appointment. Admission is free.

The *High Point Historical Museum,* 1859 East Lexington Avenue (336-885-1859; www.highpointmuseum.org), exhibits more traditional kinds of material related to the town's history, including military displays. The numbers "1859" in the phone number and the address stand for the year the town of High Point was founded. You have to admire a museum that can pull off something like that. There is also a display of old telephones that takes you back to before Ma Bell, a collection of furniture made in High Point, and, appropriately, woodworking tools that take you back to the first manufacturing in town. Also on the property are the restored 1786 John Haley House, a weaving house, and a blacksmith shop. Demonstrations are offered in these buildings on weekends. The 1754 Hoggatt House, which was damaged by fire in 2004, has been restored. The museum has also acquired the piano on which saxophonist John Coltrane composed many of his jazz pieces, including "Blue Train" and "Moment's Notice." Coltrane's mother played the piano, and later his children did. Some of the keys have words written in Coltrane's hand—"sticking," and "out of tune." Open

Tuesday through Saturday 10:00 a.m. to 4:00 p.m. and Sunday 1:00 to 4:00 p.m. Admission is free.

Another way to glimpse earlier times in High Point is by staying at *J. H. Adams Inn* (1108 North Main Street; 336-882-3267; www.jhadamsinn.com). This thirty-one-room inn is quite grand. It's a 1918 Italianate Renaissance mansion, built by the Hampton Adams family as a home and place for entertaining. It was extensively renovated in 2000, preserving such historical touches as the grand staircase and marble fireplace, while also providing all modern luxuries and amenities. The rooms are furnished with collections from the region's fine furniture makers. Each room has a private bath, telephone, TV, high-speed Internet access, and refrigerator; some have a microwave, some have a whirlpool bath. The inn has a restaurant serving lunch and dinner, but it may be closed for private parties from time to time. Inquire about specific dates when you make your reservation.

At 101 West Green Drive, the *Angela Peterson Doll and Miniature Museum* (336-885-3655) contains more than 2,700 dolls collected by Angela Peterson from around the world. She picked up everything—crêche dolls, a Shirley Temple collection of 120 dolls, and Bob Timberlake dolls, as well as enough dollhouses and furnishings to create a miniature village. Before the collection was housed here, it was in several rooms of the retirement home where Peterson lived. In fact, she said she chose that particular place to live after "auditioning" a number of possibilities because this place expressed an active interest in her doll collection. The home may have ended up being more interested than she was. Somewhere along the way, when she was in her late eighties or early nineties, she began referring to the collection as "the damned dolls," because it took so much work to keep their costumes clean and properly pressed. The dolls were moved into the building on West Green Drive after her death. The museum is open 10:00 a.m. to 4:00 p.m. Monday through Friday, Saturday 9:00 a.m. to 4:00 p.m., and 1:00 to 4:00 p.m. Sunday. Call for current admission prices.

THE UPPER PIEDMONT WEB SITES

Durham
www.visitdurham.info

Lexington
www.visitlexingtonnc.com

Greensboro
www.visitgreensboro.com

Raleigh
www.visitraleigh.com

High Point
www.highpoint.org

Winston-Salem
www.visitwinstonsalem.com

Places to Stay in the Upper Piedmont

ASHEBORO

Hampton Inn-Asheboro
1137 East Dixie Drive
(336) 625-9000
www.hamptoninn.com

DURHAM

Comfort Inn University
3508 Mt. Moriah Road
(919) 490-4949
www.comfortinn.com

Hampton Inn
1816 Hillandale Road
(919) 471-6100
www.hamptoninn.com

GREENSBORO

Battleground Inn
1517 Westover Terrace
(336) 272-4737
www.battlegroundinnnc
.com

Courtyard by Marriott
4400 West Wendover
(336) 294-3800
www.mariott.com/gsown

HIGH POINT

Biltmore Suites Hotel
4400 Regency
(336) 812-8188
(888) 412-8188
www.biltmoresuiteshotel
.com

RALEIGH

Holiday Inn Brownstone Hotel
1707 Hillsborough Street
(919) 828-0811
(800) 465-4329
www.brownstonehotel.com

The Oakwood Inn Bed & Breakfast
411 North Bloodworth Street
(919) 832-9712
(800) 267-9712
www.oakwoodinnbb.com

WINSTON-SALEM

Brookstown Inn
200 Brookstown Avenue
(336) 752-1120
www.brookstowninn.com

Courtyard by Marriott
3111 University Parkway
(336) 727-1277
www.mariott.com/intcy

Places to Eat in the Upper Piedmont

ASHEBORO

Bamboo Garden Oriental Restaurant
405 East Dixie
(336) 629-0203

CHAPEL HILL

Crook's Corner
610 West Franklin Street
(919) 929-7643

LEXINGTON

Jimmy's Barbecue
1703 Cotton Grove Road
(336) 357-2311

Lexington Barbecue
10 Highway 29/70
(336) 249-9814

SEAGROVE

Jugtown Cafe
Highway 220
(336) 873-8292

Seagrove Family Restaurant
Highway 220
(336) 873-7789

SMITHFIELD

Café Monet
302 East Church Street
(919) 989-3039

The Lower Piedmont

Statesville

In less than an hour, you can drive west on Interstate 40 from Winston-Salem to **Statesville,** a community of fewer than 25,000 people. This area was the site of Fort Dobbs, built during the French and Indian War to protect settlers. The fort is commemorated at the **Fort Dobbs State Historic Site** (438 Dobbs Road; 704-463-5882; www.fortdobbs.org) with a variety of archaeological sites, artifact displays, and nature trails. The site is open 9:00 a.m. to 5:00 p.m. Tuesday through Saturday. A variety of commemorative and interpretative programs are ongoing.

Interstates 40 and 77 meet here, and this has led to a lot of development on the periphery—hotels, chain restaurants, and service stations, along with automobile dealerships, grocery stores, and other businesses that are standard around North Carolina cities these days. Statesville doesn't advertise itself heavily as a tourist center, so you could easily drive on by and miss several appealing attractions. The downtown historic area has more than a hundred restored buildings, some dating from as early as 1860. The Statesville Convention and Visitors

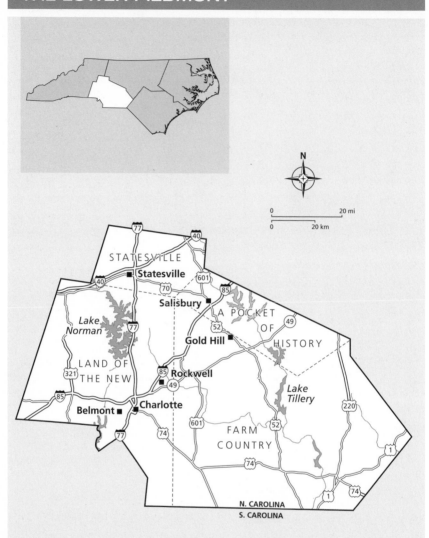

Bureau (111 Depot Lane; 704-878-3480 or 877-531-1819; www.downtown statesvillenc.org) is located in a train depot built in 1911. It's a good place to pick up brochures and local maps during normal business hours.

Statesville is especially known for its annual hot air balloon festival, a tradition that has occurred for more than thirty years. The *Carolina BalloonFest* is held every fall at the Statesville Regional Airport (704-873-2892; www.carolina balloonfest.com). A more recent entertainment in the area is *geocaching*. The town has hidden caches of trinkets in the area and provides you with latitude and longitude locations for you to use with your GPS system in order to locate a stash. When you find it, you reward yourself by taking a trinket and repay the site by leaving another trinket behind.

Mt. Airy is Andy Griffith's hometown. It's not near anything else. Although it is located a ways north, almost at the Virginia border, the most direct way to get to Mt. Airy is to drive a couple of hours from Statesville straight up I-77. (This avoids the slow, sometimes treacherous drive over the Blue Ridge Mountains.) Knowing how to classify Mt. Airy's location can be a little confusing. The National Park Service considers it part of the mountains, but the North Carolina tourism people call it part of the Piedmont. As a visitor you can approach it in one of two ways—visiting a shrine to Andy Griffith in his incarnation as Sheriff Andy Taylor, the Hero of Mayberry, or experiencing the spirit behind the Mayberry fiction.

Mt. Airy is visited by hordes of tourists these days, and it seems local people are starting to live the fiction. Griffith has always insisted that Mayberry was not really based on Mt. Airy, but it's hard to tell that to the people who create Mayberry Days with tours and contests and parades.

The *Andy Griffith Museum,* in the visitor center, 615 North Main Street (800-576-0231; www.visitmayberry.com), contains several rooms of memorabilia, including the white suit Griffith wore as Matlock. Both a walking tour of some of the town's older neighborhoods and a guided step-on tour are available.

ANNUAL EVENTS IN THE LOWER PIEDMONT

Charlotte
Southern Ideal Home Show
(mid-October)
(800) 849-0248

Gold Hill
Gold Hill Founder's Day
(late September)
(704) 279-5674

Autumn Jubilee
(early October)
(704) 636-2089

Statesville
National Balloon Rally
(mid-September)
(704) 873-2892

BETTER-KNOWN ATTRACTIONS IN THE LOWER PIEDMONT

Charlotte
Discovery Place
(704) 372-6261

Mint Museum of Art
(704) 337-2000

As for **Mayberry Days,** it's hard to give exact dates because the thing keeps growing, but they're always in late September. For specifics, call the Surry County Arts Council (800-286-6193). The Mt. Airy Web site is www.visit mayberry.com.

Now, to get a taste of a more authentic version of rural North Carolina, get out your North Carolina transportation map and look at the blue highways just off U.S. Highway 601, south of Mt. Airy. Go south on the blue highway that crosses Highway 268 at Level Cross. This takes you into rural Surry County. Comparatively speaking, you might consider Mt. Airy the "urban" part. Head for the little town of Dobson and **Old Rockford Village.** This is what country folk used to call a "poke and plumb" spot: Poke your head out the window as you drive, and you're plumb out of town.

The focal point here is **Rockford General Store.** It's a hard place to define—partly touristy, partly a local source for everything from lye soap to pickled eggs and homemade fried apple pies, as well as more than one hundred kinds of old-fashioned candy. The store, located at 5417 Rockford Road, meanders in several directions, with wooden-floored rooms filled with reminders of earlier times. Outside the store on the porch, a red wooden bench invites you to sit, and a checkerboard is set up with rocks as playing pieces, ready for anybody who wants a game. Annie Barnett died in 2003. New owners have taken it over, and it is still an important part of the community. Open Monday, Wednesday, Thursday, and Friday 10:00 a.m. to 5:00 p.m., Saturday 10:00 a.m. to 6:00 p.m., Sunday 1:00 to 6:00 p.m. (336-374-5317; www.rockfordgeneralstore.com).

Whether you actually go into the store or not, driving these back roads gives you a glimpse of rural North Carolina as it really is, not as parts of it have

Braggin' Rights

A clerk in the Rockford General Store was trading one-liners with a customer about how small the town of Old Rockford Village is. The customer won with, "This town is so small that the person who left the porch light on last December won a prize for best Christmas decorations."

been gussied up for tourists. Driving along these two-lane macadam roads with the car windows down, you can hear a "bobwhite, bobwhite, bobwhite" bird call. The warm air in summer smells of recently cut hay, although the fields are planted mostly in corn and tobacco. New orange Allis Chalmers tractors, sometimes standing right beside old ones, dot the landscape.

This stretch has as many trailers as conventionally built homes, and cable TV probably doesn't come out this far, because TV satellite dishes stand in many yards. Here and there an old log building has been restored. Others are crumbling to the ground. Driving these miles slows you down and reminds you that not everyone lives strapped with cell phones and pagers. From these roads you can drive easily over to US 601 South and head down to Salisbury.

A Pocket of History

Two kinds of people live in **Historic Salisbury**—those whose families have been in place for generations and those who have moved in recently, mostly from up north. Both share an almost smug conviction that theirs is one of the most congenial, historically interesting communities in North Carolina. I say *almost* smug because they're right. Although this is one of the oldest towns in the area, and the entire 23-block downtown community of commercial and residential buildings dating from 1820 to 1920 is on the National Register of Historic Places, it receives relatively little attention from outside. The Historic Salisbury Foundation and an active group of supporters are trying to change that (www.historicsalisbury.org).

They point to the 1898 **Grimes Mill,** a roller mill with all its original machinery in five floors; the **Civil War Salisbury Confederate Prison Site and National Cemetery,** where the largest number of unknown Civil War soldiers are buried; and the restored **Railroad Depot.** All of them are open to the public.

Then there's the Historic Salisbury walking tour, which includes the homes in the National Register Historic District. Some of these homes are open to the public. The **Dr. Josephus Hall House,** 226 South Jackson Street, for instance, is a large, 1820 antebellum house that sits among old oaks and boxwoods that have been in place nearly as long as the house. Dr. Hall was chief surgeon at the Salisbury Confederate Prison during the Civil War. After the war the Union commander used the house as headquarters. Somehow the grounds and the interior escaped the destruction typically associated with Yankee occupation in the South, and the Hall House contains nearly all its original furnishings. Open Saturday and Sunday from 1:00 to 4:00 p.m. Modest admission fee; (704) 636-0103.

Just about a block away, the **_Utzman-Chambers House_** museum, 116 South Jackson Street, is a notable example of architecture from the Federal period. It shows the life of a prominent local family during the early 1800s. An early-nineteenth-century garden features four formal beds of flowers and herbs native to the Piedmont in 1815. Open Thursday through Sunday from 1:00 to 4:00 p.m. Modest admission fee; (704) 633-5946.

The **_Rowan Museum_** has exhibits related to Rowan County history in the old courthouse, 202 North Main Street. The old courthouse building was built in 1857, for the princely sum of $15,000, and was used as a court building until 1914, when it became the community building. Since then, at one time or another, it has served as almost everything for which the town needed a building: public library, American Red Cross headquarters, chamber of commerce, and adult night school. When the flu epidemic hit the town in 1918, the community building became an emergency hospital and kitchen. Open Thursday through Sunday 1:00 to 4:00 p.m. Modest admission fee; (704) 633-5946.

The Rowan Museum includes another house a few miles outside of town that gives you a glimpse of early country life in the county. The **_Old Stone House,_** built by Michael Braun between 1758 and 1766, reflects the traditions of the German Rhinelanders who settled in the county in the early 1700s. Braun came to the area from Philadelphia, Pennsylvania, and the stone house will look familiar to anyone who has traveled the country roads in Pennsylvania and seen houses built on the Quaker plan. The house has been beautifully restored, and the museum is working to continue developing the property. The house is furnished with a collection of North Carolina and Pennsylvania pieces and looks much as it probably would have when Braun lived in it. One piece, a weaving loom in an upstairs room, has been in the house as long as anyone can remember.

To get to the Old Stone House from Rowan Museum, turn right on Innes Street, and go 4.2 miles (Innes Street becomes U.S. Highway 52 South) into Granite Quarry, and turn left on East Lyerly Street, which is also called Old Stone House Road. The house sits on the right, beside the road, about 0.6 mile farther on. Modest admission fee. The house is open from 1:00 to 4:00 p.m. Saturday and Sunday, April through November. The hours may change, and

AUTHOR'S FAVORITE PLACES IN THE LOWER PIEDMONT

Waterworks Visual Arts Center	Reed Gold Mine
Kluttz Piano Factory	Mint Museum of Art

sometimes you can arrange to see the house at another time. Call the museum at (704) 633-5946 for more information.

Moving from the historic to the contemporary, the **Waterworks Visual Arts Center,** 123 East Liberty Street, features changing exhibits of contemporary art. The outdoor sculpture garden is especially pleasant on clear, sunny days. The gallery used to be in a building that was first used as the Salisbury Waterworks and then as the city police station. Now it is in a renovated and expanded building that used to be a car dealership. Its large open spaces are especially suited to displaying art. Open Tuesday through Saturday 10:00 a.m. to 5:00 p.m. Donations are suggested. Call (704) 638-1882; www.waterworks.org.

In downtown Salisbury, which you really must see for its remarkable old factory, old train station (where Amtrak now stops), and business buildings, you can break the fast-food habit by having a bite of lunch at **Spanky's,** an old-fashioned ice-cream parlor that serves not only homemade ice-cream concoctions but also good soups, salads, deli sandwiches, and cheesecake (corner of Main and Innes Streets; 704-638-0780). Spanky's actually makes seventy-five different flavors of ice cream, but the owner explained, almost apologetically, that they keep only twenty-five flavors on hand at a time! The restaurant is in an old building that in 1859 was the tallest in North Carolina. Open Monday through Saturday from 9:00 a.m. to 8:00 p.m. and Sunday from noon to 8:00 p.m.

Of the many barbecue restaurants in the area, **College Bar-B-Que,** 117 Statesville Boulevard (704-633-9953), is a long-established place where the waitresses have known some of the regulars for years. It's almost always busy, and don't be confused by the word "College" in its name. Old-timers, families with little kids, and "just folks" all come here, though it is close to Catawba College and attracts students, too. As you approach the restaurant, sometimes you can smell the wood smoke from the barbecue fire, and inside you will hear the steady thumping sound of knives against cutting boards as the pork is chopped. The restaurant serves all the breakfast standards—eggs, biscuits, sausage—as well as sandwiches and menu specials, and you can expect your glass of iced tea to be kept full until you leave, but barbecue is the defining offering. The restaurant opens every day at 7:00 a.m. and closes at 8:00 p.m. except on Monday, when it closes at 2:00 p.m., and Saturday, when it closes at 3:00 p.m.

One eating establishment in Salisbury has become an institution that brings together people of every class in the community. **Hap's Grill** (116½ North Main Street; 704-633-5872) sells nothing but hot dogs and hamburgers, and Coke or Cheerwine in glass bottles. The original proprietor was Hap Alexander. He opened the grill in an 8½-foot-wide space (formerly an alley) the day after Thanksgiving in 1986. Greg Clup went to work there when he was fourteen, and in 1995 he bought the place from Hap. Over the years nothing has changed. Greg chops onions in the morning, pats hamburgers, cooks chili, and gets hot dogs ready for the grill. The most popular item is hot dogs "all the way" (with chili, onions, and mustard). When Greg starts cooking, the aroma draws customers from blocks away, even when they might've had other plans. People form a line that extends far down the block, but it moves fast, and even strangers talk to each other as they wait. Greg works at the grill by the counter, where Vickie Carter wraps the orders, opens the sodas, takes money, and makes change, all without breaking rhythm. There's no place to sit down. You can order to take out; eat inside, standing at a narrow shelf; or eat outside, standing at one of two rickety wood tables. Hap's is open 10:00 a.m. to 3:00 p.m. every day but Sunday.

Wink's King Barbeque and Seafood (509 Faith Road; 704-637-2410) is another intensely local place to eat that is as large as Hap's is small. And, unlike Hap's, this sprawling, old-fashioned family restaurant serves everything from the barbecue and seafood in its name to meatloaf, prime rib, and fried eggs with country ham. In fact, you can order breakfast all day. At the rear of the building, you'll see huge stacks of slab wood that are burned to make pork barbecue. The aroma of roasting pork mingled with wood smoke fills the air. Waitresses here wear jeans and loose T-shirts emblazoned with the Wink's logo. The customers are an interesting mix—older folks, groups with kids, parents and grandchildren, black and white, working men with service trucks parked outside, men in business suits. This is clearly not where club ladies go to lunch; it's where real people go for a generous plateful of real food. The restaurant has smoking and nonsmoking sections in separate rooms. Open Monday through Saturday 5:30 a.m. to 9:00 p.m.

The Blue Vine, 209 South Main Street (704-797-0093; www.thebluevine .com) is a smaller town's version of the city wine bar. Locals who patronize this place just call it "The Vine." You can stop in to enjoy a glass of wine,

Oink, Oink

As I headed back to my car after lunch at Wink's, a mooing sound attracted my attention. I saw a truck with an attached trailer cage in one of the pull-through parking spaces. A beautiful little brown calf in the cage was bleating its heart out. I just hoped veal wasn't on the menu.

The next time I went to Wink's, I ate barbecue and was happy to see no veal offered. But as I was leaving I heard baa-ing, which turned out to be goats in a trailer cage where the calf had been the previous week. I know Wink's does not serve goat. But I promise you, if that parking spot is filled with a cage of oinking pigs next time I'm there, I will order the vegetable plate instead.

It's a Carolina Thing

Q: What do folks who've had to move away from North Carolina miss most?

A: Cheerwine.

Cheerwine is a soft drink created in Salisbury in 1917 that has become such a local tradition, some people take it with them by the case when they travel. Every so often, the Cheerwine company invites people to describe how it differs from other soft drinks, and nobody can ever articulate it beyond mentioning the cherry taste. Its unique quality may be due to the fact that the flavoring is wild cherry. Don't underestimate nostalgia. Local people will tell you they like it because it's what they grew up with.

and perhaps a snack, from noon on, sitting either at the bar or at one of the tables in the room. You can also buy wine by the bottle or case to take home. The proprietor, Rose Meeks Jones, says she stocks more than 200 different wines, mostly those you cannot find in a grocery store, priced at less than $25. But even if you don't care for wine, you can have a good time here. The Vine features live music on weekends and sells a few kinds of beer as well as nonalcoholic beverages. Everything's so casual and friendly, Rose says she sometimes feels like she has friends sitting in her kitchen at home. Open Tuesday noon to 9:00 p.m., Wednesday noon to 7:00 p.m., Thursday noon to 9:00 p.m., Friday noon to midnight, Saturday 1:00 p.m. to midnight. Closed Sunday and Monday.

Almost any day you are in Salisbury, you'll see people wearing earphones and consulting booklets as they walk the streets, following one of the self-guided tours. You may borrow the brochures, tapes, and tape players for two of the tours, free, from the Visitor Information Center at 204 East Innes Street (704-638-3100 or 800-332-2343; www.visitsalisburync.com). Brochures and guide maps for the African-American Heritage Trail are available at the Visitor Information Center and also at W. J. Walls Heritage Hall on the campus of Livingstone College. You can purchase a CD for a driving tour of the African-American Heritage Trail.

The **Salisbury Heritage Tour** (audio, walking) is a 1.3-mile walking tour that provides details about the history and architecture of Historic Downtown Salisbury and the large homes of the West Square Historic District. The **Civil War Heritage Tour** (audio, driving) provides insights into Salisbury's role during an infamous time, including a Union prisoner-of-war camp where 11,700 died. Nothing remains of the Salisbury Confederate Prison. The Union soldiers are memorialized at the Salisbury National Cemetery. The **African-American**

Confederate Monument

Heritage Trail (brochure, driving) self-guided tour notes important moments, leaders, and lives of generations of African Americans who lived and worked in Salisbury.

When you are on Innes Street, orient yourself so the winged **Confederate Monument** in the center of town is to your back, turn left on Main Street (or turn right if you are facing the statue), and drive a few minutes into the neighboring town of **Spencer** to visit the **North Carolina Transportation Museum** (877-628-6386 or 704-636-2889; www.nctrans .org) on 411 South Salisbury Avenue. This is the site of what was once the largest service facility or shops for Southern Railway Company. The museum's collection includes all kinds of transportation-related artifacts—antique automobiles, railroad cars, and an airplane. The roundhouse, with thirty-seven bays, is an inevitable hit with train enthusiasts. You can watch a video about the railroad in the visitor center. Train rides in restored cars are available when there are enough people. Admission to the museum is free. Train rides are $6 for adults, $5 for children and senior citizens. Train rides and museum hours vary seasonally. It is a good idea to call ahead.

Right across the street the **Little Choo Choo Shop** (500 South Salisbury Avenue; 704-637-8717; www.littlechoochooshop.com) is a serious, well-stocked model-railroad shop handling supplies for scales from "G" to the tiny "Z." They buy, sell, trade, and repair. One room is devoted to books and videos about model railroading, and you can get top-notch advice from the people who work here, too. Another small room is filled with wooden toy trains to occupy kids while you browse among the grown-up toys. The store is open Tuesday through Saturday 10:00 a.m. to 5:30 p.m.

One interesting side trip from Salisbury is a quick jog south on Interstate 85 to **Cannon Village at Kannapolis.** Cannon Village is a shopping outlet now, but it and the town are a fascinating, almost unspoiled glimpse of a once-prosperous mill town.

Humiliation

I had just begun exploring the area around Salisbury and Spencer. People kept asking me if I'd been to the Spencer Shops yet. I wasn't in a big hurry to find them, because shopping isn't my idea of a good time, but eventually I figured that anything so many people mentioned would be worth a visit. The idea of gift shops in an old transportation museum seemed OK.

I went into the museum office and after checking all the signs, asked the receptionist where the gift shops were. Was it like a row of specialty shops in converted train buildings or what? I asked.

Her face changed from polite-receptionist to local-citizen-horrified-at-such-ignorance. The Shops at Spencer, she said, are machine shops where mechanics once repaired Southern Railway's steam locomotives. Those trains hauled passengers and such freight as furniture, textiles, and tobacco, and the shops at one time employed nearly 3,000 people.

Gift shops, indeed! Sniff.

Another interesting dimension is that Fieldcrest-Cannon was taken over by Pillowtex, which has since gone bankrupt and, finally, in 2003 closed entirely, putting several thousand local residents out of work. The building of the main plant has been imploded to make way for a new research complex dealing with food products. The area is still being redeveloped, and local residents expect many scientists and marketing people to move into the area.

The first thing you notice about Cannon Village and its outskirts is that everything matches—not sheets and towels or skirts and blouses, but the white-trimmed brick shops and brick sidewalks, bounded by the great brick walls of the Fieldcrest-Cannon mill buildings, the brick schoolhouse, the church, and even the supermarket that are part of the larger community. The buildings on the research campus are being built in the same style. About the only things that aren't brick are the mill houses—tidy, modest, mostly white frame homes that reflect pride of ownership in their neatly clipped hedges and mowed lawns. You pass these homes that run along the railroad tracks and the streets of Kannapolis on your way into Cannon Village.

Cannon Village is at the center of the town of Kannapolis. The village is a center for off-price, outlet, and specialty shopping, mainly home furnishings.

In the *Cannon Village Visitors Center and Museum,* 200 West Avenue, a museum display traces the development of textiles from some early Inca cotton to present-day fabric woven on high-speed, air-jet looms. Call (704) 938-3200 for days and hours of operation for the village and visitors center.

Here's another side trip you can easily make from Salisbury that gives you

Early Kannapolis

They say George Washington never slept here—but he could have. The area attracted many important travelers, and Washington passed through at least once. Francis Asbury, the English preacher who brought the Methodist faith to the United States, also stopped here several times. The "Great Road" between Charlotte and Salisbury in colonial days ran through the center of Kannapolis, just about where Cannon Village is now. One favorite stopping place was Murph's Inn, which stood near what is York Avenue today.

Earlier, Catawba and Waxhaw Indians traveled about the same route as they made trading trips between South Carolina and Virginia. They probably stopped at springs near what are now the South Main underpass, the east side of the North underpass, and the west side of Woodrow Wilson School.

a glimpse of earlier mill life in the area without the shopping hype. ***Cooleemee*** is a well-preserved but not gentrified mill town. To get there, go to Jake Alexander Boulevard, which becomes US 601/70. Follow US 601 North into Davie County. At Greasy Corner, turn left onto Highway 801 and drive about 1 mile to Cooleemee. Go right onto Marginal Street, then left onto Church Street. This will bring you to the ***Mill Village Museum,*** in the Zachary-Holt House at Old 14 Church Street (336-284-6040; www.textileheritage.org). It is well marked with signs. The Mill Village Museum offers an honest, down-to-earth look at life in a Piedmont cotton mill village a century ago, and the old homes in the town show how the town grew up around the ***Cooleemee Cotton Mill.*** The museum bills itself as "telling the story of Carolina cotton mill folks," and although the emphasis is on how the town developed around the Cooleemee Cotton Mill, later called Erwin Mills #3, the information about the people and the town gives you a good idea of what many mill towns in the Carolina Piedmont were like. The mill closed in 1969.

The Cooleemee Historical Society has actively collected artifacts, photographs, and stories from people who remember when the mill, which opened in 1898, was the center of life. Exhibits in the museum are organized under the categories Country Roots, Cooleemee is Born, From Cotton to Cloth, Like One Big Family, Establishing a Society, The Old Square, A New South, Honoring Their Memory, and This Old House. A detailed and engagingly written museum guide explains each exhibit.

After looking around the main museum, check out the Mill House Museum, a 1903 mill house that has been restored to what it was in 1934. It shows what life would've been like for an ordinary mill family. Then a walk or slow drive around the town, where most of the mill houses are still occupied, gives you a further sense of what a mill village was like. For instance, the addresses of the houses used to be numbered so that the lowest numbers were for the houses closest to the mill.

The historical society wants to clear up what they consider misrepresentation of Southern mill towns by some historians. Michael Myerson, in his book, *Nothing Could Be Finer,* wrote about mill hands: "Tied to their machines day and night and housed in mill-owned shanty villages, the developing North Carolina lived an existence out of a Dickens nightmare." But that's not the picture drawn by the exhibits in the museum and the stories recalled by old-timers. The museum guide says the work was hard and dirty and ran into sixty-six-hour workweeks for low pay, but it claims that wasn't out of line for rural people already used to hard work. The pace was relatively slow in the early days, and workers took breaks for drinks, snacks, or even a swim in the river. Looking around the town makes it clear the mill houses were never shanties, and old-timers' stories mention improvements such as indoor plumbing and electricity. The museum is open Wednesday through Saturday 10:00 a.m. to 4:00 p.m., or by appointment. The museum is accessible to people with handicaps. Donations accepted at the main museum. Admission to the Mill House is $4 for adults, $3 for senior citizens, free to children age twelve and under.

Another side trip, to **Mooresville,** can be pure fun for kids and exhilarating for racing fans. Like Kannapolis, Mooresville was once a textile town. Today its economic base comes from motorsports. Some forty race teams are based in Mooresville because the town is close to speedways in Charlotte, Wilmington, and Darlington, South Carolina. The town now calls itself Race City U.S.A. To dip into the race and auto culture, check out the **Dale Earnhardt Inc. Showroom,** 1675 Dale Earnhardt Highway #31 (877-334-9663; www.daleearnhardtinc.com), for displays of Dale Earnhardt Inc. drivers' achievements. Open Monday through Friday 9:00 a.m. to 5:00 p.m., Saturday 10:00 a.m. to 4:00 p.m. Admission is free.

JR Motorsports, 349 Cayuga Drive (866-576-8883; www.jrmotorsport .com), introduces you to Dale Junior, who is making a name in his own right in racing. The building houses the management company and racing operation, but for visitors, a museum called "The Dale Jr. Fan Experience" tells the story of his life and racing career. A viewing window allows you to look into the shop. Open Monday through Friday 9:00 a.m. to 5:30 p.m., Saturday 10:00 a.m. to 4:00 p.m. Admission is free.

Memory Lane Motorsports and Historic Automotive Museum, 769 River Highway (704-622-3673; www.memorylaneautomuseum.com), features exhibits showing the history of both racing and the automobile. Displays include one-of-a-kind vehicles, race cars, vintage automobiles, motorcycles,

Remembering the Intimidator

North Carolina is home to more than forty-six NASCAR (North American stock car racing) teams, more than any other state in the union. The state's focus on NASCAR racing became even stronger after the death of Dale Earnhardt, a Kannapolis native, who died in 2001 in a crash during the Daytona 500, just two months before his fiftieth birthday.

He was a high school dropout who became a racing legend, considered by experts the best ever in the sport.

When the road where Dale Earnhardt drove his 1956 Chevrolet as a teenager was named "Dale Earnhardt Boulevard" in 1993, 8,000 people turned out for the ceremony.

After Earnhardt's death, *Salisbury Post* sportswriter Mike London wrote, "Earnhardt did for racing what Arnold Palmer did for golf and Muhammad Ali for boxing."

Memorials to Dale Earnhardt stand in Cannon Village Park and in the Cannon Village Visitors Center.

---

toys, and memorabilia. Open Monday through Saturday 10:00 a.m. to 5:00 p.m. Longer hours during race weeks, shorter in winter. Admission is $8 for adults, $6 for children ages six to twelve, children under six free.

The ***North Carolina Auto Racing Hall of Fame,*** 119 Knob Hill Road (704-663-5331; www.ncarhof.com), has an art gallery of work by motorsports artists, a museum with more than thirty-five cars, a gift shop with all kinds of racing memorabilia, and the Goodyear Mini-Theater, which shows forty-five-minute films about peak moments in racing. The hall of fame is open Monday through Friday 10:00 a.m. to 5:00 p.m., Saturday and Sunday 10:00 a.m. to 3:00 p.m. Admission is $5 for adults, $3 for senior citizens and children ages six to twelve.

The only thing ***Lazy 5 Ranch*** has to do with automobiles is that the owners want you to stay inside yours as you drive around the place looking at exotic animals. The ranch is between I-85 and I-77, on Highway 150 East (704-663-5100; www.lazy5ranch.com). The ranch has about 750 animals from around the world, and you drive about 3.5 miles through pastures to see them: camels, Watusi cows from Africa with horn spreads of up to 12 feet, water buffalo, zebras, and so on. Although you have to stay in your car to see these animals, you can get out to enjoy the petting zoo and feed some of the animals there. This place is run with a sense of humor. Rules that make sense in any language are expressed with a grin: "You are not allowed to feed your children to the animals, no matter how bad they are behaving; don't honk your horn or turn on your lights unless you need help because it gives our animals heartburn; when you stop to take photos from your car, pull over to the side. This will allow other cars to drive around. It will also give the animals time to fluff their hair. So you get animal slobber all over your car . . . they're just trying to be friendly. You can wash it off later." You do need to know that you cannot take your pet here. Lazy 5 Ranch is open Monday through Saturday from 9:00 a.m. to an hour before sunset, Sunday from 1:00 p.m. until an hour before sunset. Admission is $8.50 for adults, $5.50 for senior citizens and children ages two to twelve; wagon rides $3.00 extra; horse-drawn wagon rides by appointment, $5.00.

Back in Salisbury once again, you might spend the night at ***Rowan Oak House,*** 208 Fulton Street, which offers Victorian elegance in a 1902 Queen Anne house (704-633-2086). The house is notable for its remarkably intact interior, where the original wallpaper is still in perfect condition.

Another hostelry up the street takes a different approach to the Victorian era. Karen Windate rescued an old Victorian home at 529 South Fulton Street, in the historic district, with a full-scale historic restoration that has won pres- ervation prizes. ***Turn of the Century Victorian Bed and Breakfast*** offers three guest rooms and a two-room suite, all with private baths, decorated and furnished in understated elegance with period antiques. Karen prides herself on serving a different full breakfast, on different china, each morning. Guests who've stayed for several days have sometimes made bets about how long she could go without repeating herself (704-642-1660 or 800-250-5349; www .turnofthecenturybb.com).

Leaving Salisbury, take US 52 South for an interesting drive that shows you the down-home, not the tourist, version of the Piedmont. In about 6 miles, almost before you've left Salisbury's environs, you come to Granite Quarry, where a big billboard on the left side of the road directs you to ***Kluttz Piano Factory*** (704-279-7237). They deliver free, but probably not if you live in Cincinnati. Stop in and look around, even though you probably aren't planning to buy a piano while you're out tracking unbeaten paths. Ray Kluttz Sr., the company patriarch, says they have, in fact, had customers from distant states. He loves it. This place, which advertises more than 500 new and rebuilt pianos, is awesome. The showroom, where you try out new and reconditioned pianos, looks fairly standard, but you'll be dumbfounded by the work area, which seems roughly the size of a football field, filled with pianos—whole pianos and pieces of pianos in every make, model, and size. Ten minutes of just looking will tell you more about what's inside a piano than you've ever dreamed you could know. The people who work here talk as casually about the good and bad traits of grands, uprights, spinets, Yamahas, Wurlitzers, and Baldwins as the rest of us talk about the tomatoes in our gardens.

Outsiders sometimes get a chuckle out of the name Kluttz, but around here, Kluttz is just another family name, belonging not only to the owners of the piano factory but also to architects, contractors, and art shop proprietors. Some workers get there as early as 4:00 a.m., but regular hours for ordinary mortals are Monday through Friday from 9:00 a.m. to 5:00 p.m. and Saturday from 10:00 a.m. to 2:00 p.m.

Also, on the same road, just two miles past Granite Quarry, in a long, stone building, you'll find **Old Stone Vineyard and Winery** (6245 U.S. Highway 52; 704-279-0930; www.osvwinery.com). The vineyards are beside and behind the building, while inside you'll find a state-of-the-art production facility, tasting bar, and salesroom, all managed by friendly, competent staff. Mark David Brown, the owner-winemaker, spent eight years in California, and when he returned to North Carolina, he brought a wealth of winemaking knowledge with him that helped go beyond the traditional, much-loved muscadine wines of North Carolina. Old Stone's offerings range from sweet muscadine wines, a peach wine, and a blackberry wine to cabernet sauvignon, merlot, and pinot grigio. One, a dry red blend, is popular partly because of its name, "Old Peckerhead." For three dollars, you can taste as many different wines as you wish and keep the glass as a souvenir. Depending on what is going on in the tank room, tours are offered. Even when they're not, you can see the action through large glass windows between the salesroom and the production area. Old Stone Vineyard and Winery is open Tuesday through Saturday 11:00 a.m. to 6:00 p.m., Sunday 1:00 to 5:00 p.m.

Continuing on US 52 South, which is really going east at this point, brings you to **Rockwell,** which you should pronounce *ROCKwul,* not *RockWELL.* The town bears no relationship to Norman Rockwell, but it should: Flags fly from all the porches on Memorial Day; signs advertise bait, crickets, and night crawlers; women still appear occasionally with their hair in curlers; neighbors stop each other in the grocery store to ask if the new "granbaby" has arrived yet; pink and blue bows on mailboxes announce when the new grans do come into the world. Stop for some good, authentic barbecue at **Darrell's Bar-BQ,** 117 East Main Street. If you call ahead, you can even pick it up at a drive-

From the Grape Comes the Wine

The muscadine grape is the oldest grape in America and native to this country. Muscadine wines are still a favorite among Southerners. As the state's wineries add and advertise "viniferous" wines, they refer to those made from grapes whose stock originated "in the old country," mainly Europe. And, as populations blend, the wineries are beginning to experiment with blends of muscadine and viniferous grapes.

through window, although then you'll miss the chance to mingle with the local people inside (704-279-6300). Darrell's is open Tuesday through Saturday from 10:00 a.m. to 9:00 p.m. Closed Sunday and Monday.

Continuing east on US 52, you'll come to **Gold Hill.**

Orient yourself so that the Gold Hill Post Office and a convenience store stand on your left. On the right-hand side of the road, a sign carved from wood and set in brick announces GOLD HILL. Turn right through the gate and onto Doby Road. Cross the railroad tracks, turn left onto Old 80, and go a short block to a stop sign. At the sign, turn right onto St. Stephen's Church Road, follow it just a little more than a half mile, and you'll come to a section where green banners welcome you to the **Historic Village of Gold Hill.** Gold Hill was once the largest mining district east of the Mississippi—a boomtown in the mid-1800s. But it was hard to extract ore from the soil here, and the gold rush moved on to other sites, leaving Gold Hill a sparsely populated rural community until recently, when community members began to rejuvenate the place.

The first thing you come to is a park bordered by fieldstone fences, complete with a pavilion shelter, a museum building, an outdoor stage, picnic tables, playground equipment, bike and walking paths, bridges, and information signs explaining the history of mining in Gold Hill, all the work of a community park committee. Across from the park, Gold Hill United Methodist Church, a simple white building with six columns, is a fully active church.

Boardwalks beginning here run the length of the "new" old village, past renovated, reproduced, and imported old buildings. One observer said this section looks like a Western movie set. The stores, which sell antiques, ice cream, pop, hot dogs, and Moon Pies, have varying hours of operation, but are generally open weekends. As the village continues to attract small businesses and shops, it's also attracting more visitors looking for antiques, art, and crafts. Check the Web site at www.historicgoldhill.com to see what's going on in the village. Often special arts and pottery festivals take place over long weekends.

You won't need a schedule to enjoy the spacious park, which has good play space for children and places to enjoy a picnic. It's also become popular as a meeting place for people who want to get together for a quiet chat. The work of creating the park, refurbishing its walls and buildings, has been done by local volunteers.

When you're done in the village, if you drive straight on through, you'll come to Old Beatty Ford Road, which, if you turn left, will take you back to US 52 in a couple of minutes, or you can turn right for an hour's diversion down a different kind of entrepreneurial row.

Turn left onto a road that crosses the railroad tracks and runs past a large quarry operation. You'll drive about 12 miles along this road, past a Soil Conservation Service demonstration farm on the left; a home-based sewing-machine repair shop called Sew and Sew; another home business, "Why Knot Upholstery"; and Miller Farms Racing (a track around grassy fields). Among these little businesses, many yards have for-sale signs offering produce in season, a piece of used farm equipment, a boat, a camper "like new" with tow bar and a pickup (there must be a story in that one), firewood, oil paintings—it all changes with fortune and the seasons. You'll also pass a couple of uncommonly attractive older churches, the kind with their own manicured graveyards in back. Old Concord Road intersects Old Beatty Ford Road after about 12 miles. Turn left. Drive about 3 miles more, passing Roy Cline Road and Irish Potato Road, and turn right immediately onto Goldfish Road. You're at **Greendale,** 6465 Goldfish Road, Kannapolis, which from the outside looks like one more sprawling roadside building. Inside you'll find wonder and the ultimate rural entrepreneurial enterprise.

Long rows of beautifully clear, brightly lighted aquariums gleam in the dim room, covering 44,000 square feet of display space. Here in the boonies, where if you tell your mother you're going to the fish store she assumes you're going to buy flounder, you discover gouramis and guppies, oscars, cichlids, corals, and saltwater exotics whose names you don't even know, all apparently thriving. OK, you can't keep goldfish on the road, but just looking beats watching television, and you may find the selection and prices on aquarium equipment appealing enough to tease a traveler's check out of your wallet before you leave.

Greendale started out as a goldfish farm back in 1929, when Rufus Green got laid off by Cannon Mills and decided to make his living raising goldfish in outdoor ponds to sell to dime stores. One of his first sales was to get money to buy a shirt for church. The years passed, Rufus died, and his wife maintained the business as well as she could. Rufus's son, George, returned in 1978 from another war that wasn't called one, with his wife, Gaysorn, a classical dancer from Bangkok. By now hobbyists had turned enthusiastically to exotic tropical fish, so it made sense for Greendale to develop accordingly. The whole story, in a yellowing newspaper clipping, is taped to the front wall.

It's hard to imagine there would be enough customers to keep the business going, but they come from all directions: Concord, Kannapolis, Salisbury, Albemarle. The store is closed on Tuesday, partly because new shipments of plants and fish come then. On Wednesday it's so busy that, as one employee put it, "People just come in and throw money at you." They're all there: Gay and George and local young people who work here and often get themselves hooked on the hobby in the process. You can always find someone to chat with about the troublesome habits of live bearers and how hard it is not to disrupt a gourami's bubble nest. Open Wednesday through Saturday from 10:00 a.m. to 6:00 p.m. and Sunday from 2:00 to 6:00 p.m. Closed Monday and Tuesday (704-933-1798).

When you leave, depending on which way you turn, you may see a large block-lettered sign inside a cul-de-sac in front of a mobile home: IF YOU DON'T HAVE BUSINESS HERE, THIS IS A GOOD PLACE FOR YOU TO TURN AROUND. This may be the only guy in the county who isn't looking for customers at home. The best way to return to US 52 is the way you came in. Since everything looks different going in the opposite direction, you'll see things you missed the first time and won't feel that you're backtracking.

Coming into Misenhiemer, US 52 runs through the middle of the small **Pfeiffer University** campus, where all the classroom buildings, administration buildings, dormitories, and faculty houses are made of red brick. You might think that this is the kind of place a film director would like to shoot *Who's Afraid of Virginia Woolf?,* although a director would never get approval in this Bible pocket.

Farm Country

From Pfeiffer University it's only a couple of miles to the intersection of US 52 and Highway 49 at Richfield. Go north on Highway 49 for about as long as you need to take two deep breaths and pull into the parking lot of the **Judy's Motel Restaurant** (704-463-7005). This is the breakfast and lunch spot for many of the local farmers, the people who work in the mobile-home factories, and the university. For breakfast you get two eggs, bacon, grits or hash browns, biscuits or corn bread, and coffee for less than $5. Lunch is one

Old-Timers

They still tell the story in Richfield about a bet two of the men once made. Nobody remembers for sure what it was about, though it may have had something to do with whether or not a kid could steal some chickens and then sell them back to the owner, but they do know that the loser had to push the winner to Albemarle, about 10 miles away, in a wheelbarrow.

How long did it take?

Didn't keep time, exactly, but it definitely took most of the day.

meat (meatloaf, chicken, or fried fish, maybe; the selections are written on a blackboard at the door), two vegetables, and beverage for about $6.

The Motel Restaurant waitresses know all the regulars by name, ask "You doin' OK?" as they take your order, and after the first time, remember what it is that you always have. They like a good joke. Did you hear about the prostitute who told her tax consultant that she was a chicken farmer? Well, she said. . . . Country music plays in the background, and while Willie and Waylon are appreciated, one of the waitresses says she'd really like to marry Garth Brooks, even if she is already married. But Randy Travis, now, he's one of our own, coming from Monroe and all. This is the kind of place where everybody knows everybody, and the local bank manager sits next to the local welder, who calls his regular morning trip to the restaurant "going to the office." When you've had all the coffee or iced tea you can hold, leave a dollar on the counter, pay your bill, and when someone says, "Come back," you say, "I'll do it." Open Monday through Friday 4:00 a.m. to 1:45 p.m., Saturday and Sunday 4:00 a.m. to 10:30 a.m.

Continuing south on US 52 for a few miles more brings you to **New London.** This little village of fewer than 500 people has some pretty, older houses and a small community park on Main Street. It's the kind of place you are not likely to find unless somebody tells you about it. You can't see the village from the highway, but make a left turn onto Highway 740, which brings you right to the center of town. Continuing north about 3 miles on that road, through rural countryside, you come to **Pat & Mick's Fish House** (44883 Fish Camp Road; 704-463-1366), a big sprawling place between two ponds, where local folks go mainly for fish, although the menu also includes steak, burgers, and chicken. The traditional accompaniments are iced tea and slaw. These days you can get other salads as well. The place is big and noisy, but service is fast and friendly. Portions are large. This is a place where you can clearly see how people in the area like to eat, and how the consequence often requires men to wear belts fastened below the belly. Payment is cash only. Open Thursday through Sunday, beginning at 4:00 p.m.

Between the fish camp and the center of New London, at 41697 Gurley Road, the **Cotton Patch Gold Mine and Campground** (www.cottonpatch goldmine.com) offers opportunities to pan for gold, as well as equipment for a little more elaborate prospecting. (To find the mine, turn onto Hearne Road from Highway 740 and make a left on Gurley.) Adults can pan for $10 a day, kids for $6. In really cold weather, you can work a sluice in a heated shed, but most activity is out in the open. As you drive up, the place doesn't look like much—some simple buildings and heavy equipment. This is also a working gold mine, and you're expected to follow rules about not getting in the way of that operation. From the beginning of March to December, panning is available Wednesday through Sunday 9:00 a.m. to 5:00 p.m. From the first of December to March, hours are 9:00 a.m. to 5:00 p.m. Saturday and Sunday.

The campground, open year-round, accommodates everything from tent camping to full RV hookup, and has cabins available as well. Rates are $15 for tent sites, $25 for RV hookup with 30-amp service, and $40 for cabins. You need reservations for panning (704-463-5191) and camping (704-463-5797).

Returning to US 52 and continuing a few miles south, you'll come to Austin Road on the right, right after the Mauney Feed Company. Turning onto this road and following it across the railroad tracks and through some rural countryside for a few miles brings you to the **_Uwharrie Vineyards and Winery_** (28030 Austin Road; 704-982-9463; www.uwharrievineyards.com), the fifth-largest winery in North Carolina. The sign is fairly inconspicuous and you might pass by, but you can't miss the expanse of vineyard, all neatly surrounded with white fence, or the 14,000-square-foot building that includes production rooms, salesroom and gift shop, tasting bar, and a banquet hall. Winemaker Chad Andrews is thoroughly knowledgeable about making wine and can explain in minute detail how his sophisticated equipment works; much of the process requires his close monitoring, which sometimes means minimal sleeping. Uwharrie Vineyards' wines, some of which have won prestigious awards, range from a substantial merlot and a very dry cabernet sauvignon to the sweeter Muscat, Magnolia, and Autumn Blush. Because of Chad's understanding of the relationship between quality of winemaking procedures and the quantity of sulfites needed, he can almost promise you a bottle of wine that won't induce a headache, if you're sensitive.

Returning to US 52, after just a few more miles south, you'll see signs for the town of **_Albemarle._**

learningthelingo

If a North Carolinian tells you he's ill, don't call the doctor. He means he is in bad humor. If he says he's "ill as a hornet," try not to make him mad because, if you do, he'll throw a hissy fit.

Southern Sweets

Chad Andrews, winemaker at Uwharrie Vineyards, says you can predict the kinds of wines you'll find in North Carolina by geography. "Remember the southern sweet tooth," he says. The closer to the coast you get, the sweeter beverages will be. So, while some regions have sweet and unsweet iced tea, the coastal region has sweet tea and sweeter tea. So, Chad says, "Don't expect them to drink dry wine there."

Take the US 52 business road to get into the downtown area. This is a town that is both going and coming. It celebrated its 150th anniversary in 2006, looking back to years when textile mills and related operations thrived and the downtown bustled. But as the mills closed, Albemarle, like many Carolina towns, lost a huge part of its economic base. And the inevitable bypass (Highway 24/27) attracted chain stores and fast food. Some downtown businesses closed while others moved to the bypass, a familiar pattern for many areas. With all that gone, new kinds of activity are beginning to move in. Owners of older downtown structures that survived the wrecking ball era of the 1960s, '70s, and '80s are restoring many of the remaining buildings to their original appearance, and new businesses are moving in.

One example is the shop **Wine & Roses Gift Emporium** (160 West Main Street, 704-986-6210; www.wine-roses.net), in what used to be the Cabbarus Bank and Trust Building, built in 1936. The shop concentrates largely on locally created merchandise. In what was once the bank vault, you now find more than fifty different wines, predominantly from North Carolina wineries. Another room is devoted to the work of area potters. Collections of jewelry, paintings, and gourd art, all from local artisans, are displayed throughout the store. Space on the second floor houses antiques and collectibles. (*NOTE:* At press time it was announced that Wine & Roses had closed.)

In a less glamorous, but thoroughly authentic bow to tradition, Hugh Wainwright cooks breakfast and lunch at **The Goody Shop Café,** in a small space at 241 West Main Street (704-983-7973). The shop was established in 1924, and when Hugh Wainwright took over, he decided to keep things as they'd always been as much as possible. Old signs on the wall advertise soft drinks and burgers at old prices, and today's prices haven't gone up as drastically here as they have in some places. Hugh makes the hamburgers by hand, is recognized locally for making good chicken salad, and works the grill himself. Customers sit at the counter or at a single row of small tables against the wall, and most of them know each other. Everybody pretty much talks to everybody else. It's hard to imagine anybody living in Albemarle who hasn't eaten here at one time or another—from the teenager trying to be a rock musician to an investment broker with an office down the street. This may be one of the few places left in town where people still smoke inside. No doubt it keeps some folks away, but it does add an air of authenticity.

As the community works to rejuvenate itself, preserving elements of the past has become a priority. **Stanly County Museum** (245 East Main Street; 704-986-3777; http://hpc.co.stanly.nc.us/) is definitely a work in process. The museum building also serves as a welcome center. A modest display depicts everything from the area's early American Indian culture, slavery, and the Civil

War to more ongoing development in the area. The museum also has two nineteenth-century houses, the 1873 Snuggs House and the 1847 Marks House. Both are open for tours and are furnished with period pieces and household items, many donated by local residents. The museum has a collection of about 10,000 donated artifacts kept in storage until expansion allows more room to display them.

While you're here, pick up a brochure for a walking tour of the downtown area's historic sites. Pee Dee Avenue, with a lovingly maintained old cemetery and old homes, is on the National Register of Historic Places. The museum is open Tuesday through Friday 10:00 a.m. to 5:00 p.m., Saturday 10:00 a.m. to 4:00 p.m.

On a lighter note, still almost history, **Badin Road Drive-In Theater** (2411 Badin Road; 704-983-2900; www.badinroaddrivein.com) is an attraction people associate with an earlier time, when loading pickups with people settled against bales of hay or driving in with a carful of kids was standard Saturday-night entertainment. Here it still is, although the movies are contemporary. The theater has two screens, one typically featuring a movie for kids and another for adults. Admission is $5 for adults, free for children ages eleven and under.

Going north on Highway 740 from Albemarle brings you to the little town of **Badin,** another place in the state that is reinventing itself after the loss of manufacturing. Its history goes back to 1913, when a French company, L'Aluminium Français, began building a dam on the Yadkin River, which created **Badin Lake.** Next, a town for company workers was built by the lake and named for the company president, Adrien Badin. Eventually the French company went on to other projects, and ALCOA bought the town. Badin was soon a thriving company town, with the ALCOA plant at its entrance, across from the lake. The plant shut down several years ago, but it remains the dominant

Choo, Choo

People come from all over to visit the *Albemarle Music Store* (235 West Main Street; 704-982-3815), not necessarily for musical instruments but to see the model trains. The entire second floor of the building is filled with model-train layouts, of all gauges. Jimmy and Carol Brown sell everything you'd need to set up your own layout, but a lot of people just come to play, and Jimmy's especially fond of running the trains for kids. Any upstairs space not taken up with trains is filled with model aircraft and ships, as well as some World War II pictures and memorabilia. There's no Web site, but you can find pictures taken by people who've visited with a simple Google search. The trains run Friday from 9:00 a.m. to 4:30 p.m. and Saturday from 9:00 a.m. to noon.

Picking Pickler

American Idol and Kellie Pickler have become Albemarle's claim to fame. In 2005, Kellie was just a local girl heading off to Greensboro to audition for the chance to appear on the television program. She made it, and from then until she was finally voted off the show in April 2006, Albemarle went Kellie-crazy. People of all ages gathered in restaurants and bars to watch her performances and phone in their votes. The town flashed pink bows and PICK PICKLER signs on virtually all available surfaces. Local folks wore Pickler T-shirts, and downtown stores filled their display windows with Pickler signs. After leaving the *Idol* stage, she moved on to Nashville and appearances on shows from *The Tonight Show with Jay Leno* to *Live with Regis and Kelly.* She had to teach most of her interviewers how to pronounce her hometown— *Al-buh-mar-el.* And her first CD, *Small Town Girl,* sold nearly 80,000 copies in the first week of release. Now at the little park in town, a sign on the gazebo identifies Albemarle as the home of KELLIE PICKLER.

visual feature of the area. At least until you drive on up the hill to **Badin Inn Golf Resort and Club** (One Pine Circle Drive; 704-422-3683; www.badininn .com). In an earlier time, it was the Badin Country Club and Golf Course. Before that it served as a residence hall for single males and, on another floor, female schoolteachers. Andy and Martha Kinnecom chose this place to fulfill their dream of operating an inn, and, after extensive renovation, opened it for business, complete with everything from a pro shop to an English-style pub. Spaces are large and sparkling.

The restaurant, **The Pine Circle Pub and Grille,** is open from 11:00 a.m. to 9:00 p.m. Monday through Friday and from 8:00 a.m. to 9:00 p.m. Saturday and Sunday. You can eat on the shaded porch when weather permits. In redoing the structure, the Kinnecoms kept such historical accoutrements as the original windowpanes, woodwork, and hardware in the upstairs guest rooms. The antique furnishings pay homage to the history of the place, and views of the golf course and woods from the windows seem timeless. In addition to the amusements of the inn and resort, the village offers diversion with small

ANNUAL EVENTS IN BADIN

Best of Badin Festival
Third weekend in September
(704) 422-3713

**Badin Volunteer Fire
Department Barbecues**
Second Saturday in October;
Fourth Saturday in January
(704) 422-3614

shops and pretty gardens. Town rules allow golf carts in the village, which the inn will provide. If you prefer housing with a kitchen, modern condos and renovated village town houses are available. Badin Lake has an area for putting in boats and a sandy beach area where the water is shallow and only gradually deepens. Most of the people who spend time at the lake live somewhere in the area.

Consider another side trip from Albemarle, going south on Highway 73 about 15 miles to **Mount Gilead** to see **Town Creek Indian Mound** (509 Town Creek Mound Road; 910-439-6802; www.towncreek.nchistoricsites.org). This site, which is in the middle of farmland and undeveloped countryside, deserves more attention than its remote location affords. Based on information from excavations that have been in progress since 1937, two temple buildings, a burial hut, and a stockade have been reconstructed, giving visitors a glimpse of the Pee Dee culture as it developed beginning sometime in the eleventh century A.D. It's the only state historic site in North Carolina dedicated to Native American culture. With state funds skimpy, volunteers contribute a great deal to keep the research going and to explain the site to visitors. As interesting as the outside structures are, maps and photographs inside the visitor center showing what's been learned from excavations are equally fascinating. Guides explain how as one structure collapsed it was covered with earth and another built on top of it. Each phase left behind artifacts that archaeologists use to interpret the development of the culture. The site is open Tuesday through Saturday 10:00 a.m. to 4:00 p.m., Sunday 1:00 to 4:00 p.m. Admission is free, but donations are appreciated. There's a picnic area here, which you might enjoy in good weather.

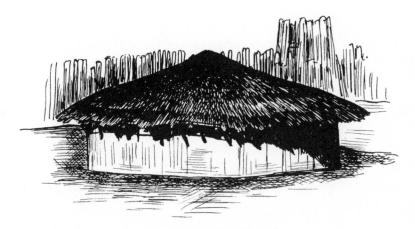

Town Creek Indian Mound

thetarheelstate

North Carolina got its nickname because of its large forests of long-needle pine trees, which were the source of tar, pitch, and turpentine. According to local lore, stepping into the tar left it stuck to the heels of your feet or shoes.

On the main street of this little community, you'll find a restaurant that is far removed from the standard "country cooking" restaurants in many small North Carolina towns. *Henry's Tonight!* (211 North Main Street; 910-439-9700; www.henrystonight.home stead.com) serves lunch and dinner, featuring a variety of dishes ranging from comfortably familiar steaks and seafood to specialties such as tandoori chicken and grilled salmon with warm pineapple salsa, as well as a variety of sandwiches and appetizers. All ingredients are fresh and top-quality. The menu changes regularly, maintaining a balance between familiar foods and newer flavors. A wine list gives special attention to North Carolina wines. The proprietors, Henry J. Antos III and his wife, Beth A. Wiese, are new to the community, which they've chosen because they "love the area." The restaurant is in a simple structure, with interior walls painted in muted colors, accentuated by dishes in the colors of old-fashioned Fiestaware. Diners sit at round oak tables. Henry and Beth are charming, low-key, and knowledgeable. Henry is a graduate of Johnson & Wales culinary school in Providence, Rhode Island, and the couple lived in Raleigh before coming to Mount Gilead. Their restaurant is more sophisticated than you'd expect to find in a town well shy of 2,000 people, but they attract people from other towns in the region, as well as travelers. Henry's Tonight! is open Tuesday through Thursday 11:00 a.m. to 8:00 p.m. and until 9:00 p.m. Friday and Saturday. Sunday brunch is served from 12:15 to 3:00 p.m. so Henry and Beth can get to church first.

The restaurant is just outside a couple blocks designated as a National Historic Site, which is still a work in progress, with many of the old buildings in good shape on the outside, but standing empty. However, you can see progress in reclaiming this street. What was once a 20,000-square-foot hosiery mill, built in 1910, has been renovated to house *Mt. Gilead Antiques* (126 North Main Street; 910-439-4641), an antiques mall and Christmas store. Although vendors will change from time to time, there is an especially good variety of china and glassware. The mall is open Monday through Saturday 9:00 a.m. to 5:30 p.m. and Sunday 1:00 to 5:00 p.m.

At 100 South Main Street, Benjamin and Celia Blake have *The Vintage* (910-439-4038), a shop filled with antiques and unusual gift items, including some of Celia's own work. She and other local artists have begun a cooperative display space toward the end of the same block, which, at the time of this

The Doctor Is In

Dr. Pressley R. Rankin Jr. has practiced medicine in the town of Ellerbe for more than forty years. The Rankin Museum is the direct result of a lifetime of collecting and studying. He began collecting birds' eggs when he was eight years old. (Although that's illegal now, it wasn't back then.) By the time Dr. Rankin was a teenager, he'd become interested in Native American artifacts. As his interests continued to expand, the items he collected filled his home, which was one impetus for starting the museum. People in Ellerbe raised money for the building, and the museum continues to be a project the community supports actively. Dr. Rankin spends time at the museum, where sometimes people who used to be his patients come in asking if the doctor is "in his office."

writing, has no sign or posted hours of operation, but represents another step in reclaiming the district.

Driving about fifteen miles farther south on Highway 73 brings you to the **Rankin Museum of American Heritage** (131 W. Church Street; 910-652-6378; www.rankinmuseum.com). The museum is attached to the library, a simple brick building that, from the outside, isn't impressive. But once you are inside and begin to study the exhibits, it's enough to take your breath away. The museum was begun more than twenty years ago with the personal collection of Dr. Pressley R. Rankin Jr. Exhibits range from a collection of Native American artifacts and a collection of South American art to the work of early potters in the Piedmont area of North Carolina. In one large display, you'll see what the museum claims is "the most well-preserved 500 gallon turpentine still on display anywhere."

Other exhibits contain relics from the Civil War, ivory carvings by Eskimos, and a fossil collection dating from the Cambrian Period, covering 500 million years. Each display is artistically arranged and accompanied by signs explaining the significance of the artifacts.

The museum is open Monday, Tuesday, Thursday, and Friday 10:00 a.m. to 4:00 p.m., Saturday 10:00 a.m. to 5:00 p.m., and Sunday 1:00 to 5:00 p.m. Admission is $4 for adults, $1 for students. Children ages four and under are free.

Back at the intersection of Highway 49 and US 52, you can also take Highway 49 North through the **Uwharrie Forest** up to Asheboro, or you could go south for an interesting drive to Charlotte.

Headed toward Charlotte, when you get to where US 601 meets Highway 49, you may decide to make a side trip on US 601 South to Highway 200 and follow the signs to the **Reed Gold Mine** at Midland, about 10 miles east of Concord (704-721-4653; www.reedmine.com). This is the site of the first

Hey Ma, Look What I Found!

The gold nugget Conrad Reed found in 1799 weighed seventeen pounds, but he was only twelve and everybody figured the kid was just hauling a big rock home. The family used it as a doorstop for three years before the boy's father sold it for $3.50.

authenticated gold find in the United States. It seems that Conrad Reed found a gold nugget the size of a brick on the family farm, and after that the family sort of lost interest in farming. We tend to associate the gold rushes with Alaska and California, but the fever burned here in North Carolina back in the late 1820s. For a time more people worked at gold mining than any other occupation except farming.

allthatglitters

Even today it's possible to find pieces of rock in the area flecked with what appears to be gold. The names of such communities as Gold Hill, Rockwell, and Richfield reflect the early influence of gold, too.

At the Reed Gold Mine State Historic Site, you can pan for gold in the spring and summer and tour the mining area year-round. In the visitor center, exhibits and a film explain the history and mining process. Admission is free, but you must pay a modest fee to pan for gold. In winter, open Tuesday through Saturday from 10:00 a.m. to 4:00 p.m.; opens an hour earlier and closes an hour later the rest of the year.

Land of the New

Charlotte's an exciting place to visit these days. In the beginning it was all about gold, and it's still about money today, having become a center for banking and commerce. The city is growing so fast that you can find something new almost every day. People seem to exude civic pride. Because they're so pleased about the way things are going, they're incredibly nice to visitors. ***Charlotte*** has reason for pride: the Charlotte Panthers NFL team; the Charlotte Bobcats NBA team; the Charlotte Knights Class AAA minor league baseball team; the Charlotte Checkers minor league hockey team; NASCAR racing at Lowe's Motor Speedway; Douglas International Airport, with direct flights to major cities around the world; a Pulitzer Prize–winning newspaper, the *Charlotte Observer;* the University of North Carolina at Charlotte; a slew of smaller colleges and universities; new skyscrapers; and a new state-of-the-art downtown arena.

Charlotte's growth brings traffic, unfortunately, along with the excitement, but it would be too bad to miss some of the city's special features because of traffic. The best advice for a visitor to minimize problems is to study a city map ahead of time and try to avoid the major high-traffic highways—I-85, I-485, I-77, and Independence Boulevard—as much as possible. Once you're actually in the city, the traffic isn't bad, except at rush hour; it's the main arteries that clog up. Don't hesitate to ask for directions if you get confused. People seem to be used to it and are good at helping, probably because the ongoing construction everywhere has forced them to figure out new routes.

The *Mint Museum of Art,* at 2730 Randolph Road, has exhibits that celebrate both local history and world culture. The name comes from the building's having been a branch of the United States Mint in the 1800s. That made sense back when the Piedmont was producing most of the country's gold.

In 1988 the museum created a huge stir with the exhibit "Ramses the Great: The Pharaoh and His Time," which featured, among other items, a gold statue of the pharaoh so large the building had to be modified to give him extra headroom. That exhibit is gone now, but permanent collections, such as "Spanish Colonial Art," along with displays of American and European paintings, African artifacts, pre-Columbian art, costumes, and gold coins minted in Charlotte are fully worth attention.

The museum is open Tuesday from 10:00 a.m. to 10:00 p.m., Wednesday through Saturday from 10:00 a.m. to 5:00 p.m., and Sunday from noon to 5:00 p.m. Closed Monday. Also closed Christmas and New Year's Day. Admission is $6 adults, $5 senior citizens and students, $3 children ages six to seventeen. Includes Mint Museum of Craft and Design (704-337-2000; www.mintmuseum.org).

The *Mint Museum of Craft and Design,* located in center city at 220 North Tryon Street, exhibits collections of ceramics, fiber, glass, metal, and wood, showing the development of handcrafts from the early days of practical use to contemporary studio art. Plans are in the works to move the craft and design displays to a new building. As this develops, you can find current information on the Mint Museum Web site. The museum is open the same

Art in the Bank

A fresco is a watercolor painting done on a wet plaster wall or ceiling. The colors sink into the plaster and become permanent as it dries.

Artist Ben Long has created much-loved frescoes in various locations across the state, including Charlotte. In the Bank of America Corporate Center lobby, on North Tryon Street, a series of scenes depict workers in North Carolina.

Hezekiah Alexander Homesite

hours as the Mint Museum of Art. Ticket price is also the same and includes both museums. Phone for both museums is (704) 337-2000.

Another museum in the vicinity worth your attention is the ***Hezekiah Alexander Homesite*** and Museum of History, at 3500 Shamrock Drive. The Hezekiah Alexander house is the oldest dwelling still standing in Mecklenburg County. It was built of local quarry stone in 1774 and has been restored. Costumed guides lead tours of the house, log kitchen, barn, and gardens. The history museum displays local crafts and artifacts. Hezekiah was a delegate to the Fifth Provincial Congress and served on the committee that drafted the North Carolina State Constitution and Bill of Rights. The site has a number of fascinating details. The house is known as "The Rockhouse." Its doors are unusually low by today's standards, a feature intended to keep heat inside when people opened the doors.

In the re-created springhouse behind the house, you can see how milk and butter were cooled in the late 1700s. Open Tuesday through Saturday from

Old Sayings

In the master bedroom of The Rockhouse, a rope bed dominates the room. In this kind of bed a latticework of ropes supported the mattress. Every so often the ropes had to be tightened—giving rise to the old phrase, "Sleep tight." Don't even think about the origins of the rest of the phrase, "Don't let the bedbugs bite."

10:00 a.m. to 5:00 p.m. and Sunday from 1:00 to 5:00 p.m. Admission is $6 adults, $5 senior citizens and students, $3 children ages six to twelve. Sundays free. For tour hours, call (704) 568-1774; www.charlottemuseum.org.

In uptown Charlotte, at 301 North Tryon Street, the kids will enjoy **Discovery Place,** a hands-on science and technology museum where they can experience some close-up encounters with fish and birds, the natural sciences, and computers. One of the most impressive exhibits is the tropical rain forest, which fills three stories with plants, rocks, waterfalls, and appropriate wildlife. The exhibits related to the human body are interesting, too. One description claims that you learn about characteristics of the human body in a "hands-on manner," which sounds risqué if you don't know about the models and machines. Open Monday through Saturday 10:00 a.m. to 6:00 p.m., Sunday 12:30 to 6:00 p.m. in summer. Sunday closing is an hour earlier the rest of the year (704-372-6261 or 800-935-0553 for rates to various areas; www .discoveryplace.org).

On the north side of Charlotte, on Highway 49, the botanical gardens at the University of North Carolina at Charlotte deserve a lot more attention than they receive. The **UNC Charlotte Botanical Gardens** have three parts: the McMillan Greenhouse, the VanLandingham Glen, and the Susie Harwood Garden. The greenhouse has one of the best collections of tropical orchids in the South, with something like 800 species. The tropical rain forest conservatory is a convincing simulation of a real rain forest. Other greenhouse rooms include a cactus room and a cool room. A great variety of carnivorous plants grow in a protected outside area by the greenhouses. The VanLandingham Glen started as a rhododendron garden in 1966 and has expanded to include more than 4,000 rhododendrons, mostly hybrids. Another interesting feature is the 1,000 species of Carolina-native plants growing in the gardens. The Harwood garden, with gravel paths, is more formal and includes exotic plants from around the world. The collection of Japanese maples is noteworthy, as is the winter garden. The greenhouse is open during normal business hours, but you can visit the gardens any time. The best way to find the gardens is to go onto campus through the main gate on Highway 49 and follow the signs to the visitor parking garage and ask for directions from there. For more information, call (704) 547-2870.

It takes about fifteen minutes driving north on I-77 to reach **Davidson,** home of Davidson College, a small liberal arts school with outstanding music and arts programs. The little town covers less than five miles and, even though it's at Lake Norman, a popular destination, the community rarely makes it into guidebooks. It's an agreeable retreat from the city atmosphere of Charlotte, though you do want to avoid graduation day in mid-May and homecoming at the end of April, when the place is packed.

Davidson Village Inn, 117 Depot Street (704-892-8044 or toll-free 800-892-0796; www.davidsoninn.com) is a comfortable eighteen-room inn directly across from the college campus, in the historic district. The building, though relatively new, was built on the site of the old Chambers Hotel, and brick sidewalks help the brick inn fit in visually. The common areas are spacious and bright, with a big library—a real one—complete with comfortable reading chairs and a fireplace. From this location you can cross the street to tour the campus, walk quickly to popular restaurants, visit an independent bookstore, and check the offerings in a knitting and needlework shop.

You're also just steps away from the Belk Visual Arts Center, which is flanked by the ***Every/Smith Galleries,*** 315 North Main Street, part of Davidson College. The galleries, completed in 1993, cover 2,000 square feet and house a permanent collection of nearly 3,000 pieces. The spaces were designed to accommodate large-scale paintings and sculpture as well as smaller work. In addition to the permanent collections, the galleries feature changing professional exhibits and also student exhibits. The galleries are open Monday through Friday 10:00 a.m. to 5:00 p.m. and Saturday and Sunday noon to 4:00 p.m. when college is in session.

A block away, at 423 North Main Street, you come to the studios of ***WDAV,*** the college's all-classical public radio station, at 89.9 on the FM dial, offering better-than-average programming, including recordings of some performances in the area (704-894-8900; www.wdav.org).

Even closer to Charlotte than Davidson, ***Belmont,*** off Highway 273, has somehow managed to avoid being swallowed up by Charlotte development and retains its distinctive feel as a community of fewer than 10,000 people. Catawba Mills, makers of knitwear, was a major employer here, and in the area around Sixth Street, modest two- and three-bedroom homes that were mill houses still show pride of ownership on properties that typically have well-clipped grass and carefully tended shrubs in the front, with the backyards variously given over to more grass or perennial gardens or vegetable gardens. The old brick mill building has been rescued and renovated and now houses upscale condominiums. From all these locations, people walk to restaurants, a library, small stores, and the post office. A small restaurant at 23 North Main Street, ***Cherubs' Café*** (704-825-0414), serves sandwiches, soups, salads, and desserts from 9:30 a.m. to 5:00 p.m. Tuesday through Saturday. It is run by the Sisters of Mercy and volunteers to provide money for care, vocational train-ing, and jobs, as well as work experience for children and adults with mental retardation and other disabilities. The restaurant has its share of church humor, with names on the menu such as "Divine Desserts," and for coffee concoctions, "Holy Grounds."

The Roman Catholic Church has another presence at **Belmont Abbey College and Monastery Historic District,** 100 Belmont-Mount Holly Road (888-222-0110; www.belmontabbeycollege.edu). The college was founded by Benedictine monks in 1876, on land that had been a plantation. Today the grounds include the oldest liberal arts college in the Southeast, a monastery, the 1892 Our Lady of Lourdes Pilgrimage Shrine, a cemetery dating to 1890, and a library with a large collection of rare books. Classes are small, typically fewer than twenty students per teacher, and although not all teachers are Benedictine monks, many are. Teachers also come from other countries, other schools, and other religious orders. But the spirit of the school is distinctly Benedictine, trying to follow Benedict's instructions to the early monks to welcome each person as Christ.

The other major attraction in the Belmont area, **Daniel Stowe Botanical Garden,** could be attributed to both divine providence and corporate generosity. In 1989 a retired Belmont textile executive, Daniel Jonathan Stowe, set aside 450 acres of land and lakefront property and $14 million to develop a world-class botanical garden. Since then, volunteers and employees have worked to develop formal gardens as well as woodland, meadow, and wetland areas. The Robert Lee Stowe Visitors Pavilion houses a gift shop and areas for displays, meetings, and classes. The garden maintains ongoing educational programs, plant sales, and seasonal exhibits. In nice weather, picnicking on the grounds is welcome. A recent addition to the property is an 8,000-square-foot orchid conservatory, billed as "the Carolinas' only glass house." In addition to a stunning variety of orchids, you'll find many other warmth-loving plants here, including bromeliads and succulents, in artfully arranged, changing exhibits set off by a waterfall. The garden is open every day from 9:00 a.m. to 5:00 p.m.; closed Thanksgiving, Christmas, and January 1. Admission is $10 for adults, $9 for senior citizens, $5 for children ages four to twelve (704-825-4490; www.dsbg.org).

About 20 miles west of Charlotte, in Gastonia, which you can reach quickly on I-85, the **Schiele Museum of Natural History and Planetarium,** at 1500 East Garrison Boulevard, attracts large numbers of visitors, especially schoolchildren, with its collection of North American mammals in habitat settings, a one-hundred-seat planetarium, a restored pioneer site of the 1700s, and a reconstructed Catawba Indian village. Other exhibits deal with everything from forestry to archaeology. A brochure maps out several self-guided tour suggestions for the outside grounds. Don't skip this one because it's popular; it has good reason for being so. Open Monday through Saturday from 9:00 a.m. to 5:00 p.m. and Sunday from 1:00 to 5:00 p.m. Call for planetarium show times, (704) 866-6908; www.schielemuseum.org. Modest admission fee. To get there, take the New Hope Road exit from I-85 and follow signs.

Places to Stay in the Lower Piedmont

CHARLOTTE

The Dunhill Hotel
237 North Tryon Street
(704) 332-4141
www.dunhillhotel.com

Hilton Garden Inn
508 East 2nd Street
(704) 347-5972
www.hiltongardeninn.com

The Morehead Inn
1122 East Morehead Street
(704) 376-3357
www.moreheadinn.com

MT. AIRY

Best Western Bryson Inn
125 Plaza Lane
(336) 352-3400
http://book.bestwestern
.com

Hampton Inn
2029 Rockford Street
(336) 789-5999
(800) 565-5249
www.hampton-inn.com

Mayberry Motor Inn
U.S. Bypass 52 North
(336) 786-4109
www.mayberrymotorinn
.com

SALISBURY

**Turn of the Century
Victorian Bed & Breakfast**
529 South Fulton Street
(704) 642-1660
www.turnofthecenturybb
.com

STATESVILLE

Hampton Inn
1508 Cinema Drive
(704) 883-8380
(800) 426-7866
www.hamptoninn.com

Places to Eat in the Lower Piedmont

CHARLOTTE

Amalfi's Pasta and Pizza
8542 University City
Boulevard
(704) 547-8651

Bombay Cuisine
230 East W. T. Harris
Boulevard
(704) 503-5558

Providence Café
110 Perrin Place
(704) 376-2008

DAVIDSON

Jasper's
127 Depot Street
(704) 896-1881

MT. AIRY

Goober's 52
458 North Andy Griffith
Parkway
(336) 786-1845

SALISBURY

Farmhouse Restaurant
1602 Jake Alexander
Boulevard
(704) 633-3276

Sweet Meadow Café
118 West Innes Street
(704) 637-8715

The Wrenn House
115 South Jackson Street
(704) 663-9978

STATESVILLE

Carolina Bar-B-Q
213 Salisbury Road
(704) 873-5585

THE LOWER PIEDMONT WEB SITES

Charlotte
www.visitcharlotte.org

Lowe's Motor Speedway
www.lowesmotorspeedway.com

Salisbury and Spencer
www.visitsalisburync.com

Statesville
www.visitstatesville.org

The Mountains

The Western Mountains

Whatever you plan in the North Carolina mountains, allow about twice as much travel time as usual. Narrow roads wind through woodland and countryside, up hills so steep you sometimes feel as though your car will peel off the road backward, from hairpin turns into switchbacks followed by more curves. The squiggles don't all show on the maps, and the maps can't allow for the time it takes if you get behind a big truck with no place to pass for 50 miles. Decide ahead of time not to hurry; relax and absorb the peerless scenery.

One way to enjoy the panoramic views of mountains and valleys is by driving some part of the **Blue Ridge Parkway.** It stretches from Shenandoah National Park in Virginia along the Blue Ridge Mountains into the southern part of the Black Mountains, through the Craggies, the Pisgahs, the Balsams, and into the Great Smokies, a total of 469 miles. The maximum speed limit along the parkway is 45 miles per hour, but in reality, traffic is often slower. It doesn't take much arithmetic to figure that it would take a long time to cover the entire length of the parkway at 30 or 40 miles per hour. The best way to

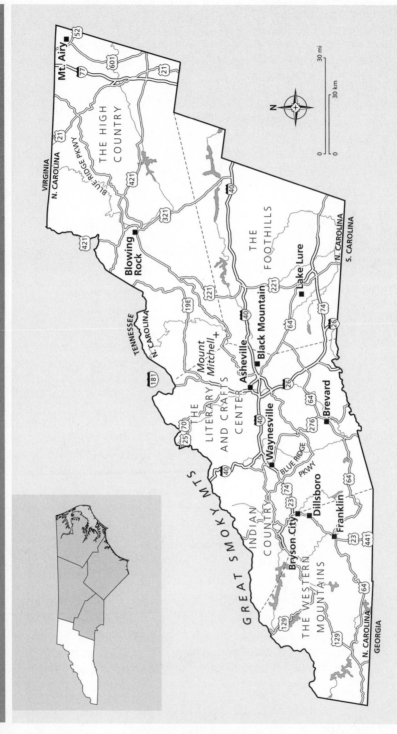

ANNUAL EVENTS IN THE MOUNTAINS

Asheville
Annual Spring Herb Festival
(early May)
(828) 253-1691

Biltmore Estate's Annual Festival
of Flowers
(early May)
(828) 274-6333
or (800) 543-2961

Banner Elk
Woolly Worm Festival
(third full weekend in October)
(800) 438-7500

Black Mountain Sourwood
Festival
(mid-August)
(828) 669-2300
or (800) 669-2301

Blowing Rock Independence
Day Festival
(July 4)
(828) 295-7851

Dillsboro
Western North Carolina
Pottery Festival
(first Saturday in November)
(800) 962-1911

Valle Crucis
Valle Country Fair
(Annual Apple Festival)
(third full weekend in October)
(828) 963-4609

plan a trip is to alternate stretches of the parkway with drives on the roads you can reach by turning off along the way. Crossovers from the parkway are marked with mileposts that are numbered and named.

To take in some of the rugged mountain scenery without driving the winding roads, you might board the **Great Smoky Mountains Railroad** (800-872-4681; www.gsmr.com) at the depot on Depot Street in Bryson City or on Front Street in Dillsboro. The tracks were first laid in the 1890s, and rail transport made it possible to establish a vigorous logging industry in the mountains. Eventually highways replaced trains, and by 1988 the state of North Carolina had taken over the tracks in this region and leased a 53-mile stretch to the Great Smoky Mountains Railroad, which runs a variety of excursion trips through the mountains. Although the main offices and depot are in Bryson City, you can also board in Dillsboro.

The **Scenic Model Railroad Museum,** 100 Greenlee Street, Bryson City (866-914-5200; www.smokymtntrains.com), next to the Great Smoky Mountains Railroad Depot, honors the area's railroading history with a 24-by-45-foot model layout, with more than a mile of track on three levels over which six trains run at once. The layout has a working roundtable with roundhouse and a 5-foot waterfall. The model includes a freight yard with at least 400 cars, a dozen animated scenes, and more than sixty buildings made by hand, not assembled from packages. This collection has 7,000 Lionel engines, cars, and accessories. Model railroad enthusiasts travel to Bryson City specifically to visit the museum. A retail store is attached to the museum, as well as an activity center for children. Open Monday through Saturday. Call for exact hours. Admission is $9 adults, $5 for children under twelve, free for children under three.

From Bryson City, drive 9 miles southwest on U.S. Highway 19 to **Nantahala Outdoor Center** at the Nantahala Gorge. The outdoor center attracts the outdoors crowd, especially rafters and hikers. This is a congenial place to hire a guide and all the equipment you need for a white-water rafting trip down the Nantahala River. It's also great for fishing, picnicking, and hiking. Part of the fun is watching the serious rafters, who, as one observer put it, seem to have a continuing contest to see who can show up in the most worn, mismatched, clothes-don't-matter outfit. The **River's End Restaurant,** right by the river, has been a popular eating place with hikers and rafters for years. Some of the most popular recipes have been bound into a cookbook, *River Runners Special,* with each recipe listed for difficulty (Class I, II, III, and so on) like the rapids on the river. Vegetarian lentil mushroom soup is Class II; amaretto cream pie is Class IV.

At River's End you'll feel perfectly comfortable in your mismatched hiking clothes and down vest, sitting at a rustic table looking out over the river while you gobble a hearty serving of spicy beef stew with the restaurant's special herb bread. Just across the river, **Slow Joe's Café** is the place for quick meals and snacks. **Relia's Garden,** near the center of the property, has a view of the mountains rather than the river. This restaurant sits in a field on the hill across from the garden, landscaped with terraced gardens of herbs, unusual

It Was Inevitable

In his younger years a good friend of mine spent most of his free time at the Nantahala Outdoor Center (they call it NOC). Several of his brothers were river guides over the years, and they finally convinced their mother, a good-natured Pittsburgh lady, to venture onto the river on a raft. She listened to the lecture about keeping her feet pointed downstream if she fell off, but she didn't take it very seriously. And she buckled into her life vest without protest but didn't take it very seriously either. She listened to the paddling instructions without getting especially serious. But she did know what to do if the raft dumped her off.

It did. And that nice lady ended up floating rapidly in icy water, with her feet pointed downsteam, buoyed by her flotation vest, shouting to her sons at the top of her lungs, "I'll never forgive you for this."

vegetables, and exotic plants. A walk through the gardens crushes fragrant bits of mint and thyme underfoot.

Staff members of the Nantahala Outdoor Center, from guides to cooks, tend to return year after year, as do visitors. The Appalachian Trail, crossing right through the center, brings many serious hikers. Moreover, the presence of the family that started the center is still much in evidence. Relia's Garden, for instance, is named for Arelia, wife of the founder and for many years director of food service. Her plants fill the terrace gardens. Spending time here feels like being part of an extended family or a close community. It is special. The center, its lodging, restaurants, and programs operate from roughly mid-March to November 1, depending on the weather. For information about operating hours when you plan to be here, call (800) 232-7238 for all attractions at NOC, or visit its Web site: www.noc.com.

Indian Country

Picking up the Blue Ridge Parkway at Cherokee brings you to some decisions about the kind of tourist you mean to be. The town, in the *Qualla Boundary Cherokee Indian Reservation,* where U.S. Highways 441 and 19 meet, maintains several features dedicated to preserving and explaining the history of the Cherokee nation, which was nearly wiped out by the infamous "Trail of Tears" forced walk in 1838, when the U.S. government tried to relocate all Indians to west of the Mississippi River. Some of the Cherokees escaped the march by hiding in the hills.

Eventually they were able to return to this area, where they were once the powerful Cherokee nation. Their story is told in **Unto These Hills,** an outdoor drama played by a cast of 130 people, beginning between 8:00 and 9:00 p.m. nightly, except Sunday, from mid-June through late August, in an outdoor theater that seats 2,800 people. The program is presented by the Cherokee Historical Association with support from the Theatre Arts Section of the North Carolina Arts Council and funds appropriated by the North Carolina General Assembly. The story begins with Spanish explorer Hernando DeSoto's arrival in 1540 and climaxes with the Trail of Tears exodus. Many of the players are descendants of the Cherokee who lived the story. Moderately high admission fee. Box office (828-497-2111) open from 9:00 a.m. to 10:00 p.m. during the summer season and from 9:00 a.m. to 4:30 p.m. in the off-season; www.untothesehills.com. The story and performances are frankly moving; it's not uncommon to see people in the audience cry.

Unfortunately, activities of this caliber are surrounded by the tourist-tacky pseudo-Indian concessions that seem to plague the areas around Indian popu-

AUTHOR'S FAVORITE PLACES IN THE MOUNTAINS

Asheville	Mount Mitchell State Park
Folk Art Center	Sylva
New River State Park	Waynesville
Hot Springs	
Carl Sandburg Home National Historic Site	

lations across the country. The matter is further complicated by the addition of *Harrah's Cherokee Casino* (800-427-7247; www.Harrahs.com) several years ago. The casino, which has 60,000 square feet of electronic gambling area with 2,800 video machines, three restaurants, and a 1,500-seat theater, attracts people by the busload. The area now has at least one hundred motels, hotels, cabins, and campgrounds, all pretty much one right next to another. Harrah's is an enterprise of the Cherokee tribe. Trying to sort out the authentic from the merely exploitative can be depressing. You can count on quality at the *Oconaluftee Indian Village,* sponsored by the Cherokee Historical Association. The village is on the Cherokee Indian Reservation. It is a living replication of a 1750s Cherokee village and shows you Indians practicing their historical crafts of basket making, pottery, canoe building, food preparations, and weaponry and, perhaps even more important, explains the culture within which these activities proceeded. Tours begin every fifteen minutes, but you are not locked into them, and there is plenty of time for exploring, photographing, and questioning. Open daily from 9:00 a.m. to 5:30 p.m., May through October. Moderately high admission charge (828-497-2111; www.cherokee-nc.com).

Qualla Arts and Crafts Mutual, Inc., the most successful Indian-owned-and-operated craft cooperative in the country, representing 350 Cherokee crafters, at the entrance of the *Unto These Hills* theater on US 441, offers you an opportunity to buy genuine Indian beadwork, baskets, wood carvings, pots, masks, and the like. Cherokee work is displayed in separate rooms from that of other tribes. Open daily 8:00 a.m. to 4:30 p.m. These hours may vary. It's a good idea to call ahead (828-497-3103; www.cherokee-nc.com).

Finally, the *Museum of the Cherokee Indian* displays traditional arts and crafts and offers a video on the history of the nation, along with displays of tools and various accounts of the Trail of Tears journey. Computer-generated images and holographic imaging bring scenes to life. Open Monday through Saturday from 9:00 a.m. to 5:00 p.m., later during the summer. Moderate admission charged. Closed Thanksgiving, Christmas, and New Year's Day. For full information about attractions, call (828-497-3481; www.cherokee-nc.com/ museum).

The Cherokee Visitor Center on the reservation is a good source of information about the village, crafts co-op, and museum (800-438-1601; www .cherokee-nc.com).

Cherokee is considered the gateway to the Great Smoky Mountains, and it seems important to mention, however briefly, the *Great Smoky Mountains National Park,* established in 1934 partly with money donated by John D. Rockefeller. The park merits a full book in itself: Elevations climb as you move along the northeast; plant life, wildlife, and scenery invite superlatives; the bears and the weather are unpredictable. About half the park falls in Tennessee, but North Carolinians, figuring there's plenty for all, forgive that. Staying on the North Carolina side, you'll find enough hiking, fishing, and camping to last most of your life without being repetitious. There are several visitor centers in the park. For information, call (865) 436-1200. The park is said to have attracted more than ten million visitors annually in recent years, mostly in the summer, although with about 500,000 acres to explore, there'd seem to be enough room for everyone. Admission is free. You'll probably enjoy your visit more if you avoid the peak summer season.

Southeast of Cherokee and Bryson City, where U.S. Highways 23/74 and US 441 come together, the little town of *Dillsboro* stretches along the banks

Mountain Greenery

Jackson County Green Energy Park is getting something good from a former landfill: methane gas for blacksmith forges. The *Blacksmith Village,* in Dillsboro, has three forges, the only ones in the United States fired using methane gas from a land-fill. Blacksmithing courses and studio spaces are offered for blacksmiths of all experience levels. For more information, call (828) 631-0271.

For the artisans living and working by a landfill at the base of the Black Mountain Range in western North Carolina, the methane is free energy. *Energy Xchange,* a nonprofit corporation formed in 1999, supports craft studios, greenhouses, cold frames, and a public gallery in Burnsville with methane gas trapped rather than released into the environment as the energy source. Potters, glassblowers, and artists using recycled and reclaimed objects are among the artists working here. The facility is open to the public Monday through Friday 9:00 a.m. to 4:00 p.m., Saturday 9:00 a.m. to noon (66 Energy Xchange Drive; 828-675-5541; www.energyxchange.org).

You Ought to Be in Pictures

The Great Smoky Mountains Railroad trains have been used in several movies, including *The Fugitive, My Fellow Americans, Digging to China, Paradise Falls,* and *Forces of Nature.*

of the Tuckasegee River. This community, with a population of only a couple hundred residents, is working actively to develop awareness of its history and to offer visitors local arts and crafts. More than fifty shops sell pottery, handmade jewelry, unusual gifts with a regional theme, wood carvings, metal works, and paintings.

This is also a ***Great Smoky Mountains Railroad*** depot, ticket office, and boarding center. The excursion line, with both steam and diesel engines, began running in 1988, on what had been the Murphy Branch Line, dating back to 1891. The trains travel through 53 miles of track in the western North Carolina mountains, going through two tunnels and crossing twenty-five bridges.

Great Smoky Mountains Railroad schedules a tremendous variety of trips, ranging from the Gourmet Dinner Train and Mystery Theatre Dinner Train to autumn scenic excursions and a Rapid Transit experience with Nantahala Outdoor Center, which offers a combination of a white-water raft trip and a 30-mile scenic train ride to explore the Nantahala River. In December the Polar Express, geared toward children, welcomes the Christmas season. Schedules and offerings change each year. For specifics, call (800) 872-4681; www.gsmr .com.

The Dillsboro Inn, 146 North River Road (828-586-3898 or toll-free 866-586-3898; www.dillsboroinn.com), is just a short walk away from the railroad terminal, but the star of the place here is the Tuckasegee River. The suites and cabins are so close to the river you can hear a waterfall rushing, even through phone calls. It's taken innkeepers T. J. and Terry Walker more than ten years to build and renovate the Dillsboro Inn to their satisfaction. The Walkers came to North Carolina via Florida and New York. T. J. says, "It's my experiences as a little kid at summer camp that brought me back here." But summer camp was never like this, except for the rustic location and nightly campfires with marshmallows. The suites are spacious, furnished with a hint of luxury and an emphasis on privacy. It's a good place to get away and rest, not a gather-round-the-breakfast-table hostelry. "We're not a bed-and-breakfast," T. J. says. The continental breakfast is delivered to the suites. The best way to spend time here, the Walkers say, is quietly, letting troubles float downstream.

The Wolf Chooses You

During one Gourmet Dinner Train trip, a couple celebrating their anniversary requested boxes to pack up the remains of generous servings of duck they were too full to finish. The woman said she would take it home to feed her wolves. She kept a dozen in a fenced field behind the house, she said. These were wolves that had sprung from dog-wolf unions. As other guests in the car began contributing their leftovers to Operation Wolf Feed, the woman went on to explain that she didn't go out to acquire wolves, they came to her house. "You don't choose the wolf," she said. "The wolf chooses you."

Another nearby lodging with a different approach is *The Chalet Inn,* 285 Lone Oak Drive (828-586-0251 or 800-789-8024; www.thechaletinn.com), a few miles west of Dillsboro on US 74/441. The Chalet is on 22 acres of wooded mountainside, surrounded by perennial gardens, streams, a waterfall, and pond. The grassy areas are groomed for lawn games, and you can follow hiking trails of varying difficulty through the woods. International travelers like The Chalet Inn because its European style feels familiar. Each room has its own balcony and is angled for privacy. Innkeepers George and Hanneke Ware play up the European theme by serving breakfast in lederhosen and including whole-grain breads, cheese, and German cold cuts along with standard American egg dishes. Breakfast is served by candlelight in the dining room outside on an open, but heated, patio. You can pretty much communicate in your language of choice here. Hanneke was born in the Netherlands and George served in the army there at NATO headquarters. In addition to German and Dutch, they manage a little French. When Hanneke knows guests with foreign backgrounds are coming, she takes the trouble to learn at least a few phrases to greet them. The inn is between Bryson City, Dillsboro, and Cherokee, about fifteen minutes away from the beginning of the Blue Ridge Parkway, the Nantahala River Gorge, and Great Smoky Mountains National Park.

People go to the *Jarrett House,* 100 Haywood Street (800-972-5623; www.jarretthouse.com), to eat, but the old inn also has eighteen guest rooms, each with private bath. Jarrett House is famous for its food, which includes huge servings of country ham or fried chicken, your choice, accompanied by unlimited amounts of old Southern classics—green beans, slaw, pickled beets, baked apples, potatoes—and heaps of little light biscuits. The proprietors, Jim and Jean Hartbarger, and Jim and Jean's sons, Scott and Buzz, with their wives, Mary and Sharon, work actively in the community to revitalize a sense of history and continue the inn's tradition of hospitality. Jarrett House, standing on the corner in the center of town, has been an inn since back in the 1800s.

The inn opened as the Mount Beulah Hotel in 1884 and was a stopping place for trains of the Western North Carolina Railroad traveling between Asheville and Murphy. The inn's name came from Frank Jarrett, who bought the place in 1894, when tourists began coming to the area to get away from summer heat in the lowlands. The Hartbargers have kept the place fastidiously clean, white on the outside, with such antiques as old sewing machines and oak pieces in the halls upstairs. In the downstairs Victorian parlor, an old Bacon & Raven piano that belonged to Jim's grandmother holds pride of place in one corner. The inn is open May through December; the dining room is open April through December.

Just fifteen or twenty minutes farther east via US 23/74, the town of **Sylva,** which once would've been only a quick stop on the way to other attractions, has become the kind of community where people wish they could live, and it's full of quirky and interesting spots, beginning with the historic downtown area, which has been in the process of revitalization since about 1998. On Main Street, a variety of thriving shops—outfitters, bookstores, music stores, and specialty shops—attract both local and tourist traffic. When you get into the downtown area, park. Traffic tends to be slow because the streets are narrow, and you can walk the town easily, to see more with less aggravation.

Two old structures hold special interest, and you'll have no trouble seeing either one. First is the **Hooper House,** 773 West Main Street (828-586-2155; www.mountainlovers.com), where offices of the Jackson County Chamber of Commerce, the Jackson County Travel and Tourism Authority, Sylva Partners in Renewal, and the **Jackson County Museum** are headquartered. The building is open Monday through Saturday from 9:30 a.m. to 5:30 p.m. and Sunday from 1:00 to 4:00 p.m. This Queen Anne Victorian structure was designed from plans that came from Sears, Roebuck & Company. Completed in 1906, the building became the home of Dr. Delos Dexter Hooper, one of the first medical doctors in Jackson County.

It had fallen into disrepair and was scheduled for demolition when a group of local citizens in 1999 began a drive to raise money for its restoration, which cost more than $347,000. Much of the passion for the project came from Julie Spiro, the chamber's director and a great-niece of the doctor. She not only worked on fund-raising but also did much of the physical work on the building herself. Renovation involved scraping away fourteen layers of old paint, analyzing and duplicating the colors of the original coats, and removing more than 800 nails from the walls.

On a hill above Main Street, the **Jackson County Courthouse** attracts photographers and fitness nuts. It's a 1913 neoclassic revival building that sits so high above the town it appears on a foggy day to be floating. If you want

Jackson County Courthouse

to climb from the street to the entrance, you've got 107 steps to negotiate. Locals say this is the most photographed courthouse in North Carolina. It's no longer being used as a courthouse and is under renovation, but it's still a good photo-op.

Should all that climbing steps and walking along Main Street work up your appetite, Sylva has a number of good places to eat. *Lulu's Café,* at 612 West Main Street (828-586-8989; www.lulusonmain.com), has attracted not only local diners but also those from nearby towns with an offbeat menu the owners call "eclectic." They emphasize fresh ingredients and offer everything from black bean vegetarian chili to grilled salmon with mustard and sour cream sauce on saffron couscous. Sandwiches include a white albacore (dolphin free) tuna salad, a grilled portobello mushroom, and a huge ground-chuck burger on a French bun. A children's menu offers peanut butter and jelly on whole-wheat bread from Annie's Bakery and pasta dishes. Lulu's maintains an extensive wine and beer list. The restaurant serves lunch and dinner, Monday through Saturday, beginning at 11:30 a.m. By the way, there's no Lulu. Never was.

Walking a block up the hill from Main Street, on Spring Street, you'll come to *Spring St. Café,* 3 East Jackson Street (828-586-1800), a restaurant tucked into the bottom floor of the building that houses City Lights Book Store. It features locally grown organic produce, locally raised trout, hormone-free meats, and fresh seafood. The menu here is also widely varied, with such choices as Indonesian Gado-Gado, roast turkey sandwich, and jumbo shrimp on a rosemary skewer. The cafe serves locally roasted coffees, bakes its own desserts, and has good beer and wine lists. It has two entrances, one from the sidewalk on the hill, where there's a small outdoor serving area for nice weather, and another down the stairs from the bookstore above. Work by local artists lines the stairway and walls in the restaurant. Spring St. Café is open for lunch and dinner Tuesday through Saturday 11:00 a.m. to 9:30 p.m. and Sunday brunch 10:30 a.m. to 2:30 p.m.

In contrast to the relative sophistication of Spring St. Café and Lulu's, the **Coffee Shop,** 385 West Main Street (828-586-2013), almost at the edge of town, is one of those places where working people eat, day after day. Men meet in small groups early in the morning or at lunch for a little gossip to break up the workday, and old-timers come in knowing a waitress has started getting their regular order ready as soon as she sees them park. The restaurant has been in operation since 1927 and probably doesn't look much different now than it did then, with red booth seating and round stools at the counter, which stands in front of the grill and stove burners. This is a meat-and-three place, specializing in such meals as meatloaf with green beans, mashed potatoes, and slaw. You can get a sandwich here and a slice of homemade pie. The restaurant serves breakfast, lunch, and dinner from 6:00 a.m. to 8:00 p.m. Monday through Friday, until 4:00 p.m. Saturday. Closed Sunday.

Both Lulu's and Spring St. Café, as well as more than thirty other restaurants and stores in North Carolina and Georgia, sell baked goods from **Annie's Naturally Bakery,** 506 West Main Street (828-586-9096; anniesnaturallybakery .com). This bakery produces its goodies in a large, commercial French stone-hearth oven in the basement of the building. At street level, customers come in steadily to buy coffee, croissants, cookies, breads, pies, and cakes. All the products are made with organic and natural ingredients, with no artificial sweeteners, fats, or preservatives. One of the most popular items is a multigrain bread. Other choices include an authentic French baguette, focaccia, Jewish challah bread, and a huge assortment of pastries. The retail shop is open Tuesday through Friday from 7:00 a.m. to 5:00 p.m., Saturday from 8:00 a.m. to 9:00 p.m.

Culturally, this area is influenced by the Tuckasegee River, which runs through it. It is popular for trout fishing, rafting, kayaking, and canoeing, and has the advantage of being gentle enough, at least in areas, to be appropriate for young children and beginners who'd like to try rafting. The main fish in the river are rainbow and brown trout, which are stocked, as well as catfish and smallmouth bass near the dam at Dillsboro.

The Usual

"He's coming now," a Coffee Shop waitress called to a cook behind the counter. The cook began frying a couple of eggs, sunny side up, poured a mug of coffee, popped two slices of bread into the toaster, and spooned applesauce into a side dish. By the time an elderly man in a plaid flannel shirt got inside the door, his breakfast was set up for him in front of the end stool at the counter.

In addition to a number of standard motels, **Mountain Brook Fireplace Cottages,** 208 Mountain Brook Road (828-586-4329; www.mountainbrook .com), has twelve cottages, each with fully equipped electric kitchen, private bath, and fireplace; some with whirlpool and sauna. The proprietors of Mountain Brook have pulled off an unusual accomplishment. They've taken a group of cottages built in the woods in the 1930s and renovated them without losing the rural feel of the original buildings. No two are alike. They're built variously of log, stone, brick, and frame. The cottages called "Romancers" have a whirlpool-sauna area and a bedroom from which you can see the fireplace in the living room. Guests in all cottages may use the whirlpool spa and cedar sauna in a separate building surrounded by mountain laurel and rhododendron. In another building, the game room includes a pool table, pinball machine, some sports equipment, board games, and a lending library. Other amenities on the property include a picnic area, charcoal grills, nature trails, and a stocked trout pond. You don't need a license to fish here. The Mountain Brook folks provide bait and tackle, charge a nominal sum for each fish you catch, and expect you to keep the fish, not throw them back. Rates include wood for the fireplace.

Just south of Sylva, on Highway 107, Western Carolina University is another significant influence on the area. For visitors, a stop at **Mountain Heritage Center,** on the university's campus, provides a detailed and graphic glimpse of the region's history. A permanent exhibit depicts the migration of the Scottish and English migrants whose descendants came from Northern Ireland to settle in western North Carolina. Other exhibits are built around such themes as early mountain skills and culture, mountain trout, and Appalachian handicrafts. A collection of thousands of western North Carolina artifacts from mountain families illustrates old mountain life. The center also publishes books, tapes, and shorter printed material about mountain culture based on academic research. On the last Saturday in September, some 35,000 visitors congregate in **Cullowhee** for Mountain Heritage Day, a celebration of music, storytelling, food, and crafts. The center is open, free of charge, Monday through Friday

8:00 a.m. to 5:00 p.m., Sunday 2:00 to 5:00 p.m., from June through October. The center operates on the university's holiday schedule. Call (828) 227-7129 for specifics; www.wcu.edu/mhc.

At Cullowhee, the **River Lodge Bed and Breakfast,** 619 Roy Tritt Road (828-293-5431; www.riverlodge-bb.com), sits at a bend in the river, with views of the Blue Ridge Mountains on all sides. The lodge was built from one-hundred-year-old hand-hewn logs found in old barns and cabins around the area. In addition to six guest rooms, it has a large great room dominated by a stone fireplace and decorated with antiques and Native American artifacts. It's filled with books and art and games such as chess and billiards. Each of the guest rooms is decorated according to a mountain theme, such as mallards in flight and the trout and creel. A hideaway suite with a private entrance has a whirlpool for two and a cathedral ceiling. But the real pleasure of this place comes with the innkeepers, Cathy and Anthony Sgambato, a couple of Italians originally from the Bronx who intended to open an inn in the Adirondacks and ended up here instead. They love to laugh and tell stories, and their breakfasts go beyond the ubiquitous grits and sausage to include such treats as lox and bagels, sugar waffles, fresh fruits, and ham.

giddyup!

The Bunk House Tuckaseigee Valley Vacation Cabin is done in a cowboy theme, with saddles and cowboy pictures. Horseshoes serve as everything from towel holders to a wine rack. One guest left a note on the refrigerator: "There are 108 horseshoes in here."

And almost directly across the road are the **Tuckaseigee Valley Vacation Cabins,** at 897 Roy Tritt Road (828-293-5131 or 888-906-7409; www.tuckcabins.com). Each of the cottages is decorated thematically, in a Western motif or Native American, for instance, and has a fully equipped kitchen, lots of sleeping space, a fireplace, and a television. These are fairly new structures, designed to look rustic. The property is hilly, with lots of grass and fruit trees that were once used by the family on the homestead. Although the river for which the cabins are named is the Tuckasegee, the owner of the cabins has retained the Cherokee spelling, "Tuckaseigee." It can mean "long man" or "slow turtle."

For a pretty authentic mountain experience, you might try **Fox Den Cottages,** 142 Silver Fox Drive, Cullowhee (828-293-0828 or toll-free 800-721-9847; www.foxdencottages.com). The innkeepers, Genie and Brent Dore, came originally from New Iberia, Louisiana, but they settled into this mountain town among lifetime residents of the place on the side of the mountain. Each of the three cottages is well furnished, with a fully equipped kitchen, telephone, satellite TV, washer, dryer, and fireplace, but to get to them you have to drive up a steep, narrow road with hairpin turns, past a variety of mobile homes and small houses, all inhabited by Foxes—that's people in the Fox family, not the four-legged wild creatures. These people are the most open, friendly, helpful folks you could ever hope to find. Talking with them is part of the fun of staying here. And if you're not necessarily looking for a private getaway, it's good to know each of the cabins can sleep at least four. Your pets are welcome here, too.

Heading toward Waynesville, you come to the little community of Balsam, which isn't much more than a dot on the map. Here, ***Moonshine Creek Campground,*** 7 Moonshine Creek Trail (828-586-6666; www.moonshinecreek campground.com), offers RV sites, tent sites, and camping cabins. The RV sites have water, electricity, and sewer. Tent sites have water and electricity. The first thing you notice is how quiet everything is. Moonshine Creek Campground is tucked into a wooded cove off a rural road that winds up and down several hills and around curves from US 441, between Sylva and Waynesville. The facility includes a sparkling clean bathhouse and laundry facilities, as well as a children's playground, camp store, and walking trails. The sites are level and well maintained, with woodland growth providing an unusual degree of privacy between sites. The tent sites are clustered in a grassy creek-side area a bit apart from the RV sites. One RV site, more secluded than the others, sits on a rise next to a waterfall with its stream running down to the creek, so you hear the continuous sound of flowing water. The creek is good for fishing. The camping cabins are simple wood shelters with doors, windows, and beds, but no other facilities inside. The campground also offers a few furnished rentals with bathrooms and kitchens. It is open April 1 to November 1.

A Mystery Carved in Stone

Lying in a grassy field about 7 miles from Cullowhee, a big gray soapstone boulder known as the Judaculla Rock mystifies locals and visitors alike. It is covered with markings that people have variously identified as stick figures, pictographs, and hieroglyphics. The rock is named after a giant Cherokee monster, and one popular legend is that he made the marks when he jumped off a mountain. Others speculate that the rock marks the location of a hidden treasure, that it is a space aliens' map, or that it was an ancient community bulletin board. To find the rock, drive about 4 miles south from Cullowhee on Highway 107. Turn left at Highway 1737, Caney Fork Road, and follow the signs about 3 miles more, through a farm where the rock is protected by an open shed. A wooden observation deck is in place as well (828-586-2155 or 800-962-1911).

Galvladi Mountain Inn, at 1498 Branch Falls Trail, Balsam, is an entirely different kind of hostelry. *Galvladi* is the Cherokee word for "heaven." In this case, it's fitting in more than one way. The newly built inn is at the top of a drive steep enough to feel as though you're going to heaven, and once you get up there, elevation 4,000 feet, it's a heavenly place to be. Innkeepers Dave Stubbs and Terry Matre have created a kind of retreat, where you can look out over mountains in every direction. The inn has five generously sized guest rooms, a complete fitness room, lots of deck area, and an inviting great room where you can chat with other guests over evening hors d'oeuvres. You could treat this place as your sole destination since three tasty, healthful meals a day are included in the rate. The inn sits on 250 wooded acres, with hiking trails and walking paths for whatever level of strenuousness you prefer. For that matter, you can cozy up in a chair and enjoy a good brisk sit. And at the end of the day, you can have a massage. Galvladi is open April 1 to November 1 (828-631-0125 or 877-631-0125; www.galvladi.com).

From this area it's a drive of approximately 30 miles down Highway 107 to **Cashiers,** a community of fewer than 2,000 people at an elevation of nearly 3,500 feet. The drive will seem longer because the road is narrow, steep, and twisting. But it's also beautiful, as is Cashiers itself, with scenic views of even higher mountains, the Blue Ridge Parkway, waterfalls, and multifingered Lake Glenville. This is the home of many waterfalls, including **Whitewater Falls,** which has a total drop of 800 feet. Kevin Adams, author of *North Carolina Waterfalls—Where to Find Them, How to Photograph Them,* calls Whitewater Falls "the most spectacular cascade east of the Rockies." The Whitewater Falls Scenic Area turns off Highway 281. This is also home of the smallest U.S. post office, still standing on Whiteside Cove Road. It was in operation from 1903 to 1953.

On Highway 107 South, the **Zachary-Tolbert House,** built by Mordecai Zachary in the mid-1800s and virtually unchanged today, is a great opportunity to see a little truth-in-history. Zachary built the house on land that had been Cherokee hunting grounds until the Trail of Tears forced them away. The house had eight rooms, with no electricity, plumbing, central heat, or paint on the inside walls. Mordecai Zachary also built the home's furnishings, using lumber from trees cut on the property for both the house and its furniture. He married Elvira Keener, daughter of a Methodist minister who lived among the Cherokee. They moved into the new home and ultimately had thirteen children, who were taught to speak Cherokee. Only three other families ever lived here.

Robert Tolbert bought the house in 1909, and until 1997 Tolbert used the place as a summer home before selling it to people who listed it on the

National Register of Historic Places and donated it, along with everything in it, to the Cashiers Historical Society. Much of the original furniture built by Mordecai Zachary remains in the house, along with basic household goods. According to the Cashiers Historical Society, this may be "the world's largest collection of Southern Plain Style furniture made by a single identifiable furniture maker." The

sayitthisway

You don't pronounce "Cashiers" the way it looks. Proper pronunciation is *CASHers*. Local wisdom says the difference was the result of an early misspelling by a map-maker.

historical society has compiled a detailed and fascinating history of the property and its families. They offer guided tours beginning at 11:00 a.m. Friday and Saturday, June through September. Tours take about forty-five minutes, and the last one begins at 1:00 p.m. Call the historical society or check their Web site for more details (828-743-7710; www.cashiershistoricalsociety.org).

Just north of Cashiers, off Highway 107, you'll find a bed-and-breakfast as different from standard motels as it could be, and as unlikely for the area as well. ***Innisfree Victorian Inn and Garden House*** (write to P.O. Box 469, Glenville 28736; 828-743-2946; www.innisfreeinn.com) has five rooms in the main house and five luxury suites in the Garden House, each with private bath, some with Jacuzzi or garden tubs for two, some with fireplace. The garden house rooms have wet bar, private phone, and TV with VCR.

This is not a place where you expect to find an old Victorian structure. In fact, although Innisfree is the perfect representation of old Victorian mansions, it is actually a new building. Henry Hoche bought the land in 1981, had the inn built there, and opened for guests in 1990.

Innisfree is not at all about the comforts of home. Home was never like this. Innisfree is a place of luxury, romance, and exotic furnishings, a special-occasion place. Depending on your room, you have window or veranda views of the mountains and valleys, elaborate bed and window treatments, fine art, and Victorian-period furnishings. In the Garden House you can look out over the green landscape from the showers and tubs. All these rooms carry the names of Victorian writers, and their books are included in each room, so that, for instance, you can lounge in Lord Tennyson's suite and read his work. Breakfast at the inn is served by candlelight, on fine china, accented by antique silver pieces in the room. The inn's common rooms are filled with collections of crystal, silver, and Victorian-esque decor. Innisfree overlooks Lake Glenville, in the Blue Ridge Mountains—the highest lake east of the Rockies. The place seems isolated but is close to the attractions of Cashiers, as well as places for hiking, horseback riding, waterfalls and boating. The landscape in this area is

noshadesofgray

Watch for the Belgian white squirrels scampering up trees and across roofs around town. This area is noted for these squirrels, which are not albinos—they have normal eyes—and don't seem interested in other kinds of squirrels.

filled with Christmas tree farms, which have replaced the many fields of cabbage that used to be grown here.

Even though it is away from major highways, in a remote mountain setting, Cashiers has its share of local crafts and specialty shops and tourist attractions. During the peak season, May through October, the area is very, very popular, which means lots of people.

In the off-season, some of the businesses won't be open, but your experience will be much more off the beaten path. One place you can count on any time of year is *Tree House Pottery,* a gallery at 148 Front Street (828-631-5100), owned and operated by Joe Frank McKee and Travis Berning, who met in graduate school at the University of North Texas. This is a working studio, as well as a nice gallery, and part of the fun of stopping in is the chance to talk with one or both of these potters. These guys can chat while they work, and they seem to enjoy it. They feature functional raku and horsehair pottery, both of which are more complicated to make than a simple clay pot. If you're interested in pottery, they'll teach you a lot. In addition to their own work, Frank and Travis carry pottery, woodwork, photography, and glass from other crafters. The shop represents seven other potters, too. Six of them went to graduate school in Texas with Frank and Travis. The shop is open year-round, Monday through Saturday 10:00 a.m. to 5:00 p.m., Sunday 11:00 a.m. to 4:00 p.m.

From here you can drive to *Brevard* on U.S. Highway 64. The town's big claims to fame are its proximity to the Pisgah National Forest, the many waterfalls in the area, and the Brevard Music Center. *Brevard Music Center,* 1000 Probart Street (888-384-8682 or 828-884-2011; www.brevardmusic.org), holds a festival each summer from late June through mid-August during which almost nightly concerts, from opera to chamber music to jazz, are offered. At the center, which has been operating since 1936, 400 students, ages fourteen to post-college, study and play with professional musicians each summer. The main auditorium, Whittington-Pfohl Auditorium, is an open structure that seats 1,800 people, with additional seating on the lawn on both sides of the building. In good weather, audience members are invited to bring a bottle of wine and a picnic basket to enjoy on the lawn. Concerts are held also in several smaller auditoriums on the grounds.

On Main Street, Brevard's center, you'll find a variety of specialty shops, an antiques mall, a variety of eating places, and a fine arts co-op. The co-op,

Number 7 Arts, run by the *Transylvania County Arts Council,* has show-rooms at 7 East Main Street (828-883-2294; www.number7arts.com). The work of the artisans includes pottery, jewelry, wood, and fabrics, often reflecting a western North Carolina mountain influence. The shop is open Monday through Saturday 10:00 a.m. to 5:00 p.m.

Brevard Antique Mall, 57 East Main Street (828-885-2744), has more than 20,000 square feet of shopping space in a former department store. Booths have a great variety of antique furnishings, china, maps, magazines, and vinyl recordings. The mall is open 9:30 a.m. to 5:30 p.m. every day but Sunday, when it is open 1:00 to 5:00 p.m.

Of the possibilities for eating, *Jason's Main Street Grill,* 48 East Main Street (828-883-4447), serves breakfast, lunch, and dinner every day, beginning at 7:00 a.m. You can get everything from a burger to macadamia-crusted trout here. For a more old-timey experience, *Rocky's Soda Shop,* 36 South Broad Street (828-877-5375), claims to be Brevard's original lunch counter and serves up soups, sandwiches, shakes, sundaes, and homemade ice cream. Rocky's is open Monday through Saturday 10:00 a.m. to 6:00 p.m., Sunday 11:30 a.m. to 5:00 p.m.

As you might expect in an area so full of forests and parks and lakes and rivers and waterfalls, the services of all kinds of outfitters and guides are avail-able, as are maps for hiking and touring. Check with the Transylvania tourism offices and Brevard Chamber of Commerce (35 West Main Street; 800-648-4523; www.visitwaterfalls.com; www.brevardncchamber.org) for brochures and details.

When you are ready to head north, to Waynesville, allow enough time to make the drive up U.S. Highway 276. It's winding and slow but also a lot of fun, and what you see going up this route, except for a couple of sites, is

Oh Tannenbaum

Around Christmas time each year, the Aluminum Tree and Aesthetically Challenged Ornament Museum and Research Center invites visitors to see its collection of alu-minum Christmas trees. The trees come in all sizes and colors, including pink, and some are thematically decorated: the Elvis tree, the bathroom tree, the Jim and Tammy Faye Bakker tree, for instance. The collection has more than sixty trees and keeps growing as people find old oddities in the attic. One such oddity is the Marilyn Monroe ornament, complete with a little fan that blows her skirt up as she plays paddleball. The museum doesn't have a permanent home, but you can find out how to see the collection by calling curator and founder Stephen Paul Jackson (828-884-5304; www.aluminumtree.com).

authentic, not gentrified, mountain country. The **Sliding Rock Recreation Area** in the Pisgah National Forest is just north of Brevard, about 7.5 miles from the junction of US 64 and 276. This is nature's version of a commercial waterslide. It is a slippery rock slide of about 60 feet that drops you into a 6-foot-deep pool. Wood steps, places to sit, and a small park office make the spot a little more comfortable, but pictures of injuries that can happen in such a slide and bulletins about how to treat hypothermia make it clear that rock sliding is not without risk. The rushing water in here is beautiful, though, and you don't need to get into it at all to enjoy it.

Continuing north on US 276, you'll come to the entrance to the **Cradle of Forestry in America National Site** (828-877-3130; www.cradleofforestry .com). The first forestry school in America was founded here in the early 1900s, and the National Historic Site stands today as a commemoration of the importance of forests in the North Carolina mountains. Paved trails take you down to old cabins and a logging train. In the Forest Discovery Center, hands-on exhibits and an eighteen-minute film explain early forestry in detail. From spring through autumn, the center has a variety of tours, programs, and crafters on site. Open in season 9:00 a.m. to 5:00 p.m. daily. Hours may change. Admission is $5 for adults, free for children ages fifteen and younger, and free for everyone on Tuesdays.

After this you'll pass an entrance to the Blue Ridge Parkway, the Big East Fork Trailhead into the Pisgah National Forest, and some spots for camping and fishing. Farther north, churches, a trout farm, and some accumulations of junk on private properties dot the roadside. At the community of Cruso, a handmade sign tells you this is "9 MILES OF FRIENDLY PEOPLE, PLUS 1 OLD CRAB."

Following US 23 East from Sylva brings you quickly to **Waynesville,** a town of Scotch-Irish and English founding, at an altitude of 3,000 feet. It is doing an outstanding job of revitalizing its downtown with art galleries and shops selling the work of local crafters, as well as a bookstore, the popular Mast General Store, a high-quality cooking store, a wine shop, and a number of good restaurants and bakeries. In addition, the town holds an ever-increasing number of street fairs, dances, and celebrations, including the **International Folkmoot USA** in July. This international festival of dance and music brings groups from more than ten countries each year to perform in their national costumes. Call (828) 452-2997 for performance dates; www.folkmoot.com.

Waynesville is the home of the annual **Ramps Festival.** The ramp is a rank, onionlike, wild plant of no particular virtue, except that every summer the American Legion throws a big party to cook it all the ways they can think of: steamed ramps, braised ramps, ramps a la king, ramps fritters. Presumably, folks eat the results, but that is not as conspicuous as the cooking, which leaves a garlicky odor heavy on the town all day. For some reason it's a popular time and place for politicians to appear. The festival is always held on the first Sunday in May, at the American Legion Park, 171 Legion Drive. A ramp-eating contest is the high point of the day, unless you're one of the contestants, in which case it may be the beginning of a big bellyache for the rest of the day. For more information, call (828) 456-3517; www.downtownwaynesville .com. Other ramp festivals are held in nearby counties, but an American Legion representative says, "Ours was the first one, and it's the real one. The others aren't like ours."

Here's a place to stay and dine that you probably wouldn't find unless you were specifically looking for it. The *Old Stone Inn* (109 Dolan Road; 828-456-3333 or 800-432-8499; www.oldstoneinn.com) has been owned and operated by Cindy and Robert Zinser for fifteen years. It was known in earlier years as Heath Lodge. The Zinsers upgraded the inn in many ways, improving the rooms, making the dining room more attractive, and best of all, moving from old-style Southern all-you-can-eat meals served at huge round tables to more sophisticated and very good food served at tables appropriate for the size of your party. Passing the baton, the Zinsers have sold the inn to David Gardener, an experienced innkeeper. He has brought along executive chef Terry White, who has more than twenty years of experience. The shady site, comfortable rooms, and good food make this a great rejuvenating spot. It's a larger operation, technically an inn rather than a bed-and-breakfast, tucked under lots of shady foliage and rhododendron on top of a hill at the edge of Waynesville. This isn't a place to make new friends around a breakfast table so much as one for retreating from a noisy life for a while. The inn has passed the sixtieth anniversary of its founding, and is now open year-round.

For the smaller bed-and-breakfast experience where you mingle with other guests, try *Herren House,* 94 East Street (800-452-1932 or 828-452-7897; www .herrenhouse.com), run by Jenny and Tom Halsey. This beautifully restored Victorian used to be a boardinghouse. As a bed-and-breakfast, it has six guest rooms. The house has wraparound porches and a gazebo in the perennial gardens, both good places for socializing, as is the dining room, where guests eat breakfast and later can help themselves to homemade baked goods on the sideboard. A five-course candlelight dinner is available in the dining room by reservation most Thursday and Saturday nights for guests and the public. The house is in a quiet residential neighborhood just a block from downtown.

Another place to eat in Waynesville is *Maggie's Galley III* (828-456-8945), at 22 Howell Mill Road. The building housing the restaurant was made from primitive log cabins. An earlier owner had an antiques business here, and as his need for space grew, he just kept tacking on additional old cabins. He

Elvis Is in the Building

As you go into the ladies' room at Maggie's Galley, the first thing you see is Elvis's reflection in the mirror. After the initial shock, you realize it's one of those life-size cardboard figures, strategically placed. As you sit to do what you went into a restroom for, Elvis talks! It takes a minute and a couple repetitions of his message (he thanks you for coming) to figure out it's a hidden recording.

used five cabins to make the building as it is today. Each of the cabins has a story and a bit of history attached. The restaurant has a flyer with all the information. The food at the restaurant includes fresh seafood, steaks, and a good selection of sandwiches. The atmosphere is zany, and a meal here, in addition to being good, is a lot of fun. Many people miss it because it's a little off the highway and looks so odd from the outside it seems an unlikely place. Local people recommend it enthusiastically. Open for lunch and dinner. Sometimes closed on Monday.

Lomo Grill, 44 Church Street (828-452-5222; www.lomogrill.com), has been going full steam since 1995. Ricardo and Suzanne Fernandez have earned a reputation for serving interesting and unusual Argentine food with Italian and Spanish influences, much of it cooked on an open-flame grill. Ricardo is a master gardener. The restaurant participates in the Appalachian Sustainable Agriculture Project, growing many of the fruits, vegetables, and herbs they use on their own Wildcat Ridge Farm. A good wine list is part of the appeal here, too. Hours vary seasonally.

The Windows on Main, 122 North Main Street, Waynesville (877-258-0008; www.windowsonmain.com), is a new lodging concept in the heart of Waynesville's downtown, just steps away from brick sidewalks, shops, coffeehouses, and restaurants. The Curé family have taken a 1919 building on Main Street and renovated it to create seven furnished rental condos on the second floor, with a common area in a wide hallway. Guests have parking privileges on Main Street as well as in the rear of the building. Those units on the street side have minibalconies at the windows from which you can watch the activity on the street. Yet when you close the windows, you can't hear any of the street noise. The furnishings in the units, which sleep anywhere from two to four people, depending on the unit, are an eclectic mix of leather, tapestry, and designer items in muted tones. Jorge Curé has collected more than 500 old window frames, and these figure in the rooms' decor as well. The kitchens are small but completely equipped with full-size refrigerators, stoves, and such appliances as coffeemakers. Linens and towels are provided, and a one-time cleaning fee is added to your bill. Weekly rates here add up to less money per night than most accommodations in the area.

Another inexpensive alternative is *The Lodge of Waynesville,* 909 Russ Avenue, (828) 452-0353 or toll-free (888) 213-2666. The Lodge is an older forty-unit motel that sits atop a hill just off the highway, looking down on Russ Avenue, which is an area with commercial development—grocery stores, restaurants, and chains—that heads directly into the historic downtown area. But you can't hear any of the noise from this location on an acre of nicely land-scaped grounds, with an outdoor swimming pool, a courtyard including picnic tables and a swing, and nice views of the mountains. Joseph Sutton owns the place; his daughter, Cindy Smith, serves as innkeeper; and the people who work at the desk are mostly family friends. The feeling in the office is quite jovial. Smith says the property was once part of the family home place. The guest rooms are simply furnished with basic motel furniture and bathrooms in good repair. Everything is spotlessly clean. From here it's a drive of five minutes or so to everything from a good Chinese restaurant, Maggie's Galley, or fast food on Russ Avenue to the specialty shops and the more trendy restaurants downtown. Because of the swimming pool, courtyard, and picnic area, it's a good place to stay with kids.

One spot in the area has a Waynesville address but is actually out of town and 5,000 feet up, and offers fine food, rustic lodging, hiking trails, and an entry to the Great Smoky Mountains National Park. *The Swag,* 2300 Swag Road, comprises a collection of pioneer buildings that were hauled up the mountain about thirty years ago. Innkeeper Deener Matthews has managed to combine rustic elements such as the rough wood interior walls of the rooms with luxurious amenities, including handmade coverlets on the beds, coffee grinders, coffeemakers, hair dryers, and terry-cloth robes in the rooms. She's managed something similar in the dining room, where guests sit around hand-made tables to enjoy first-rate food professionally prepared and served. And although the other recreational facilities are tucked unobtrusively into the prop-erty, you can find everything from a racquetball court and sauna to a library. For more details, call (828) 926-0430 or (800) 789-7672; www.theswag.com.

All that is up on the mountain. Down in the valley you'll find some other interesting attractions. *Maggie Valley* is a year-round resort town between Cherokee and Waynesville. On both sides of US 19, or Soco Road, which runs through the valley, you'll see one motel after another, every kind of eating place, and souvenir shops galore—generally not the kind of places an off-the-beaten-path traveler wants to visit at all. But you'll also find a place worth the drive because it began as a labor of love.

Let's Get Lost

Being able to walk through the backyard of The Swag and right into the forest of the Great Smoky Mountains National Park was an opportunity too good to ignore. The hiking trails were all there, well marked and shown on a large map on the grounds. Sorry to say, I forgot to look at it. But figuring that all the trails would loop, I just got onto one and started walking. After walking a couple of hours, I was on a road I had never heard of, with no money in my pocket and no place to spend it anyway.

I asked an old man in a pickup truck where I was. He told me, but I was still disoriented. He gave me a ride to a campground where he introduced me to some friends with a trailer. Within minutes, I was sitting at a picnic table, digging into hot roast beef sandwiches, sliced fresh tomatoes, and mashed potatoes. We were all laughing and chatting so much, it was like a party.

Eventually, the idea of getting back where I belonged came up. Everyone knew right where The Swag was, because a swag is a dip in the mountains. It was about 30 miles away by road, a substantial drive for a stranger to make for another stranger.

The old man not only drove me, but he had fun doing it, telling me all about his family, life in this area, secrets you can learn on back roads, and who lives on them. When we got back to The Swag, he got out of the truck to look around. "Always wanted to see the view from up here," he said. Then we hugged, and he was gone.

That's why I love North Carolina.

The **Stomping Ground** is a huge building on US 19 with a massive dance floor and seating for 2,000 people. Kyle Edwards hopes to make it the world center for clogging. The Edwardses are a clogging family, but they've always thought of it as "mountain dancing." Kyle thinks the word *clogging* came into use in 1935, in Chattanooga, Tennessee. His mother and his uncle performed with a Maggie Valley team in the 1920s that performed in the White House for President Franklin D. Roosevelt and the Queen of England. Kyle and his wife, Mary Sue, also danced on teams. Their son, Burton, was a world champion clogger in 1981, when he was eighteen. (He is running the operation now.) And their daughter, Becky, had won two championships by the time she was thirteen. It doesn't take a rocket scientist to figure out that if you go to the Stomping Ground, you're either going to clog or watch clogging. Dances and shows are held every night from April through November. A number of large display cases related to clogging give you a lot of information about the history, contests, and fun of the dance. Call (828) 926-1288 for details about times, shows, and admission fees. Don't hang up if you get what sounds like a private home instead of a business, with a recorded message telling you that you've reached 926-1288. The telephone rings at the Stomping Ground, in Mary Sue's beauty shop, and in the family's residence. Just leave a message. They'll get back to you.

As you drive along Soco Road in Maggie Valley, you'll find all kinds of shops, businesses, tourist attractions, and eating places on either side of the road; a bit of a clutter, really, but in the Market Square Shopping Center, at 3483 Soco Road, one little store is worth a stop. *The Chocolate Shoppe* (828-926-0113; www.maggievalleyfudge.com) has been in business here since 1997. The owners, Sherry White and Donna Rector, sell a huge assortment of candies made right there in the back room of the shop. They have ten different kinds of fudge, made the old-fashioned way, as well as peanut brittle and pecan brittle and pecan pralines, but the star of this show must be the hand-dipped chocolates, truffles, and cherry cordials. They have a good assortment of sugar-free candies, too.

If you're in the area sometime between the end of April and the end of November, you might make *Cataloochee Ranch,* 119 Ranch Drive, Maggie Valley (828-926-1401 or toll-free 800-868-1401; www.cataloocheeranch.com), a destination and spend a few days in its laid-back atmosphere. This is the kind of place to which some families return year after year. It has twelve rooms and twelve cabins, each with private bath, some with Jacuzzi and fireplace. Rates include breakfast and dinner and activities except horseback riding, all on about 1,000 acres. You can look down on the town and meadowlands and over at many ranges of the Great Smoky and Blue Ridge Mountains, with meadowland vistas below. The rooms and cabins, which are all different, are set up for everyone from couples looking for a romantic getaway to families with children. Some guests who started coming here soon after Tom Alexander and his wife, Judy, opened the place in 1933 (it's still family-owned and -operated) have brought their children and then their grandchildren here. The mix is lively, and one staff member says part of the pleasure in working at Cataloochee is watching the children grow up. Guests eat family-style in the dining room, where the food is hearty and relies on locally grown produce, homemade breads and jams, and favorites like trout, baked ham, and prime rib. Four nights a week, the resort has a cookout featuring such entrees as steak and chicken. A cookout is a big production, but they've been doing it so long it's down to a smooth-running science. In addition to tennis, swimming, and hiking, the ranch has entertainment a couple of nights a week. This might be storytelling, a magician, bluegrass music, or a hands-on presentation about the timberwolf by a local animal keeper.

Timberwolf Creek, which runs along the valley, apparently got its name from the presence of the animal in earlier times. *Timberwolf Creek Bed and Breakfast,* at 391 Johnson Branch Road (828-926-2608 or toll-free 888-525-

4218, ext. 2681; www.timberwolfcreek.com), is snuggled alongside Timberwolf Creek, surrounded by old-growth hardwoods and rhododendron in Maggie Valley. Innkeepers Sandee and Larry Wright run an intensely romantic, small B&B focusing on giving guests a special experience with everything from a candlelight breakfast indoors or, when it's nice out, breakfast on a deck over the creek, to Jacuzzi tubs with rose petals for the water. No matter which room you choose in Timberwolf's two refurbished buildings, the sound of the creek running briskly fills the air in a way that wouldn't be possible in a recently built facility, because new construction is no longer allowed this close to the water. It's so quiet back here you can hardly remember the busy main road.

The Literary and Crafts Center

It's only 25 miles from Waynesville and the Maggie Valley area to Asheville. *Asheville* is crammed with arts, crafts, antiques, literary and musical people, and a healthy assortment of free spirits deeply involved in the unique Appalachian culture.

After a long period of time during which the downtown area seemed to be going downhill, this part of the city has made a marvelous recovery. The downtown *Asheville Historic District* has an interesting assortment of early-twentieth-century architecture, much of it being restored or renovated and filled by specialty shops, galleries, and restaurants. Walking the district, you encounter a rich mix of old and young hippies, artists, entrepreneurs, intellectuals, shopkeepers, businesspeople, tourists, and just folks.

One outstanding example of a renovation that works is right in the heart of the downtown area. The *Haywood Park Hotel* (One Battery Park Avenue; 828-252-2522 or 800-228-2522; www.haywoodpark.com) is in a building that once housed Ivey's Department Store. This small independent hotel is luxurious, with fine furnishings, spacious, bright rooms, and such niceties as valet parking and turn-down service. Haywood Park Hotel emphasizes local products, from the handmade soap dishes in the bathrooms and the hand-stitched bedding, to the chocolates on your pillow and the art on the walls.

In the hotel's atrium, independent, local restaurants and shops offer everything from fine dining to flowers to shoes. The chocolates placed on your pillow each night are made fresh daily, with no preservatives, at *The Chocolate Fetish,* a shop where you can watch the candy being made. All the chocolates are handmade, in small batches, with top-quality ingredients and no added vegetable oils (36 Haywood Street; 828-258-2353; www.chocolatefetish.com). The shop is open Monday through Thursday 11:30 a.m. to 6:00 p.m., Friday and Saturday 11:00 a.m. to 9:00 p.m., and Sunday noon to 5:00 p.m.

Also without going farther than the hotel atrium, guests can enjoy fine dining at the ***Flying Frog Café and Wine Bar,*** a restaurant run by veteran restaurateurs with a flare for fine dining. The restaurant is open for dinner Wednesday, Thursday, and Sunday 5:30 to 9:30 p.m., Friday and Saturday until 11:00 p.m. Reservations are "strongly recommended" (One Battery Park Avenue; 828-254-9411; www.flyingfrogcafe.com).

A more casual atmosphere in the atrium for food and fun is the ***Bier Garden,*** with a choice of more than 200 different beers from all over the world and an appropriately casual menu. Open daily 11:00 a.m. to 2:00 a.m. (46 Haywood Street, 828-285-0102; www.ashevillebiergarden.com).

Other eateries in the atrium offer a great variety of possibilities as well.

From the hotel, a walk in any direction takes you through parts of the historic district, with galleries and arts and crafts shops.

Also downtown in Asheville, at 40 Wall Street, ***Laughing Seed Cafe*** (828-252-3445; www.laughingseed.com) serves vegetarian and vegan meals in an atmosphere that calls to mind the days of tie-dyed shirts and Volkswagen vans. But don't be fooled by the funky atmosphere. This is a sophisticated restaurant that offers creative entrees and wine and beer to go with them. Laughing Seed also prepares a variety of smoothies using soy milk and organic fruits. The restaurant is open Monday through Thursday (closed Tuesday) from 11:30 a.m. to 9:00 p.m., Friday and Saturday until 10:00 p.m. Sunday brunch is served from 10:00 a.m. to 2:00 p.m., with the regular menu in place the rest of the day until 9:00 p.m.

One massive undertaking you can't miss in downtown Asheville is the renovated ***Grove Arcade,*** 1 Page Avenue (828-252-7799; www.grovearcade .com). This structure, with 269,000 square feet of floor space, is western North Carolina's largest commercial building. It was built in 1929, housing shops on the ground floor and offices above. The arcade was one of the first indoor public markets in the country, and it thrived as the center of Asheville commercial activity until 1942, when the U.S. government took it over to use for activities related to World War II, displacing 74 shops and 127 offices in a single month. Later the building began to fall into disrepair, and the space was too big and expensive for a commercial investor. But local opinion persistently demanded restoring the building to its original appearance and use.

In 2002, with funding and direction from a foundation, the renovation was completed, and the building's cream glaze terra-cotta facing gleams once again. Restaurants and shops selling everything from antiques and art to bread and meat, ice cream and candy have been moving in. It will probably be a while before all the available space is rented to businesses and offices stable enough to stay there, but there will be plenty to see and do anytime you visit.

The Grove Arcade Building

Outside the building, bordering on Battery Park Square, artisans and farmers in outdoor market stalls, open 10:00 a.m. to 6:00 p.m. Monday through Saturday, sell directly to the public. Some businesses are open on Sunday as well.

Also in this part of town, the **Basilica of St. Lawrence,** at 97 Haywood Street, has the largest unsupported tile dome in North America. It was designed by Rafael Guastavino in 1909.

At the edge of town stands an attraction so well known it has become an almost obligatory stop for anyone who wants to say they have seen the area— **Biltmore Estate.** George Vanderbilt liked Asheville, and he had money. He bought a lot of Asheville, about 125,000 acres, and had a 250-room private home built on the property. (Today only 7,500 acres belong to the estate. The rest is part of the Blue Ridge Parkway or Mount Pisgah National Forest.) The home was famous from the beginning for the beauty of its design and workmanship. The master builders were brought from Europe. The home was also famous for being ahead of its time in its modern conveniences, having early forerunners of washing machines and dryers. Art in the mansion includes originals by Boldini, Ming dynasty china, and antiques that belonged to Napoleon.

It will take you the better part of a day to see the place properly, especially if you go beyond the mansion to explore the gardens and visit the winery. Admission fees to the Biltmore Estate are high. The estate is open daily from 9:00 a.m. to 5:00 p.m. (828-274-6333 or 888-804-8258; www.biltmore.com).

If you're feeling literary, visit the **Thomas Wolfe Memorial,** 52 Market Street. This is the novelist's boyhood home, described in his novel *Look Homeward, Angel* as "Dixieland." In real life it was called "The Old Kentucky Home." Wolfe's mother, Julia, ran a boardinghouse in the rambling Victorian house, and its various rooms and furnishings, along with local people, were all incorporated into Wolfe's novel, mostly in unflattering terms. The people of Asheville didn't like that one bit, which led to Wolfe's second novel, *You Can't Go Home Again.* After Wolfe died, the townspeople relented, as they often do when a troublesome celebrity stops being troublesome and remains merely famous, and bought the house to turn into a memorial for him. It is now a North Carolina State Historic Site. Visiting the house, which has been kept the same as it was when the Wolfes lived in it, and has descriptions from Wolfe's writing in appropriate places so you can compare the words with the reality, goes a long way toward explaining the often gloomy tone of his writing. Nominal admission fee. The Wolfe house was damaged by fire in 1998, and restoration continues, so call ahead for viewing and tour schedules and rate details (828-253-8304; www.wolfememorial.com).

One thing you might not expect to find in a mountain city is the ***Botanical Gardens at Asheville,*** 151 W. T. Beaver Boulevard, located on a 10-acre site next to the campus of the University of North Carolina at Asheville. The gardens were begun in 1960 by the Asheville Garden Club and designed by Doan Ogden, a landscape architect of repute. The gardens are open all year, and no matter when you visit, you'll find something in bloom, bud, or fruit.

The Botany Center is open from March to December. Other parts of the gardens include a library and gift shop. You can arrange for garden tours or use a map to explore on your own. Special places in the property include a springhouse, a garden for the blind, a rock garden, an azalea garden, and an herb garden. For more detailed information about the gardens, contact the Botany Center at (828) 252-5190; www.ashevillebotanicalgardens.org.

You will find many appealing places a little removed from the downtown area of Asheville, too. For instance, a long-established and reputable place to see and buy regional arts and crafts is the ***Folk Art Center,*** just east of town at milepost 382 on the Blue Ridge Parkway, about a half mile north of U.S. Highway 70. It has been operated by the Southern Highland Handicraft Guild since 1980 and houses permanent and traveling exhibits and the Allanstand Craft Shop, where you can buy items similar to those in the exhibits. Crafts represented include weaving, pottery, basketry, quilting, jewelry, wood carving, stitchery, and musical instruments. Admission is free; donations are welcome. Open every day except Thanksgiving, Christmas, and New Year's Day from 9:00 a.m. to 5:00 p.m., except that it stays open until 6:00 p.m. April through December. Closed occasionally for inventory and changing exhibitions (828-298-7928; www.southernhighlandguild.org).

Just about 10 miles outside Asheville, near Weaverville on Reems Creek Road off U.S. Highway 25 North, is another state historic site, the ***Zebulon B. Vance Birthplace.*** Vance was a Civil War officer, a U.S. senator, and governor

Rootball at the Rootbar

The Rootbar is about ten minutes from downtown Asheville. It's a bar started by Max Chain, who invented the game Rootball, which has been described as a cross between horseshoes and boccie. Add Frisbee into the mix and you're getting close. Max Chain opened the bar as a place where people could gather to play the game on white-sand courses out back, listen to music, and drink really good beer. As the bar's own publicity says, the place "looks like hell" from outside, but inside it's pleasant. The Rootbar features live acoustic music, booking only original bands, and sells bottle conditioned, unpasteurized, unfiltered beer. One way to order is to focus on your country of choice and then pick a beer from there. The staff know their beers, and they can help. The crowd here includes many local regulars—bright, articulate, lively, and fond of live music.

As for the game, in Rootball men, women, and even people in wheelchairs can compete equally. The Rootbar is open most of the day and night in spring, summer, and fall to allow ample outside playing time. In winter the hours usually begin about noon. Live shows begin at 9:00 p.m. This is the kind of place where it's a good idea to check hours if you're hoping to go there. Take exit 55 off I-40. The Rootbar, which has a sign with a big "R" in front and is across from a BP service station, is so unassuming you'll probably just pass it before you realize you need to turn around (1410 Tunnel Road; 828-299-7597; www.rootbar.com). Learn more about the game: www.rootball.com.

of North Carolina. In fascinating contrast to the splendor of the Biltmore Estate, this restored pioneer farmstead has only a five-room log house and some outbuildings. The log house was reconstructed around the original chimneys. The outbuildings, including a loom house, springhouse, toolshed, smokehouse, corncrib, and slave cabin, are furnished as they would have been between 1795 and 1840. Displays instruct you further in life of the times. Admission by donation. Hours of operation vary because of budget constraints, so call ahead (828-645-6706).

The **North Carolina Arboretum** is outside the city, at milepost 393 (off Highway 191). It features southern Appalachian landscape plants on a 426-acre site, as well as hiking and nature trails. The arboretum also has a state-of-the-art greenhouse complex. Call (828) 665-2492; www.ncarboretum.org.

The Sourwood Inn, also outside Asheville, has been praised by OBP readers as a great place to stay (810 Elk Mountain Scenic Highway; 828-255-0690; www.sourwoodinn.com). People love the inn's location at 3,200 feet, its cedar and stone construction, and its warm, relaxing atmosphere. It's been in operation since late in the 1990s, but it might never have been here at all. Construction was almost complete when a fire destroyed it. Determined to have an inn at this location, the owners started over, and the result is a place that radiates warmth and deep satisfaction with being here, reflected in every-thing from the food to the attitude of the inn's staff. The inn has several com-mon areas, a lobby with a fireplace, a library, and a game room. Each of the twelve guest rooms has a wonderful view of the Blue Ridge, and the 100 acres on which the inn sits include gardens and hiking trails. A cabin with a fully equipped kitchen and two full baths is heated by a Jotul woodstove. Sourwood serves dinner Thursday through Sunday, prepared by Chef Kacia Duncan, a graduate of the New England Culinary Institute who has had experience every-where from France to Oregon. She brings a traveler's flair and an appreciation for fresh, local, organic, seasonal ingredients to the kitchen; hence, such spe-cialties as benne seed fried trout over lemon-scented orzo with a fresh tomato slice and homemade bread. The inn does not have an ABC license, but guests are welcome to bring their own spirits. Sourwood is open year-round except from the week before Christmas to February; open weekends in February, and every day after that.

And just 4 miles north of downtown Asheville, *Old Reynolds Mansion,* 100 Reynold Heights (828-254-0496 or 800-709-0496; www.oldreynoldsmansion .com), a bed-and-breakfast in a brick antebellum mansion on a high ridge, may be a testimony to the strength of people from Minnesota. Fred and Helen Faber bought the place in 1977 and moved here from Minnesota in 1981 to restore it. It was in sad shape, and the operative word is "restore," not "cause to be restored." The Fabers did virtually everything, including the gardening and construction work, with their own hands. The place has become consistently better and better. It stands in the middle of an expanse of gardens, grass, and pines atop a ridge with a magnificent view, secluded and rural. The rooms are furnished with comfortable antiques. Children over six are welcome during the week, over twelve on weekends. In warm weather the 25-by-62-foot cement swimming pool, the courtyard, and the gardens appeal to adults as well as children. And in cold weather, the fireplace in the great room is a popular attraction. Since Fred Faber passed away, Helen, with friends and family, con-tinues to maintain their hands-on innkeeping tradition.

Camping is another popular option around Asheville. At *Campfire Lodgings,* 116 Appalachian Village Road (800-933-8012; www.campfirelodgings .com), on a wooded mountaintop, elevation 2,270 feet, you can camp in any-thing from an RV or simple tent to a luxury cabin or an exotic yurt, just 6 miles north of downtown Asheville and 10 miles from the Blue Ridge Parkway. The facility includes a bathhouse with laundry facilities and private bathrooms with showers—an unusual feature in a campground. Beyond that, it all depends on what you want. Pets are welcome here; a courtesy phone/modem hookup is available; and the 120 acres include hiking trails, a private fishing pond, and meditation spots. Some of the RV sites have phone/modem hookups, and all the RV sites have water, sewer, electric, and cable.

The yurts are large, round, domed tents of insulated canvas set up on a large wooden deck. The screened walls and dome can be opened in good weather or closed against rain. Inside, a bed is made up with luxurious bedding. The yurts have air-conditioning, gas fireplaces, cable TV, and kitchens; two have bathrooms. The deck is large enough to put up a tent for families with children. The luxury cabins, which sleep seven, have two bathrooms, a gas log fireplace, a fully equipped kitchen, air-conditioning, a washer and dryer, a telephone, cable TV, and linen service. Not exactly roughing it. The views from this campground are stunning, and the wooded sites are large enough to afford considerable privacy.

Asheville makes a good center from which to go in several different directions. Following the parkway takes you to *New River State Park.* A drive of about 20 miles down Interstate 26 takes you into the southern mountains, where Flat Rock, Hendersonville, and Saluda offer many rural pleasures and some interesting crafts and antiques shops. Driving northeast from Asheville along the Blue Ridge Parkway takes you higher into the mountains to Blowing Rock and environs. And a scenic ride east along Interstate 40 and Highway 226 to Polkville brings you back into the lower elevations of the Piedmont.

If you follow the parkway almost to the Virginia border, getting off to drive north on U.S. Highway 221, you come to the oldest river in North America and the second oldest (the Nile is older) in the world. It's the only major river in the

BETTER-KNOWN ATTRACTIONS IN THE MOUNTAINS

Asheville
Biltmore Estate
(828) 274-6333
(888) 804-8258

Blue Ridge Parkway
(828) 298-0398

Blowing Rock
The Blowing Rock
(828) 295-7111

Cherokee
Cherokee Indian Reservation
(828) 497-9195
(800) 438-1601

Harrah's Cherokee Casino
(828) 497-7777
(800) 427-7247

Chimney Rock
Chimney Rock Park
(828) 625-9611
(800) 277-9611

country that runs south to north. Paradoxically called New River, it meanders peacefully through more than 100 miles of northwestern North Carolina. The name was the result of surveyors' surprise when they finally chanced upon the river they hadn't known about in this remote part of the state in 1749.

You'll enjoy good access to the river from New River State Park (336-982-2587), an area of breathtakingly lovely mountains, valleys, woods, and fields, 8 miles southeast of Jefferson off Highway 88 on Highway 1588. Compared to other state parks, New River shows up infrequently in travel books and articles, probably because it is in a remote part of the state and because the facilities are primitive. This is the river to find if you like placid canoeing rather than wild races through white water and want fishing spots not bothered by heavy powerboat traffic. There are canoe landings and campgrounds. The woods are great for hiking and are full of spots that cry out for a simple picnic.

Behind the peaceful scene lies the story of a dramatic struggle that isn't anywhere near being over. It started in the 1960s, when the Appalachian Power Company planned to build a dam there, eliciting tremendous public objection. In protective response Congress designated the area a National Wild and Scenic River in 1976, effectively stopping the power company.

But little funding was ever forthcoming to actually buy and protect the land, and a new force is changing the scene along the river: subdivision and development. New houses, roads, and lots are appearing on what was once farmland or woodland. Although none of it is in the state park, of course, people who like their countryside bucolic and unspoiled are getting nervous, whereas those who value economic development for the area are digging in their heels and sending out the bulldozers.

Given the usual inclination of those who can afford to build in the prettiest places—high on mountain summits, on beaches and islands, and along rivers—it's hard to say what will happen along the New River in the coming decade. The good news is that the state park is, as locals like to call the river, "a national treasure," and should remain a special place to visit for a long time to come. It has four access sites, three for camping and one with a canoe launch for day use.

About thirty-five minutes north of Asheville, in Madison County, you'll find an interesting cluster of places near the *French Broad River.* This river is a step above the Nantahala River in difficulty for white-water rafting, but the water is warmer and far fewer users come into the area, so your experience will be considerably more off-the-beaten-path than it is on the Nantahala. The greater part of Madison County is part of Pisgah National Forest, and the Appalachian Trail passes through the county, offering short segments of trail for day hikers. In the little town of *Hot Springs,* you can soak in outdoor tubs along the banks of the river. Hot mineral water, flowing constantly from natural springs at a temperature of about 100 degrees, has often been considered therapeutic and is certainly relaxing, the more so if you indulge in a massage while you are there. Spa rates are figured by the hour and vary depending on the time of day. Massage rates are calculated by the half-hour and become proportionately slightly less expensive per half-hour the longer the time you reserve. For information about the hot springs and massages, call (828) 622-7676 or (800) 462-0933. For information about white-water rafting tours and hiking, contact the Visitors Information Center at (828) 680-9031 or (877) 262-3476.

Because the town is known for attracting hikers from the Appalachian Trail and bikers, *Mountain Magnolia Inn and Retreat,* 204 Lawson Street (828-622-3543 or 800-914-9306; www.mountainmagnoliainn.com), comes as a bit of a surprise in Hot Springs. But this inn sits above the town, on a hill, looking directly at the rises of several mountains in the Pisgah National Forest, secluded from the rest of the community by shrubbery, old magnolias, and perennial gardens.

When owners Pete and Karen Nagle bought the house, it had only one floor, though it was built in 1868 with three floors and enough rooms and Victorian furniture to accommodate a family with eight children. In the 1950s the top two floors, a failing roof, and an observation tower were removed to reduce the cost of maintaining the place.

Once the Nagles learned more of the property's history, they engaged an architect and restored the house. The new rooms of the top two stories fit nicely with the first story, which still has the original wood floors and plaster molding. All guest rooms are spacious, with high ceilings and plenty of daylight.

In season, the inn serves dinner every night, and on weekends the rest of the time. The menu changes often, with such entrees as oven-roasted duck breast and seared Asian marinated salmon fillet. Trout and Black Angus filet mignon are always offered. The restaurant also has a nice, moderately priced wine list.

On the drive down I-26, one of the most interesting stops is the *Carl Sandburg Home National Historic Site,* a 240-acre farm called *Connemara,* a bit south of Hendersonville in Flat Rock. Sandburg spent the last twenty-two years of his life here, mostly writing, while his wife and daughter managed the place as a goat farm. His collection of poems, *Honey and Salt,* was written here when he was eighty-five. The poems contrast with such earlier works as "Chicago," reflecting not only the work of an older man, but also of one living in different surroundings. For instance, in the poem "Cahokia," Sandburg writes about an Indian watching a butterfly rise from a cocoon, flowers sprouting in spring, and the sun moving. The Indian, Sandburg writes, doesn't worship the sun but dances and sings to the "makers and movers of the sun." It takes on added significance when you know that Flat Rock was named for a large granite plateau that had once been a Cherokee sacred ground. Sandburg's life here was influenced not only by the early cycles of nature but also by Cherokee Indian lore. Similarly, looking across the mountains, it's easy to understand how Sandburg might have arrived at his poem, "Shadows Fall Blue on the Mountains."

enoughofa goodthing

North Carolina has nearly 600 golf courses scattered across the state. For a free copy of the *Official North Carolina Golf Guide,* call (900) VISIT-NC, or check the Web site: www.visitnc.com/what_to_ do_golf.asp.

When you visit Sandburg's study at Connemara, both the man and his poetry seem alive. The study is said to be exactly as he left it, with a shawl tossed over the back of his desk chair, a clunky manual typewriter standing on an upended crate, and stacks of paper and disorderly piles of books everywhere. A fascinating aspect of the entire home is the simplicity of its furnishings. To say the interior is plain puts it mildly. The furniture resembles what you find in a summer camp, functional but not decorative. Also fascinating is the fact that every room is crammed with books, all of which appear to have been well used. Similarly, the rooms where Helga kept records about breeding her goats are functional and were apparently furnished with no thought to decoration. What you find outside seems more carefully designed. You may also walk along trails on the grounds, where you'll see the kinds of plants and wildlife from which Sandburg must have drawn many of his images. Open daily except Christmas from 9:00 a.m. to 5:00 p.m. Tours begin at 9:30 a.m., and the last tour departs at 4:30 p.m. Tours are $5, free for children under sixteen. Inquire about some special seasonal activities (828-693-4178; www.nps.gov/carl).

The town's **_Historic Flat Rock District_** (www.historicflatrock.org) is on the National Register of Historic Places. It began about 150 years ago as summer estates for wealthy people from Charleston, South Carolina. Flat Rock has a wonderful place to enjoy a good dinner and spend the night. **_Highland Lake Inn,_** on Highland Lake Drive, is a complex with inn rooms, cabins, and cottages scattered on a wooded property that also has a lake, a swimming pool, and 100 acres of walking trails. The Lindsey family's objective was to create a self-sufficient compound, and although they didn't manage that entirely, they came close. They've sold the property to Jack and Linda Grup, who continue in the same spirit, while providing more luxurious accommodations and emphasizing the country-retreat aspect of the place. The restaurant, *Seasons,* serves vegetables and herbs organically grown on the property and provided by local gardeners. The food is simply wonderful. Offerings range from an herb-stuffed free-range chicken breast to some elaborate pasta and seafood dishes, as well as vegetarian dishes. Every bite you take bursts with flavor. Seasons offers a good wine list and full bar service. If you are traveling with children, this is a place where you can take them to see vegetables growing in a garden, look at honeybee hives, and watch a goat being milked. Phone (828) 693-6812 or (800) 762-1376; www.hlinn.com.

From Flat Rock you can head over onto U.S. Highway 176, driving about 12 miles to *Saluda,* a little town of less than 1,000 people, with a notable concentration of antiques and artisans. Walking around in the little town itself, you'll find several shops selling local crafts and antiques and a general store run by a pair of women reminiscent of the sisters on *The Waltons* television show, except, of course, they aren't offering Mason jars full of the "recipe"—as far as anyone knows.

The town is at the crest of the steepest mainline railroad in the country. The business district is on the National Register of Historic Places.

Like Asheville, Saluda has a bakery that comes as a surprise. *Wildflour Bakery and Café on Main Street,* 173 East Main Street, concentrates on flavor and nutrition. The owner and her friends have created all the recipes, including a variety of vegetarian soups, salads, and sandwiches, all from original recipes that use stone-ground flour, ground fresh as needed from untreated wheat. Ingredients are measured and mixed mostly by hand.

Wildflour offers a variety of loaves, ranging from the regular oatmeal bread and the nutritious Boogie Bread (seven grains) to gourmet choices such as roasted walnut and English cheddar bread. Open Wednesday through Saturday 8:00 a.m. to 3:00 p.m., Sunday brunch 10:00 a.m. to 2:00 p.m. (828-749-9224).

A few miles into the country, in a totally different mood, the *Orchard Inn,* on US 176, sits atop the Saluda rise on 18 wooded acres at an elevation of 2,500 feet. The inn comprises nine rooms in the main house plus five cottage suites, each with private bath, some with fireplace and whirlpool tub. Cottages have telephones. Kathy and Bob Thompson, their son Robert, and his wife, Charley, are the innkeepers. Robert is the chef. Kathy is one smart lady. She says some people come to the inn for a private getaway and others for a social experience as part of the inn. She and Bob took over Orchard Inn after ten years of visits as guests in the main house, but she understands why some people prefer the cottages. "Our job is to create a place for people to come and be together differently than they do in the real world," she says. The inn removes you from the real world with its quiet atmosphere and its mix of good art, antiques, and books. Orchard Inn serves a four-course dinner Tuesday through Saturday, with white linens, fresh flowers, and candlelight, on a glassed-in porch.

The inn has a good wine cellar and serves wine and beer. Jackets are suggested for men at dinner, furthering the sense of escaping the real world (828-749-5471 or 800-581-3800; www.orchard inn.com).

A stop suggested by several readers of this book is *Pearson's Falls,* 2720 Pearson Falls Road. This nature and wildlife preserve is a gift to the public

nina'ssecret

The late jazz/soul singer and piano player Nina Simone was born February 21, 1933, in Tryon. She was one of eight children, four boys and four girls. Simone was playing the piano and singing before she reached the age of five and developed her talent in the early years singing in the local church with her sisters. She left home for Philadelphia when she was seventeen and later studied at Juilliard in New York. Some of her earliest gigs were in a piano bar in Philadelphia, a job she kept secret from her churchgoing family in North Carolina.

owned and maintained by the Tryon Garden Club since 1929. More than 200 different species of flowering plants, algae, and mosses grow here. The preserve includes the 90-foot falls, which you get to by a short trail of less than a half mile. The area is ideal for a picnic, a photo session, and a little walk. Admission is $3 for adults, $1 for children ages six to twelve. From March 1 to November 1, the preserve is open Tuesday through Saturday from 10:00 a.m. to 6:00 p.m. Closed Monday except on holidays. During the winter months the preserve is closed Monday and Tuesday, open Wednesday through Saturday 10:00 a.m. to 5:00 p.m. No pets are allowed in the preserve. To get to the falls from Saluda, head toward Tryon on US 176. Just a couple miles past Orchard Inn, as you head down the mountain, you'll see a giant sign identifying Pearson Falls Road and Pearson's Falls. Turn right. The entrance to the preserve is a mile farther in (828-749-3031; www.pearsonsfalls.org).

The 10-mile stretch of road from Saluda to *Tryon* is the *Pacolet River Scenic Byway,* which gives you glimpses of the Pacolet River, wonderful vistas, and historic sites as well as more waterfalls. Tryon is known as an equestrian center. The *Foothills Equestrian Nature Center,* 3381 Hunting Country Road (828-859-9021; www.fence.org), is a nature education and recreation center with 5 miles of trails for hiking and riding, horse stables, and family-oriented nature education programs and outdoor concerts. The programs are often seasonal, such as a kite-flying day and a Mother's Day celebration, and most are free. The center is open during normal business hours, Monday through Friday. Admission is free.

Not far from the center, **Pine Crest Inn,** 85 Pine Crest Lane (828-859-9135 or 800-633-3001; www.pinecrestinn.com), has thirty-five rooms in a variety of buildings including the main inn, as well as a restaurant and business meeting rooms. The overall theme here is the English Country Hunt, probably due at least in part to the influence of earlier owners who were British. The restaurant serves new American-style cuisine, emphasizing locally available ingredients, and all spirits are available. All rooms have private bath, television, telephone, and VCR players. Some have fireplaces and whirlpool baths.

Downtown Tryon is filled with quaint stores and antiques shops, many of them also reflecting the local interest in horses.

The High Country

The next drive you might make from Asheville continues north on the Blue Ridge Parkway to **Mount Mitchell State Park,** elevation 6,684 feet, the highest point in the eastern United States. You'll leave the parkway at milepost 355.4 to take Highway 128 to the 1,500-acre wilderness park. It's a 5-mile drive to the peak, but it will feel a lot longer. The park has hiking trails, picnic areas, a visitor center with maps, camping areas, and a lookout tower from which you can see what must be the most stunning mountain views east of the Mississippi. There are also a restaurant and a refreshment stand. Be careful while you're here. Mount Mitchell is named for Dr. Elisha Mitchell, who fell off the summit and died. Your falling off too probably wouldn't lead to getting the mountain renamed in your honor. Park hours vary depending on the weather and time of year. You can call ahead (828-675-4611).

The next stop you might try along the parkway is at milepost 331, where Highways 226 and 1100 take you to Emerald Village near Little Switzerland. At Emerald Village, established on the site of the Old McKinney and Bon Ami mines, you can visit the **North Carolina Mining Museum,** which displays the tools used at the height of gem mining in the area. Outdoor displays and a printed trail guide explain the entire mining process, and you'll have the opportunity to look for your own emeralds, rubies, aquamarines, and the like. If your gem hunting doesn't go well, you can pick up something at the shop or have a rough gem cut, polished, and set into a piece of jewelry. Open daily from 10:00 a.m. to 4:00 p.m. in April, longer hours May through October, weekends only in November. Modest fee for mining tour (828-765-6463; www.emeraldvillage.com).

The Orchard at Altapass, close by at milepost 328, provides an experience more at one with nature, rich with history, and just plain fun (888-765-

9531; www.altapassorchard.com). The apple orchard was originally created by the Clinchfield Railroad, beside its tracks, in the early 1900s. Those tracks had been laid following what was probably an old buffalo and elk path. Eventually the railroad ceased to run through the area, and the same route was chosen for the Blue Ridge Parkway. It was bitterly contested in the North Carolina Supreme Court, but ultimately went right through the orchard, dividing it in half. The orchard went into decline. In 1994 Kit Truby bought it, and with her brother, Bill Carson, and his wife, Judy, began working on its restoration and preservation. It's now a family enterprise supported by a nonprofit foundation. It's not just the apple trees you can enjoy here now, but also butterflies, and all kinds of activities celebrating earlier crafts, music, and food. In season, you can pick your own apples, choosing from eight varieties. You can go on hayrides, listen to old-time music, buy fudge, and learn about the history of the area going back to the time of its earliest inhabitants, long before the British came along. If history were taught this way, more people would enjoy studying it. Open mid-May through September, 10:00 a.m. to 6:00 p.m. Closed Tuesday, Sunday noon to 6:00 p.m. Open daily 10:00 a.m. to 6:00 p.m. in October.

Also nearby, you can take US 221 to get to **Linville Caverns** and **Linville Falls,** just beyond the caverns. If you're back on the parkway, exit at milepost 317.4 and turn left on US 221. Linville Caverns lie under Humpback Mountain and were believed to have been forgotten by the white race until about one hundred years ago, when fish that seemed to be swimming out of the mountains caught the attention of explorers. During the Civil War, deserters from troops on both sides hid in the caverns. Today the caverns are lit electrically, showing stalactites and stalagmites and trout that, having always swum in the dark, can't see. Guides lead the tours 2,000 feet underground, pointing out important features and answering questions. Admission is $6.00 for adults, $4.50 for senior citizens, $4.00 for children ages five through twelve, free for children under five. Open daily, March through November, beginning at 9:00 a.m. (828-756-4171 or 800-419-0540; www.linvillecaverns.com).

Linville Falls comprises two waterfalls at Linville Gorge and a primeval canyon in the sizable wilderness area given to the Blue Ridge Parkway by John D. Rockefeller. The gorge is the deepest cut east of the Grand Canyon. There are hiking trails and picnic spots.

At a convenient spot where the Blue Ridge Parkway and US 221 meet, **Parkview Lodge** (Blue Ridge Parkway and US 221, 800-849-4452, www .parkviewlodge.com) is a most unchainlike place to stay. This is the full-time home of innkeepers Cindy and David Peters. Parkview Lodge consists of a series of knotty-pine-paneled rooms in a long stone building and three cabins in the woods, all furnished with locally purchased pieces, old family items, and bed headboards David built by hand. The atmosphere fits with the inn's Blue Ridge Parkway mountain location while offering more comfort than a tent or camper. Some of the lodge accommodations are especially designed for private, romantic getaways. Other rooms are basic, with recognizably old heaters and close quarters. But they're not boring. Rates include breakfast: homemade quiche made from eggs gathered at the Peters's henhouse, which is open for children to see, and coffee made with beans ground on the premises. The lodge's main room, where breakfast is served, also has a wine shop, a cooler with forty brands of cold beer, and local arts and crafts.

Across the highway and back along a gravel road into the woods, *Linville Falls Trailer Lodge and Campground* (Gurney Franklin Road, 828-765-2681, www.linvillefalls.com) has nice sites for RVs of all sizes as well as a section for tent sites. The bathhouses are clean, with plenty of hot water, and laundry facilities are available at the small campground store and office. In warm months, each campsite is marked with a hanging basket of blooming flowers.

A little jog off US 221, onto Highway 194, leads into the little community of *Crossnore,* with a population of just a few hundred friendly people. This is not a place that generally makes it into guidebooks, because it is not tourist-oriented, but it is known for the *Weaving Room and Gallery* (100 D. A. R. Drive; 828-733-4660; www.crossnoreschool.org), a hand-weaving center with a gift shop featuring Appalachian crafts as well as woven goods. The operation was founded in 1920 as a way to raise money for the Crossnore School. This school was run by several committed women as a way to educate children in Appalachia, for whom few opportunities existed. The school had a boarding section as well as classrooms. In addition to weaving, the sale of old clothes was a source of revenue for the school. Today sales from the weaving room and a large thrift shop still benefit Crossnore School students. Ben Long has created a fresco at the chapel on the campus, open to the public. The theme is "Suffer the Little Children to Come unto Me." Many of the models were children who live on campus. (See entry on Ben Long Frescoes later in this chapter.)

Still moving north along the parkway, you'll come to *Grandfather Mountain,* where, if you've got the nerve for it, you can walk across the *Mile-High Swinging Bridge,* a 218-foot suspension bridge between two peaks that sways in the wind. Should you quite sensibly prefer to put your feet on something more solid, Grandfather Mountain has lots of hiking trails, as well as indoor exhibits and habitats for black bears, otters, cougars, eagles, and deer. You'll need to pick up a moderately priced permit and a trail map at the entrance. This is the area where the *Scottish Highland Games,* open to the public, are held the second weekend in July every year. Admission is $14 for adults, $12 for senior citizens, $6 for children ages four to twelve (828-733-4337 or 800-468-7325; www.grandfather.com).

A few minutes farther brings you to U.S. Highway 321 and the ***Blowing Rock,*** a cliff 4,090 feet above sea level that overhangs Johns River Gorge, 3,000 feet below, at the town of Blowing Rock. Because of the way the gorge is shaped and overhung, air blows upward, making snow appear to fall upside down and throwing upward light objects tossed over the edge. According to the legend of Blowing Rock, a Cherokee brave leaped to his death here to keep his tribe from making him return to the plains, leaving his Chickasaw wife behind. She prayed to the Great Spirit until the sky turned red and the wind blew her brave back up onto the rock. A wind has blown up from the valley ever since. A moderate admission is charged. Hours vary with the season and the weather. For details call (828) 295-7111; www.theblowingrock.com.

By the time you get to Blowing Rock, the children will probably have heard of ***Tweetsie Railroad,*** a family theme park that has been operating in North Carolina since 1956. It's touristy but kind of fun. Coal-fired steam engines pull the train of open cars through 3 miles of staged events: a train robbery, an Indian raid, and so on. Also, a chairlift carries you up to Mouse Mountain, where you can pan for gold and walk through the petting farm. Another section of the park duplicates a country fair of the early 1900s, right down to the cotton candy. Among other features are an ice-cream parlor, a jail, and a firehouse. Moderately high admission is charged. Open daily from

Tweetsie Railroad

May through October from 9:00 a.m. to 6:00 p.m., with shorter hours and some features closed weekdays after Labor Day. The days and hours of operation here can, as one employee put it, "change at any time," so do call ahead (828-264-9061 or 800-526-5740; www.tweetsie.com).

When you see **Crippen's Country Inn and Restaurant** at 239 Sunset Drive in Blowing Rock (828-295-3487 or toll-free 877-295-3487; www.crippens .com) from the outside, nothing about it particularly catches your attention; it's easy to walk on by. But people who stay here go home and tell others about it as an outstanding place to eat, with unassuming but perfectly comfortable lodging right there. Jimmy Crippen says it's a place to slow down and kick back. The menu changes every day according to what's in season and good quality. This means organic, homegrown salad greens and fresh produce, fresh seafood and meats. The "nouvelle cuisine" label typically gets attached to food here, but that seems too limiting. An appetizer might be pan-seared Hudson Valley foie gras. A splendid pasta concoction, "Italian pie," includes tomatoes, herbs, and mozzarella. For entrees, choices could include everything from Vietnamese grilled pork tenderloin or rack of lamb with goat cheese to a whole grilled free-range chicken, all with appropriate herbs and sauces that you'll never see in Grandma's kitchen. It's a restaurant in the mountains, not a mountain restaurant. Beer and good wines are available, and Jimmy Crippen says that guests appreciate the proximity and comfort of their rooms after all the food and drink have been consumed. The place has eight rooms and one cottage.

Just outside of town, **Cliff Dwellers Inn,** 116 Lakeview Terrace (800-322-7380; www.cliffdwellers.com), offers some of the best vistas in an area known for great mountain views. The inn is just a mile south of the Blue Ridge Parkway, off US 321. But this place has none of the closed-in feel of many mountain cabins. The inn has twenty rooms, each with private bath, TV, telephone, and refrigerator, plus three suites, all with gas log fireplaces. Two suites have whirlpools. The guest rooms are unusually spacious, with large windows to take advantage of the mountain views, and airy, cheerful furnishings that emphasize the light. Balconies with rocking chairs run the length of the building. Look down from the sundeck onto the rock garden; from various other perches see Lake Chetola and the outlet Shoppes on the Parkway, across US 321. From here it's a quick drive into Blowing Rock. You are also just 8 miles south of Boone.

Off the main highways outside Blowing Rock, on Shulls Mill Road, **The Inn at Crestwood** (828-963-6646; www.crestwoodnc.com) comes as a surprise—a center of luxury secluded in the woods on a winding rural road. This was originally the private summer home of the Moberg family. In 2004 the inn

The British are Coming—Hurray!

The night I dined at Dominic's Table at the Crestwood Inn, I heard the stories about Dominic, the chef, and how much his kitchen staff liked him. I enjoyed a splendid meal. Dominic came to say hello, and then let me see the kitchen! When I found out he was English, I told him about my Brit Grandma Edith's Cornish pasty. The next day, he delivered one to my room. While he was there, he admired my guitar, which I got him to play briefly; then he insisted I play. I was too self-conscious to do more than a few chords, but he said, "Wonderful. Marvelous. Don't give up." He headed back to the kitchen and I settled down to pasty. No wonder his staff loves him.

opened with an addition that preserved the old home and increased space for rooms, balconies, and dining. The decor includes framed renderings of many of the senior Moberg's architectural drawings. In its current ideation, the inn comprises a variety of luxurious rooms and suites, the restaurant, ***Dominic's Table,*** and the ***Dawg Star Bar.***

On the same property, new villas accommodate families and larger groups. A spa offers massage, skin treatments, and access to a lap pool, steam bath, Jacuzzi, and fitness center. This is a pricey place to stay, although dinner in Dominic's Table, open to the public, is in the moderate range. The rooms are luxurious, but their greater charm is views of mountains in all directions. In the dining room, which has walls of windows and spectacular views, British chef Dominic Geraghty offers a sprightly menu mix of new approaches and European touches. His lobster pie is a favorite appetizer. He prepares an unusual and very successful entree of sea bass wrapped in thin slices of lightly grilled zucchini that diners often recommend to new guests.

The restaurant serves dinner Monday through Saturday 5:30 to 9:00 p.m. Call (828) 963-1417 for reservations. The bar opens at 4:30 p.m. Service there includes a lighter bar food menu.

For a fun little diversion, stop at 175 Mystery Hill Lane in Blowing Rock to visit the ***Appalachian Heritage Museum,*** in what used to be the home of the Doughertys, who founded Appalachian State University. This is on US 321/221 North. The home is decorated authentically in turn-of-the-century furnishings and shows how mountain families lived in the early 1900s. Sometimes the museum holds demonstrations of mountain crafts or cooking. There's a separate exhibit of Native American artifacts. The museum is open every day, year-round, beginning at 9:00 a.m. It closes at 8:00 p.m. in summer, and 5:00 p.m. September through May. Museum admission includes ***The Hall of Mystery*** and ***The Mystery Platform and Mystery House,*** where you can experience varied optical illusions and scientific oddities (828-264-2792; www.mysteryhill-nc.com).

Breakfast in downtown Blowing Rock, at **Sonny's Grill,** 1119 Main Street, is an intensely local experience. The area has more popular tourist restaurants, but Sonny's, in the center of town, is where you're most likely to find the folks who actually live in Blowing Rock. The cafe is in a small cinderblock building painted gray with no visible street address. Inside, diners sit at Formica tables or, if alone, on red stools at the counter, from where they can watch the bacon frying and the eggs flipping. This is the kind of place where people gossip about local events, talk about who went to Cherokee to play the slot machines over the weekend, and joke among themselves. And they welcome strangers, at least those who come in smiling. Sonny's starts serving breakfast early in the morning—an exact time isn't posted—and continues into lunch.

At the center of the activity, Robbie Cheeves acts as some mix of cook, social director, and manager. While he's scrambling eggs and brewing coffee, he's also introducing people to each other. A customer wonders where to get Italian Cypress. Robbie scribbles the question on the back of a blank guest check along with a phone number. Next day when a professional gardener perches on a red stool, Robbie hands him the slip. A tourist wonders where to buy a dulcimer. Robbie draws a little map on the back of a slip, directing him to a craftsman's shop in Foscoe. The action goes on, moving from biscuits and eggs to lunch. Robbie says he flips burgers until about 2:00 p.m. Call (828) 295-7577.

Boone is a little college town about 10 miles from Blowing Rock. You will miss it if you just keep on driving along US 321, because the traffic and peripheral development are off-putting. But the town itself, best known as the home of Appalachian State University, typically called "App" by its students, is a lot of fun. King Street, running through the center of town, has a variety of funky stores with some good arts and crafts, books, music, motorcycles, vintage clothing, and antiques. Walking along King and some of the side streets, you'll find small restaurants with the quirky names that seem to go with college towns.

Melanie's Food Fantasy (664 King Street; 828-263-0300; www.melanies foodfantasy.com) is popular with college students and their visitors. The people

Running Away from Home

Jan Karon, author of the best-selling Mitford series of books, based her novels on her hometown, the village of Blowing Rock. Sometime after she became famous, she moved away from Blowing Rock because, she said, tourists kept wanting to come see her house. Locals sort of forgive her, though. They arrange Mitford festivals in the fall.

Ribbit, Ribbit

I stopped at **The Tomato Shack** on Highway 105, just outside Boone, to buy apples and Ashe County cheese curds. This is one of those places that has everything from hot boiled peanuts to sourwood honey and apple butter. I had to put on my glasses to read labels, which led the proprietor and I to joke about going to buy apples then forgetting that you even wanted apples, and about how you can't see to find your glasses without your glasses—that kind of stuff. Then he said, "Where are you from?" Well, gee, I was driving my red muscle Nissan Frontier—a mountain vehicle, surely.

"What?" I said. "You don't think I can pass for local?"

"It's not that," he said. "If you came here often, I'd remember you."

I made a joke as I headed to the door. "Whoooeee—does that mean I'm in trouble?"

Before I could get out the door, he said, "Well, I am getting older, but my daddy always said you don't know from looking at a frog how high it can jump."

who work here are mostly young and seriously dedicated to providing healthful food that also tastes wonderful. The variety of the menu is substantial. The restaurant is open from 8:00 a.m. to 3:00 p.m. Tuesday through Saturday for breakfast and lunch, and from 9:00 a.m. to 3:00 p.m. for Sunday brunch.

A fun and friendly restaurant in an unlikely location, **The Coyote Kitchen** is just past the end of King Street, around the corner in the Wal-Mart Shopping Plaza, off US 321 (200 Southgate Drive; 828-265-4041; www.thecoyotekitchen .com). The owner, Ben Whitehead, who is also the chef, calls Coyote's food "Southwest Caribbean Soul Food," but adds that it's basically Tex-Mex taken a bit upscale. The menu is extensive, the portions large, and the wine and beer choices are pretty good, too. The restaurant is popular with an interesting assortment of people—from rock climbers to businessmen. The atmosphere is quirky. You could well encounter a waiter wearing a straw hat with his Coyote Kitchen T-shirt. Ben says he uses local and organic products to the degree it's possible, and willingly accommodates vegans, vegetarians, and others with special dietary requests. This restaurant is an area leader in the green movement. They've installed spiral energy-saving bulbs in all the ceiling lights and are using compostable paper products for take-out containers. The Coyote Kitchen is open Sunday through Thursday 11:00 a.m. to 9:00 p.m., Friday and Saturday to 9:30 p.m.

You can stay at any of a couple dozen standard motels in the area, but for about the same price and the best sense of the App kids, **The Broyhill Inn and Appalachian Conference Center** (828-262-2204 or 800-951-6048; www.broyhillinn.com) is choice. It's on the university campus, on top of a

silly, silly sara

A big hotel with only two stories takes some getting used to. After I absentmindedly signed my dinner check "Room 410," a grinning student waiter asked if I were planning a construction project.

hill overlooking campus. The university owns the inn, and it's a place where students work alongside professionals, learning the hospitality business. This older stone lodge has been renovated; its eighty-three rooms are spacious and comfortable. Each has private bath, TV, telephone, microfridge, and free wireless Internet connection. Although the inn has extensive conference and special events areas, the place doesn't feel like an anonymous hotel, partly because it is only two stories high. Special events don't have much impact on regular guests because of the way space is allotted. The award-winning executive chef, Bill Morris, is perhaps best known for his elaborate Sunday brunch, which runs most of the day. Whatever else is on the buffet, you'll always find fried chicken, looking a little out of place. "People complain if it's not there," Morris says. Staying here you are away from downtown traffic. The dining room and guest rooms have glorious landscape and mountain views. The dining room serves three meals a day, with wine and beer available. But the unique appeal of Broyhill Inn is in its staff and service—the youthful energy of students, including dining-room musicians, working with professional staff, is pure joy. There's a hint of the personality behind the uncommon atmosphere here when one of the students mentions that Doug Uzelac, the general manager, has a university degree with dual majors, physics and theater.

Beech Mountain is close to Boone and Blowing Rock, but in a sense it's far away, or will feel like it as you negotiate the mountain road curves. It's about 23 miles west of Boone, more or less straight up, at a peak elevation of 5,506 feet. The town covers only about 6½ square miles, with a year-round population of 381, although this occasionally must change a little with a birth or death. The town advertises itself as the highest incorporated town in America. Much of the community's economic base comes from tourist activ-

The AppalCART

AppalCART is the public transportation authority serving all of Watauga County. Buses and shuttles run from The Broyhill Inn to points around campus and town, serving students and anyone else who boards at no charge. Other routes may require a fee. For a map showing routes and details of the service, call (828) 264-2278, or check the Web site: www.appalcart.com. This is a good, easy-to-use service.

Yearly Fun at the Beech

- Annual Roasting of the Hog and Fireworks Display, Fourth of July weekend

- BJ's Annual Dog Show and Dancing in the Streets at Town Hall, mid-July

- Annual Barn Dance, mid-August

- Annual Mile-High Kite Festival, last weekend in August

Call (828) 387-9283 for exact dates when you make your travel plans.

ities—hiking, skiing, fishing, or just relaxing in a vacation condo—"A week at the Beech." Your first stop probably should be at the ***Beech Mountain Chamber of Commerce,*** 403-A Beech Mountain Parkway (828-387-9283; www.beechmountain.com), to pick up maps, events schedules, and brochures. In that vicinity you'll see a large brick building and a modest building beside it. Contrary to what one might expect, the smaller one is the chamber. "Hiking on Beech" maps trails of varying length and difficulty, along with verbal descriptions and even history. Townspeople are especially proud of a little booklet, "Bike Beech Mountain," which lays out the route of Lance Armstrong and the Tour DuPont. Seems Lance said this is the best place to train in the United States.

The town is now offering an alternative to skiing, too—guided winter hikes. These hikes are scheduled ahead of time, so you can find news about them each season on the Web site or by calling the chamber. And one of the surprisingly successful winter innovations here is the sledding hill, where kids twelve and under may sled on a safe course for free. If the snow is a little skimpy, a machine blows on some artificial frozen stuff. The children must use plastic sleds, be supervised by adults, and not yield to the temptation to build snowmen on the course. A slope supervisor keeps a watchful eye on the proceedings. As it's turned out, this isn't just a spot for locals; families come from considerable distance, from places where there is little snow, to give their kids a sledding experience.

If you need to buy anything in Beech Mountain, ***Fred's General Mercantile Co.*** (501 Beech Mountain Parkway; 828-387-4838; www.fredsgeneral.com) is the place to go. Fred Pfohl coined the motto, "If you don't see it, ask for it—if we don't have it, you don't need it," back when he and his wife, Margie, opened in 1979. The store has been open every day since, and it's hard to imagine what you might want that isn't here, from hardware and tools to winter clothing to patent medicines to wine and beer. If you want breakfast, lunch, or dinner, you can get that here, too. ***Fred's Backside Deli*** invites you to

notinkansas anymore,toto

The **Land of Oz Theme Park,** in the Beech Mountain ski area, west of Boone on Highway 184, was popular several decades ago but has since fallen out of fashion and closed, except for the first weekend in October, when visitors come into the park to mingle with the Tin Man and Dorothy and the other Oz characters wandering along the Yellow Brick Road, investigating the old Kansas farmhouse that still has remnants of its 1930s decor, and indulging in quirky nostalgia. For details call (828) 387-9283.

"dine in or carryout." Breakfast eggs are served scrambled and come with toast; the Southern classic biscuit with sausage gravy is on the menu, along with hash browns, grits, country ham . . . all the Southern favorites with a few additions such as bagels thrown in. Lunch and dinner offerings include soup, hot and cold sandwiches, pizza, salads, grilled meats, barbecue, and cookies, pie, and cake. Drinks range from iced tea and milk to wine or imported beer.

Fred and Margie raised their five children in living quarters above the store. Consequently, none of the kids wants anything to do with running it, so Fred and Margie expect to keep on indefinitely. Because they've always been so flexible in accommodating customers at any time of day or night, it's hard to give specific hours of operation, but breakfast starts at 7:00 and ends at 11:00 a.m. Locals have been known to come at 2:30 in the morning "because the baby needs medicine," picking up a six-pack and cigarettes while they're at it. As visitors, it would be courteous to observe normal business hours.

The Brick Oven Pizzeria (402 Beech Mountain Parkway; 828-387-4209) is also a family operation. It started as a modest pizza place, and as business took off, the restaurant expanded its menu to include salads, wings, oven-baked pastas, sandwiches, a coffee/cappuccino bar, a candy and dessert counter, and a full bar. Seating includes wooden booths and a front dining room with tables. A family game room has various blinking and winking games, and, since it gets cold in winter, fireplaces where you can warm up. The Brick Oven is open for lunch and operates on into the night as business requires.

Northeast of Boone, it's well worth your time to make a trip to West Jefferson and Glendale Springs, off Highway 194 at the juncture with Highway 163, to see the **Ben Long Frescoes** in two Episcopal mission churches, St. Mary's Episcopal Church and Holy Trinity. The paintings in St. Mary's include an image of Mary pregnant with Jesus and a depiction of Christ on the cross, with a second view of the transfigured Christ behind it. The paintings in the Holy Trinity church include *The Lord's Supper* by Ben Long, as well as works by his students. The churches, which are only a few minutes apart, are not

Ben Long's Frescoes

Ben Long is a native of North Carolina who studied the art of fresco painting in Italy and has worked in several venues around North Carolina. Frescoes are created by mixing sand and lime, applying it to a surface, and then painting on it while it is still wet. Michelangelo's paintings on the ceiling of the Sistine Chapel in Rome, Italy, are frescoes.

tended, and visitors may go in any time (336-982-3076; www.churchofthe frescoes.com).

In a completely different mode, West Jefferson is also the home of the **Ashe County Cheese Company** (106 East Main Street, 336-246-2501; www.ashecountycheese.com), where visitors can see cheese being made and buy a variety of cheeses, including mild, medium, and sharp cheddars. One of the most popular items here is fresh cheese curds, which are soft, chewy curds before they're pressed and aged into hard cheese. Cheese-making schedules vary, so it's a good idea to call ahead if you want to see the process.

West Jefferson is becoming quite an art and antiques center, too, with lots of shops all within easy walking distance downtown. This arts district also has three restaurants; one of them, Sweet Aromas, is a bakery and cafe.

Another drive on US 421, which is an easy highway these days, brings you to Wilkesboro, where you can find connections with topics as diverse as wine and racing and gardens and the jail where Tom Dooley was held after being accused of murdering Laura Foster. **Wilkes Heritage Museum** (100 East Main Street; 336-667-3171; www.wilkesheritagemuseum.com) includes exhibits in what used to be the courthouse about everything from the relationship between moonshine and stock-car racing to stories of Native Americans and the Civil War. The museum includes the 1860 Wilkes Jail. The museum is open from 10:00 a.m. to 4:00 p.m. Tuesday through Saturday. Closed major

Hang Down Your Head, Tom Dooley

His real name was Tom Dula, pronounced *Dooley*. The Confederate soldier who was held in the Wilkes Jail before being executed in Statesville for the murder of his fiancée, Laura Foster, claimed his innocence until the moment he was hanged. He rode to the gallows sitting on top of his coffin, playing his banjo, and joking with the executioner that he'd have washed his neck if he'd known the rope would be so nice and clean. Many musicians have sung "The Ballad of Tom Dooley," including the Kingston Trio.

holidays. Admission is $5 for adults, $4 for students and senior citizens over fifty-five, and free for children ages four and under.

At **St. Paul's Episcopal Church** (200 West Cowles Street; 336-667-4231) you'll find two frescoes painted by Ben Long (see sidebar and entry earlier in this chapter) about St. Paul the Apostle on the road to Damascus, and in prison writing his epistles to churches. The Web site for the Cultural Arts Council of Wilkes (www.cacwilkes.org) offers an especially clear explanation of the fresco process, along with Ben Long's biography. The Wilkesboro Tourism Development Authority is promoting tours for those who'd like to see many more of Ben Long's frescoes (www.benlongfrescotrail.org). The trail includes twenty-five counties in western North Carolina.

For those who find religion in gardens, **Wilkes Community College Gardens** will be a special treat (1328 South Collegiate Drive; 336-838-6100; www.merlefest.org/gardens.htm). The gardens are incorporated into the landscape of the college's 150-acre campus, with rose, Japanese, and native gardens. But it's the Eddy Merle Watson Garden of the Senses that truly attracts attention and inspires visitors. Eddy Merle Watson (son of legendary blind acoustic musician, Arthel "Doc" Watson) died in 1985, about the time he was fully recognized for his guitar picking in bluegrass country music and the blues. He rolled his farm tractor on a steep hill near his home and was killed instantly. In tribute to him, Wilkes Community College began the Eddy Merle Watson Garden of the Senses, creating a garden that people who cannot see might enjoy, emphasizing fragrance and texture, with sculptured alphabet walls, and plants labeled with Braille signs. MerleFest was begun as a way to raise money to continue developing the garden, but the festival has taken on a life of its own and is now a huge musical event each year. Much of the money it raises still goes to the gardens, while the influx of music lovers swells the local economy. The event is alcohol-free, suitable for families.

Yet another attraction in the area is a testimony to love. **Benny Parsons Rendezvous Ridge Tasting Room and Racing Museum** (172 Benny Parsons Road, Purlear; 336-973-7375; www.bennyparsons.com) represents the determination of his widow, Terri, to carry out the dream they shared of having not just their own wines, but also their own vineyards. Benny was a much-loved race-car driver, the 1973 NASCAR champion, with a string of other racing triumphs to his name, and then a trusted name in racing broadcasting. He and Terri planned to move back to the land where he grew up, build a home and winery room, and establish their own vineyards. He died in January 2007, before the project was completed. He's buried in a family graveyard on the property. Terri decided to go ahead with their plans, and the recently planted grapes are taking hold. The house has been built, and the museum, filled with pictures and mementos of Parsons's career, also houses the tasting room. It will be a while before these vines produce grapes for wine, but Benny and Terri Parsons had already been producing several wines, which Terri still offers. Race fans and, perhaps, wine lovers, were lining up at the new location almost before the paint in the museum and tasting room was dry. The wines range from a hearty cabernet franc to a soft blush that is 85 percent cabernet and 15 percent muscadine. The tasting room is open 11:00 a.m. to 7:00 p.m. Wednesday through Saturday, but hours may change, so call ahead.

Valle Crucis is close to the Blowing Rock–Boone area, but totally unlike it in nature. Although the little town sees hundreds and hundreds of visitors, it manages to continue operating and looking like a small town except for the visiting hordes. It's a good off-season stop. The town's history dates back to 1780, when Samuel Hix, the first known white settler in Valle Crucis, staked a claim to 1,000 acres. Later he traded the land for a gun, a dog, and a sheepskin. Eventually it became an Episcopal mission, named Valle Crucis because three creeks came together in the shape of a cross. Today the mission serves as a retreat for many church denominations.

People stop most often at the *Mast General Store,* on Highways 112/194, listed on the National Register of Historic Places as one of the best remaining examples of an authentic, old country store. Here you can still buy penny candy, seeds, leather boots, Woolrich sweaters, flannel shirts, long johns, and just about anything else you can think of, mostly stacked, not too neatly, along wooden shelves. The Mast General Store has a couple of other locations now, but this is the original 1883 landmark (828-963-6511; www.mastgeneralstore .com).

The Foothills

Instead of heading north from Asheville, you may choose to start east toward the foothills and the Piedmont. A drive of about forty minutes on US 74, heading southeast from Asheville, takes you to the little vacation community of *Lake Lure.* Everything centers on the 1,500-acre lake, which has 27 miles of shoreline. The area is surrounded by the Blue Ridge Mountains. It's in the heart of the thermal belt, where the climate is almost always a bit milder than the extremes of heat and cold found in the rest of North Carolina. The temperate climate makes Lake Lure excellent for boating, fishing, hiking, and horseback riding year-round. Lake Lure, Chimney Rock, and Bat Cave, three tourist towns, run together one after another along the narrow mountain road.

For hiking you have your choice of hundreds of trails. Organized hikes leave from *Chimney Rock Park* (828-625-9611 or 800-277-9611), located on

US 64/74 in Chimney Rock, a private park with hiking trails, easier paths, and even an elevator to the top. From the top you can look down and see Lake Lure and mountains in all directions. Hickory Nut Falls, one of the highest waterfalls in the East, is on the grounds. The park is open daily from 8:30 a.m. to 5:30 p.m. during summer months but closes at 4:30 p.m. as days grow shorter. In bad weather the park closes. Rates vary seasonally. For simpler hiking you can ask almost any local person to recommend a favorite trail. These personal favorites are loosely kept secrets because no one wants them to become overrun with "lookey-loos" and littered with aluminum cans, but locals gladly share the information with anyone who cares enough to ask personally. The town marina, on the lake and right next to US 64/74A, has boats for rent, and *Lake Lure Tours* runs hourly tours and twilight and dinner cruises (877-386-4255 or 828-625-1373; www.lakelure.com).

From here it's an easy drive up either US 74A or Highway 9 to I-40, where you'll come to *Black Mountain,* an interesting village that was once a Cherokee Indian center and now is a thriving community specializing in all kinds of top-quality arts and crafts. The town has taken to calling itself "the front porch of western North Carolina," a name that seems to suit the peaceful but interesting atmosphere of the community.

In May and October, Black Mountain sponsors the Mountain Music Festival, during which musicians play the old mountain music on dulcimers, fiddles, bagpipes, and mandolins. In August the Sourwood Festival features more music and dancing and a large arts and crafts show. These events are fun; they're also well attended, so if you have any notion of being in Black Mountain when they occur, you will need to arrange for lodging well ahead of time. (For details call 800-207-8759 or check the Web site: www.explore blackmountain.com.)

The Black Mountain Inn, 1186 West Old Highway 70 (800-735-6128 or 828-669-6528; www.blackmountaininn.com), has seven guest rooms. The building was once a studio and retreat where artists and writers such as Norman Rockwell and John Steinbeck spent time. The decor is casual country; the breakfasts include a main course plus fruits, home-baked breads, and homemade granola.

The Red Rocker Inn, 136 North Dougherty Street (888-669-5991 or 828-669-5991; www.redrockerinn.com), is a long-established, seventeen-room inn long known for its food, served in portions that leave guests needing a walk after dinner. The rooms all have private baths. In cool weather, gas fireplaces add warmth to the public rooms and some of the guest rooms. The proprietors take special pride in the long row of red rocking chairs on the porch and go so far as repainting them regularly to keep them looking bright and shiny.

When the Red Rocker Inn is full, the folks there recommend the ***Inn around the Corner,*** 109 Church Street (800-393-6005 or 828-669-6005; www.innaroundthecorner.com). This is a more recently established bed-and-breakfast operation in a residential part of town, in the same block as a church. The restored 1915 Victorian inn has five rooms and two luxury suites, all with private baths, as well as sleeping space on the upstairs porches. This place is ideally set up for families. It has a full kitchen available for guests, and the downtown restaurants and shops are a quick walk away. Rates include an ample breakfast.

Visiting the ***Song of the Wood,*** at 203 West State Street, a workshop and salesroom devoted to dulcimers and unusual string instruments and their music, leaves you feeling exhilarated and refreshed. Jerry Read Smith makes hammered dulcimers and the even more unusual bowed psaltery, a small tri-angular instrument played with a violin-type bow, similar to a medieval bowed harp. JoAnn, Jerry's sister, manages the showroom. Everything about the shop is devoted to keeping the old music alive, producing fine-quality handmade instruments, and surrounding you with music.

You'll first be attracted by the music coming through outside speakers. When you get inside, they'll play lots more music for you. You may hear the music from their independent record albums, *The Strayaway Child, Homecoming, One Wintry Night,* and *Heartdance.* The shop sells a highly personal selection of other tapes and albums, mainly hammered dulcimer music, piano music, and Celtic music. The shop is light and airy, with instruments on the walls, a fuel-efficient wood-burning stove, and a mountain rocker. You're invited to sit down and try any of the instruments or listen to the recorded music. If you're interested and ask, you can almost always manage to be shown through the design studio and workshop in a building about twenty minutes away and have the whole process explained to you. Open from 10:00 a.m. to 5:00 p.m. Monday through Saturday (828-669-7675; www.songofthe wood.com).

As for shopping, the streets are lined with crafts shops, antiques shops and antiques malls, and a craft co-op.

In the old Black Mountain Fire Department building, the ***Swannanoa Valley Museum,*** 223 West State Street (828-669-9566; www.swannanoavalley museum.org), focuses intensely on local history from the Stone Age to the present. For instance, exhibits depict the lives of Native Americans, early settlers, the coming of the railroad, and Billy Graham and other famous valley personalities. One of the museum's most popular programs is a series of hikes to points of historical interest in the valley. To participate in a hike, call for details. The museum isn't open in winter because it's too costly to heat the big building. It is open April through October, Tuesday through Saturday 10:00 a.m. to 5:00 p.m., Sunday 2:00 to 5:00 p.m., and by appointment in winter.

Immediately after Black Mountain, you come to **Old Fort,** an area that was still considered Cherokee Indian land for some time after white pioneers began pushing in during the mid-1770s. At the beginning of the American Revolution, General Griffith Rutherford assembled 2,500 troops to attack the Cherokees, who seemed to be siding with the British. Afterward the Indians conceded a huge portion of land, a pattern that was repeated often up to the time of the Trail of Tears in 1838. In subsequent years the Western North Carolina Railroad became important here. The **Mountain Gateway Museum,** in the 100 block of Water Street, tells the story, as do the Stepp and Morgan cabins that were moved here later. The site is a branch of the North Carolina Museum of History. It's not a big, splashy place and deserves your attention for that very reason. Admission is free. Open daily from 9:00 a.m. to 5:00 p.m., except opens at noon on Monday; Sunday from 2:00 to 5:00 p.m. (828-668-9259; www.mcdowellnc.org).

Places to Stay in the Mountains

ASHEVILLE

Campfire Lodgings
Appalachian Village Road
(800) 933-8012
www.campfirelodgings
.com

Cedar Crest Inn
674 Biltmore Avenue
(828) 252-1389
(800) 252-0310
www.cedarcrestvictorianinn
.com

Old Reynolds Mansion
100 Reynold Heights
(828) 254-0496
(800) 709-0496

Sourwood Inn
810 Elk Mountain Scenic
Highway
(828) 255-0690
www.sourwoodinn.com

BLACK MOUNTAIN

Black Mountain Inn
1186 West Old Highway 70
(828) 669-6528
(800) 735-6128
www.blackmountaininn
.com

The Red Rocker Inn
136 North Dougherty Street
(828) 669-5991
(888) 669-5991
www.redrockerinn.com

BLOWING ROCK

**Crippen's Country Inn
and Restaurant**
239 Sunset Drive
(828) 295-3487
(877) 295-3487
www.crippens.com

CULLOWHEE

Fox Den Cottages
142 Silver Fox Drive
(828) 293-0828
(800) 721-9847
www.foxdencottages.com

**River Lodge Bed and
Breakfast**
619 Roy Tritt Road
(828) 293-5431
(877) 384-4400
www.riverlodge-bb.com

Tuckaseigee Valley Vacation Cabins
897 Roy Tritt Road
(828) 293-5131
(888) 906-7409
www.tuckaseigeevalley
cabins.com

DILLSBORO

The Chalet Inn
285 Lone Oak Drive
(828) 586-0251
www.thechaletinn.com

The Dillsboro Inn
146 North River Road
(828) 586-3898
(866) 586-3898
www.dillsboroinn.com

The Jarrett House
100 Haywood Street
(825) 586-0265
(800) 972-5623
www.jarretthouse.com

HOT SPRINGS

Mountain Magnolia Inn and Retreat
204 Lawson Street
(828) 622-3543
(800) 914-9306
www.mountainmagnoliainn
.com

LINVILLE FALLS

Parkview Lodge
US 221 and Blue Ridge
Parkway
(828) 765-4787
(800) 849-4552
www.parkviewlodge.com

MAGGIE VALLEY

Cataloochee Ranch
119 Ranch Drive
(828) 926-1401
(800) 868-1401
www.cataloocheeranch
.com

SALUDA

Orchard Inn
Highway 176
(828) 749-5471
(800) 581-3800
www.orchardinn.com

SYLVA

Mountain Brook Fireplace Cottages
208 Mountain Brook Road
(828) 586-4329
www.mountainbrook.com

TRYON

Pine Crest Inn
85 Pine Crest Lane
(828) 859-9135
(800) 633-3001
www.pinecrestinn.com

WAYNESVILLE

The Old Stone Inn
109 Dolan Road
(828) 456-3333
(800) 432-8499
www.oldstoneinn.com

The Swag
2300 Swag Road
(828) 926-0430
(800) 789-7672
www.theswag.com

The Windows on Main
122 North Main Street
(828) 734-6429
(828) 508-2786
www.windowsonmain.com

THE MOUNTAIN WEB SITES

Cherokee History
www.cherokee-nc.com

Great Smoky Mountains
www.visitsmokies.org

List of Movies Shot in North Carolina Mountains
www.ncfilm.com

Official North Carolina Web Site
www.visitnc.com

Transylvania Waterfalls
www.visitwaterfalls.com/travel

Places to Eat in the Mountains

ASHEVILLE

Gabrielle's at Richmond Hill
87 Richmond Hill Drive
(828) 252-7313

Laughing Seed Café
40 Wall Street
(828) 252-3445

BLOWING ROCK

Blowing Rock Café
Highway 321 at Sunset Drive
(828) 295-9474

Sonny's Grill
Main Street
(828) 295-7577

BREVARD

Jason's Main Street Grill
48 East Main Street
(828) 883-4447

Rocky's Soda Shop
36 South Broad Street
(828) 862-4700

DILLSBORO

Jarrett House
100 Haywood Street
(800) 972-5623

FLAT ROCK

Highland Lake Inn
Highland Lake Road
(800) 762-1376

HOT SPRINGS

Mountain Magnolia Inn
204 Lawson Street
(828) 622-3543
(800) 914-9306

SALUDA

Wildflour Bakery and Café
173 East Main Street
(828) 749-9224

TRYON

Pine Crest Inn Dining Room
85 Pine Crest Lane
(828) 859-9135

WAYNESVILLE

Lomo Grill
44 Church Street
(828) 452-1515

Maggie's Galley III
22 Howell Mill Road
(828) 456-8945

Old Stone Inn
109 Dolan Road
(800) 432-8499

Indexes

Entries for Inns, Bed-and-Breakfasts, Potteries, and Botanical Gardens and Arboretums appear in the special indexes on pages 198–99.

General Index

About the Author

Sara Pitzer is a transplanted Yankee who has been roaming and writing about the South since 1983. She can't go back north, where it's cold and people talk too fast. In 2006 she received the Charles Kuralt Award from the North Carolina Travel Industry Association. When she isn't on the road, Sara lives in the woods with a yard full of birds and a house full of pets. Visit Sara's Web site at www.planetpitzer.com.

Travel Like a Pro

To order call 800-243-0495 or visit thenewgpp.com

The Cheap Bastard's Guide™ to
NEW YORK CITY
MORE THAN 1,000 **FREE** LISTINGS

100 BEST
Resorts of the Caribbean

OFF THE BEATEN PATH®
VIRGINIA A GUIDE TO UNIQUE PLACES →

The Luxury Guide to
Walt Disney World® Resort *Second Edition*
How to Get the Most Out of the
Best Disney Has to Offer

shifra stein's
day trips®
from kansas city
fifteenth edition

NINTH EDITION JOHN HOWELL S III
CHOOSE COSTA RIC
FOR RETIREMENT

FUN WITH THE **FAMILY**
Hundreds of Ideas for Day Trips WITH THE Kids
Connecticut

INSIDERS'GUIDE®
Florida Keys and Key West

SCENIC DRIVING
COLORADO
STEWART M. GREEN
THIRD EDITION